WHAT NEEDS T

GILES RADICE, Labo
Chairman of the Co
Committee, is one of p̶₋...₋ᵤₘ₉ thinkers. As
an expert on European affairs, he is Chairman of the
European Movement and was a Parliamentary Fellow
of St Antony's College, Oxford, from 1994–5. His
Fabian series on attitudes in southern marginals was an
important influence in Labour's modernization. He
writes frequently for newspapers, and broadcasts on
television and radio. His most recent book was the
highly praised *The New Germans*, an authoritative
account of the united Germany.

WHAT NEEDS TO CHANGE

New Visions for Britain

EDITED BY GILES RADICE

With an introduction by Tony Blair

▉ HarperCollins*Publishers*

HarperCollins*Publishers*
77–85 Fulham Palace Road,
Hammersmith, London W6 8JB

This paperback edition 1996

1 3 5 7 9 8 6 4 2

First published in Great Britain by
HarperCollins*Publishers* 1996

ISBN 0 00 638761 6

Set in Sabon

Printed and bound in Great Britain by
Caledonian International Book Manufacturing Ltd, Glasgow

Contents

PAST AND PRESENT

Preface

This book of essays is not a political manifesto nor a set of party policies. Indeed most of the authors are not party political and some are not committed Labour Party supporters. Rather they have been chosen for their intellectual distinction and authority on the themes and issues covered in this work. I believe that the book maps out a new and distinctive agenda for Britain which could unite a broad spread of centre-left opinion and help inspire a new government.

I am grateful to all the essayists for their cooperation in responding to editorial suggestions and in meeting tight deadlines. Thanks to Penny Cooper and Lisanne Radice for commenting on drafts, to Michael Fishwick and Rebecca Lloyd of Harper Collins for their ideas, which have improved the text, to Penny Cooper for her editorial assistance and to the partners and staff of Gregory and Radice for their help. I am especially indebted to Denyse Morrell for her patience, skill and dedication in making sense of my handwriting and transcribing successive drafts of essays.

Giles Radice, March 1996

WHAT NEEDS
TO CHANGE

INTRODUCTION:

My Vision for Britain

Tony Blair

Leader of the Labour Party since 1994.

I said in my 1995 party conference speech that I wanted to see Britain become a 'young country' again. I meant that instead of trading off our past, we needed to develop the energy, the enthusiasm and the ideas to match the challenges of the future. We need to be proud of our history, but not bound by it; judicious in embracing new ideas, but open to new thinking; above all aware that we live in a radically changed world from that left by our grandparents, we need to construct a new and radical politics to serve the people in the new century ahead.

My vision is of a Britain that is truly one nation, where we work together to prepare ourselves for massive economic and technological change; to extend opportunity in a world of deep insecurity; to create a genuine civic society where everyone has a stake, where everyone has a responsibility, and where power is pushed down towards the people instead of being hoarded centrally; and to secure our place in the world as a nation cooperating with others in Europe and elsewhere.

I emphasize the idea of Britain as one nation. Without social justice, there will be no modernization, without mutuality and solidarity there will be no prosperity; without shared values there will be no progress; without responsibility there is no society. A high level of social cohesion is not just urgent in itself; it is essential for an efficient and prosperous economy, which is why we have to bring together a drive for economic efficiency with that for social justice.

Labour is the only party with the aim of doing this. But I have believed for some time that only a changed Labour Party could do it. That is why the first year of my leadership was dominated by modernizing the Labour Party; only then could it be the vehicle for modernizing Britain. Already much has been done. Our constitution has been rewritten; our relations with the trade unions have been changed; our democratic structures have been renewed. We are opening up the party so that members can play a much greater part in policy making. Many more people have been attracted to join and the party is in touch with the voters.

In 1945, Labour was truly representative of the nation as a whole. In 1964, it summoned up a spirit of national progress. Today I want the party to capture the spirit of national renewal. We need new thinking because the old, all-embracing ideologies have given way to a more complex, uncertain world. Labour is now in a position to offer that leadership. We have as members the self-employed and the unemployed, small business people and their customers, managers and workers, home owners and council tenants, skilled engineers as well as skilled doctors and teachers. In touch with the communities we want to serve, we can articulate the realities of daily life, and show how it can be improved.

VALUES

My politics is in essence quite simple: it is rooted in my values. Values provide a compass with which to navigate one's way through the political jungle. They help define the objectives and character not only of political parties but also of society.

My value system is based on a belief about individuals and the society in which they live. It is only in a strong and active community that the individual thrives. People must have a stake in society – the essence of social justice. They need to work together for what they cannot achieve alone. And they should all fulfil responsibilities to the wider community. These are the principles of practical and popular socialism championed by Keir Hardie and Clement Attlee. And they are the source of Labour's enduring appeal.

I have always thought that its underlying system of values was one of the Labour Party's greatest strengths. It is what makes many people join the party in the first place. The rejection of injustice, the commitment to solidarity and democracy, the embrace of mutual responsibility motivate members of the Labour Party and resonate in the country. The modernization of Labour has been in part about trying to get the party back to these traditional values and removing from it the dead weight of an ideology which had very little to do with its basic purpose.

What happened to the Labour Party in the late 1970s and early 1980s is that its intellectual temple was stormed and captured by a generation of politicians and academics who thought that values and concepts like community and social justice were too weak to guide the party. Since the 1950s, Left and Right, in the party and in politics more generally, were defined by the battle for state control of industry. As a result, the party went through a period when, because for many it justified itself solely in terms of nationalization, it became divorced from the people it claimed to represent and at the same time subjected itself to continual debate about betrayal. Tragically, it turned its back on an entire strain of thinking within the Labour Party – the tradition of ethical socialism. Yet it is socialism as ethics which has stood the test of time: if it teaches us nothing else, experience in Eastern Europe should teach us that.

With the revision of Clause IV, the Labour Party has reclaimed its basic values. We say that socialism is based on the moral assertion that individuals are interdependent, that they owe duties to one another as well as themselves, and that power, wealth and opportunity should be held by the many not the few. This moral credo shows itself in our practical commitment to a mixed economy, with public and private sectors both working in the public interest, a fair society that is judged by the condition of the weak as well as the strong, a more democratic politics that diffuses power, and a realization that we must conserve the environment for the benefit of future generations. I sum it up by saying that we need a society in which ambition is matched by compassion, success by social justice, and rewards by responsibility.

For all the so-called radicalism of the Thatcherites, they wanted not to break up the establishment but to buy it out. Their recipe has not worked. They have cut public spending on investment, but the result is higher taxes to pay for higher spending on the costs of economic failure. They have privatized utilities, but created powerful and unaccountable private monopolies in the process. They said markets would overcome the failures of government, but they created the most centralized and heavy-handed state in peacetime history.

Radical politics, by contrast, is about giving many more people the opportunity to share in the nation's wealth and power. In John Smith's words, it is about developing 'the extraordinary potential of ordinary people'. Labour has always succeeded when it has been the party of popular aspiration and opportunity. In the end, the Tories remain the party of privilege, and as long as that basic dividing line exists, we will be speaking to the needs of the majority in Britain.

ONE NATION

The best politics always aspires to the creation of a country which feels itself as a cohesive and united unit, where there is a strong sense of purpose and justice and where people have obligations to each other as well as to themselves.

For far too long we have defined ourselves as a nation not by what unites us but by what divides us. We have a class-ridden and unequal society; a social fabric which is tattered and torn; and a politics where centralization and secrecy drives out democracy and accountability. The majority of Britons are insecure and unsure of their future. We still have two education systems – one public, one private. We have what amounts to a new 'underclass', cut off and alienated from society.

Part of our job is to ensure that the people frozen out of Tory Britain are brought in from the cold, their talents used, their potential developed. But citizenship is about duties as well as rights. The freedoms won by ordinary people over the last hundred years are what makes this a civilized society today. T. H. Marshall described the process as the century-by-century accretion of civil, political and social rights. The assumptions of hierarchy, deference and status are broken down, and progress to full citizenship is gradually achieved. But full citizenship requires that people take on new responsibilities too.

That is why I talk of the need to build a new social order in which there is respect for both rights and responsibilities. Not the old social order of hierarchy and repression, but a new one that combines freedom and responsibility in a modern way. In the 1970s and the early 1980s, the Left sometimes spoke as though it was possible to divorce rights from responsibilities. It was in a way a social forerunner of the economic individualism of the new Right. It rightly fought for racial and sexual equality but it appeared to ignore individual responsibility and the need for family stability. I believe that was an aberration.

When we talk about strong families, responsibility and duty we are not aping the Tories but recapturing values in which our forebears and supporters believe. Similarly when we talk about being tough on crime and tough on the causes of crime, it is a message warmly welcomed in housing estates across the land, where people, often trapped by poverty or unemployment, are tormented by criminal behaviour, antisocial or violent neighbours, and drugs. This is not a Tory agenda, but a Labour one. And in a world of massive change – economic, social, political – it is more important than ever, because without it, people become victims of change not masters of it.

The Conservatives have failed to provide security for this new world. In fact, they have fought to use insecurity as the only spur to progress. Their economic liberalism has often lapsed into greed, selfishness and moral irresponsibility, while much of what they have done in power has actually helped accelerate social breakdown.

The only way to rebuild social order and stability is through strong values, socially shared, inculcated through individuals, family, government and the institutions of civil society. This is not a lurch into authoritarianism or an attempt to impose a regressive morality. It is, in fact, about justice and fairness, freedom and responsibility. The strong and powerful can protect themselves. Those who lose most through absence of rules are the weak and vulnerable. Unless we act together, the rewards will be hoarded at the top.

PATRIOTISM OF THE LEFT

It was always short-sighted of the Labour Party to allow the Conservatives to wrap themselves in the national flag and to monopolize and distort the idea of patriotism. Now they run the government not for the nation but in the narrow interests of their party, as their behaviour over the Nolan Committee report on corruption in parliament, their policy over the European Union and the partisan 1995 Queen's Speech demonstrates.

In 1945 and in 1964 Labour was the party which brought the nation together and gave it a sense of purpose. In the party's publication *The Spirit of 1945*, there is a letter from a colonel writing home at the end of the war. He predicted that the Labour Party would win by a landslide because, in contrast to the Tories who represented only the 'moneyed interests', Labour was for the 'common man'. It is this idea of the Labour Party as the party of the people, as an inclusive, one nation party, reaching out to people and bringing them together which is so relevant today.

The concept of one nation is powerfully patriotic. When Michael Portillo exploited the professionalism and bravery of the SAS and tried to whip up anti-European feelings at the Conservative Party conference in October 1995, he revealed not patriotism but xenophobic nationalism. Not surprisingly it was deeply resented by many people in the armed forces. Patriotism is about pride in British achievements, in the National Health Service, in the sciences and the arts as well as in the professionalism of our forces, but it is also about a belief in the capacity of the British people to improve themselves and be a force for good, by deed and example, in the wider world. The carer who gives up her time to look after elderly people, the committed teacher who improves standards at school, the devoted civil servant who provides a service to the public, the business executive who wins export orders by developing new products – that too is patriotism. A country with high ambitions and high ideals for itself but also outward looking and tolerant of others: that is patriotism for the new millennium.

NEW LABOUR – NEW BRITAIN

Today's Labour Party – 'New Labour' – is the heir to a proud tradition in the party's history. The 1945 government combined practicality and idealism in equal measure. It changed Britain in a way that was relevant to the postwar world. It was 'new' Labour. In 1964, Harold Wilson was a modernizer, as his speeches and programme demonstrate. But despite the considerable achievements of that government he was unable to carry through his project in full. The Wilson government did not fully succeed in modernizing the economy or establishing Labour as the natural party of government. Without change within the party there was bound to be a tension between what he wanted to do and the culture and politics of the party that had to do it. The modernizing edge was blunted.

In the 1990s, a renewed Labour Party is in a much stronger position to lead national renewal. I would highlight four key issues that will be of lasting importance to this country: the creation of a stakeholder economy based on the contribution of the many and not the few; the rebuilding of social cohesion and social justice; the dismantling of unaccountable power, vested interests and class hierarchies; and a new role for Britain in the wider world, and in Europe in particular.

Our economic performance determines the way we can afford to live. But today, four years on from the last recession, we are suffering from the long-term neglect of economic fundamentals. The failure of economic management has caused the Tory government's failure on employment, spending and tax. We have slipped from thirteenth to eighteenth in the world prosperity league because of our failure to modernize and invest.

I believe in a 'stakeholder economy' in which everyone has the opportunity to succeed and everyone the responsibility to contribute. It is based on the idea that unless we mobilize the efforts and talents of the whole population, we will fail to achieve our economic potential, and continue to fall behind. A stakeholder economy is one in which opportunity is extended, merit rewarded and no group of individuals locked out.

In a global economy, transformed by a revolution in the way we work and communicate, the opportunities are great but so are the risks. If a few prosper but the majority suffer, then the country will fail to stem its economic decline. The old ways will not work, and we should not be afraid of new ways of looking at things. The stakeholder economy is a new way for the left-of-centre to look at the creation of wealth, rather than just its distribution. It is an economic rationale for a fairer and stronger society. For Labour, it provides a unifying theme for the policies which we have already got, and a framework for thinking about policy development in the future.

A stakeholder economy has as its foundation the economic stability that is necessary to plan and invest. That is why we are committed to balancing the government books over the cycle, and borrowing only for investment. It requires more investment and better investment – notably capital spending through public–private partnership to regenerate our infrastructure, investment by industry, funded by patient and committed provision of capital from the financial sector, and we need to make the most of new technology, not just because industries like telecommunications and media are the industries of the future, but because all organizations can become more productive by using the enormous advances in technology.

Our greatest investment should be in education and skills. We have always offered high-class education to those at the top, but education and training for the majority has been inadequate. The rise in higher education participation is a welcome first step, though we need a more equitable and secure funding regime for the future. But in truth, the knowledge race has only just begun. There are 60 million undergraduates in India; South Korea has 80 per cent of eighteen-year-olds reaching university entrance standard; and yet in Britain millions have trouble with basic reading and writing. To develop the capabilities of our people, we will need to combine reform and vision in education. Reform means a new combination of pressure and support in schools, so children and teachers are stretched to achieve all they can and give all they can. The best local authorities are already pioneering personalized learning in primary schools, weekend schools, new links with the world of work. We need to build on them but we need a national lead as well. Hence Labour's proposals for wiring up schools, libraries and hospitals, and for developing plans to give every child access to a laptop computer. We also need to open up the world of learning to more people already in work. We are well on the way to the development of Individual Learning Accounts and we are proposing a University for Industry – exciting initiatives for the information age.

With investment and education comes partnership at work – industrial relations that help employers and employees join their common interests and resolve their differences. The foundation of that partnership must be minimum standards of pay and conditions. But it means too a culture of respect, trust, cooperation and team-working that is essential to productive and competitive industry. That partnership can then stretch to cooperation between government and business in regional development, infrastructure, science and innovation and technology.

The second pillar is the rebuilding of social cohesion in Britain. The counterpart of a stakeholder economy is a stakeholder society. Social justice is inconceivable while millions of people have no stake in society. That is why we have placed such stress on tackling unemployment, and especially long-term unemployment, which is the cause of social decay and disintegration in many communities. Our objective is not to keep people on benefit but to give people the financial independence that comes from having a job. The world has changed enormously since the Beveridge Report of 1942, which formed the basis of our social security legislation – unemployment is often long-term, women go out to work, part-time work must be properly recognized. We need a new settlement on work and welfare for a new age, where opportunity and responsibility go together. If we can substantially reduce unemployment we will bring hope to the unemployed but also relief to those left paying for it.

One nation also means building security for a new age. In relation to pensions for example, the old assumption that all pensioners were penniless without state help is obviously wrong. The rise of second and third private pensions needs to be recognized. That is why we are looking at the Commission on Social Justice's innovative idea of a Minimum Pension Guarantee for pensioners, that integrates tax and benefits and effectively abolishes the stigmatizing and ineffective means test.

But security is not just about old age and unemployment. It is about freedom from the fear of crime, and freedom from the fear that if one becomes ill the health service will not be in a position to provide the necessary care. Crime has always been a Labour issue. Apart from anything else, it is often Labour voters who are the most persistent victims of crime. That is why it is so ironic that the Conservatives claimed to be the party of law and order. They have always offered more in the way of rhetoric than solutions.

On health, the challenge is slightly different. Labour is justly proud of the NHS. It is the most visible symbol of popular socialism. Under the Tories, it is direly threatened. Privatization is not just on the agenda. It is happening. Academics who saw merit in some of the government's reforms also say that the private finance initiative may be the backdoor route to large-scale privatization of clinical services. Labour has to counter the Tories by making health a major issue at the next election, and also by promoting our own ideas for reform, detailed in a policy paper agreed at the 1995 conference. The NHS may have been battered in the Tory years, but it has survived. Labour's job will be to revive it for the next century, devolving power downwards to hospitals and doctors and nurses but setting it within a service that is cooperating and not competing as if it were a commercial enterprise operating in the marketplace.

The third area is political reform and modernization, to make our government fit for the twenty-first century. If we want to create an active civil society, the system of government has to be one that shares power and responsibility with the people. Centralized government, such as we have in Britain, is inefficient, unjust and fails to give people power over their lives. Decentralization of government is essential if power, wealth and opportunity is to be in the hands of the many rather than the few. Devolving power and democratizing power is an idea whose time has come.

There is no place for hereditary voting in the House of Lords. There should be no assumption of government secrecy, which is why a Freedom of Information Act is essential. We have made clear our proposals for a Scottish Parliament and a Welsh Assembly. London, our great capital, will be run by a directly elected authority like any other capital. If, in time, the regions of England want a greater say in their health, education, police and transport, then that too can come. And there should be no scope for the abuse of people's rights, which is why we are committed to the incorporation of the European Convention on Human Rights into British law. The trust that people had in government fifty years ago no longer exists, which is why political renewal is integral to economic and social renewal.

One of the keys will be the rebirth of accountable local government. The concentration of power in Whitehall has been one of the most harmful consequences of the sixteen years of Tory rule. But despite the pressures on them, many

Labour local councils have pioneered excellent innovations in service delivery, and at the same time turned themselves into the catalysts of local renewal, working with the business sector, voluntary organizations and the local community to improve the economic and social environment. The good work they have done – from job creation and economic development, to education reform, to leisure and other public services – will be an enormous source of expertise and good practice for a future Labour government.

Institutional reform will not revive faith in politics in and of itself, but it will help. To be fair, disillusion with politics is not just a British phenomenon, but a more generalized one. People have learnt not to trust their leaders: they have come to think politicians are in it for what they can get out of it. We want to change this.

It is crucial for the Labour Party to build up trust and then retain it. That is why it is so important only to promise what we can deliver. People often say to me that we must seek to generate excitement with big promises. But that is a recipe for disillusion in government. I want a government that lasts because it is in tune with the people, and because the people understand the priorities and strategies of their government. The reason why we changed the policy on the minimum wage, so that it would be set with reference to the state of the labour market and not according to a preset formula, is that we needed a policy that could be carried out for the good of the country. The policy we now have is the one we shall be proud to adopt in government. The same applies to our position on tax and spending, and also on regional government.

Radical policies require patient politics. The last thing the British people want is for me to say 'vote Labour' because of this and that and then on the Friday afterwards to go back on what I have said. That is why I take an unashamedly long-term view of political strategy as well as economic and social change.

LABOUR AND INTELLECTUALS

That climate of optimism, the belief that we can do better as a nation will, I hope, give those who may have become disillusioned over the last sixteen years, a new lease of life. One of the tasks for the party in the run up to the election and beyond is to start building a common thread between the ideas of academics, thinkers and intellectuals on what Labour is trying to do. I believe Labour's project is exciting and relevant. But it needs to be built, developed, carried forward into new areas. That requires constant engagement in the battle of ideas.

One of the most corrosive aspects of political debate is the use of negative campaigning which makes a rational discussion of serious issues difficult and, to some extent, inhibits our relations with academic thinkers. If somebody connected with the Labour Party writes or says something controversial, then the Tories will misrepresent it, especially during the election campaign, as Labour Party policy. But despite this, we need to address the fact that for far too long the Left has been on the defensive, partly because it confused medium-term policy prescriptions with underlying values and partly because it lost its intellectual self-confidence under the onslaught of the Thatcherite Right. But there is now an emerging common agenda, shared by many thinking people, around two points which I made earlier: first, that we have to navigate our way through a world of great economic, social and political change, and this makes new demands on the policies as well as the style of government; and second that, unless we can unify our country, we will not be able to modernize it in the way that international and domestic change demands. Renewal and cohesion go together; they are two sides of the same coin.

The role of intellectuals and thinkers is crucial to changing the political climate. It is in fact critical to the regeneration of politics. I want Labour to be able to draw on a coalition of thinkers, including people outside the party. We should never forget that the 1945 Labour government's programme was based on a broad centre-left tradition of ideas. In the 1990s, we should be similarly eclectic. The Labour Party has shown that it is back in business and ready to provide the leadership this country needs. We must show the confidence and open-mindedness to join together with others to map out a new course for Britain.

This book is an important part of that process. The insights of the contributions brought together in this volume are testimony to the rebirth of confidence and new thinking on the left-of-centre of British politics. It is reflected in the enormous interest in new Labour around the world. There is a great opportunity in Britain today to show that there is an alternative to the divisive and inefficient remedies of the new Right, and I am determined that we seize it.

PART ONE

Values and Perspectives

1 People and Change

Charles Handy

Independent writer and thinker and a
former Professor of London Business
School, he is author of *The Age of
Unreason* and *The Empty Raincoat*.

The most significant changes that are shaping our world do
not appear in the headlines nor in the news bulletins but
are going on under the surface and over time – the changes
in technology; the changes in organizations; the information
revolution; the fact that we now lead longer and healthier
lives. These changes will have a major impact on the economy, on society and on politics. We will be forced to reshape
the way we organize our lives; we will have to reinvent
what we mean by work; to reinvent education; to reinvent
capitalism; and we will have to reinvent our democracy.

THE DEFINING TRENDS

The pressures of technology are inexorable. It knows no
boundaries. Increasingly what the British can do, somebody
else can do cheaper, not only in Southeast Asia but also
now in Eastern Europe. That means that we cannot rely on
doing the same old things. We have to change the things
we do and perform better and quicker in order to earn our
way in the world. The chairman of a large pharmaceutical

company has a formula to describe the effects of these changes: $1/2 \times 2 \times 3 = P$. This says that any organization, which seeks to remain competitive, plans to employ half as many full-time workers being paid twice as much and producing three times as much as they do today. In other words, there will be good, expensive, productive jobs but there will be many fewer of them. The chairman's formula is fine for productivity but it also means that half the original employees are no longer required – they have to find something else to do. That creates a problem not only for individuals but for society as a whole.

Technological change also means that increasingly brains are replacing brawn. Intelligence, the ability to acquire and apply knowledge and know-how, is becoming the new source of wealth. In January 1992 Microsoft's market value, for a time, passed that of General Motors. In the future, organizations will be based as much on intellectual property as on plant and machinery. This has enormous implications for conventional ideas of company ownership and the way we run our economy.

The organization will look different. In the old days there were layers of people in organizations whose main job was to filter out information – the middle managers and clerks. Now, with communication by telephone or increasingly by computer, they are not needed. Nor do you have to have all the people in the same place at the same time to get the work done. People will no longer really need to commute from all over the southeast to London offices in order to communicate with each other. So offices are no longer going to be designed like factories where everybody can see and meet each other. It's called the 'virtual organization' in the sense that you cannot actually see it but, at the same time, it still functions and delivers products and services.

Linked to the impact of technology are changes in work. What is happening is that increasingly organizations are no longer places of employment but places of organization.

That is to say that they will no longer buy up to fifty years of someone's time and then tell them what to do with it. Nor are they any longer promising to give everybody a guarantee of employment. Organizations will increasingly be made up of a core of well-paid, highly skilled and highly committed employees, while much greater numbers of people will be temporarily employed or organized to work on fixed-term projects. As a consequence, the word 'job' will change its meaning. For most people, a job will no longer mean a role in an organization, but a task, which could often be of quite a short duration.

Indeed by the end of the century over half the working population in Britain is likely to be outside the organization and that is going to make a big difference to people because no longer will a single institution be responsible for their livelihood. Most people will increasingly live 'portfolio' lives. Instead of being in full-time employment and having one employer, they will look for a series of jobs and clients. The disturbing conclusion is that the majority of people will no longer be employed in the old sense.

The impact of the information age of the 1990s can be compared to that of the Gutenberg printing revolution of the fifteenth century. Then for the first time ordinary people could read what before was only available in the monasteries and to the great men of society. The Reformation that followed was no accident. In the same way, we no longer respect leaders and politicians as we used to because we have access to as much information as they do. The good side of that is that we now have the opportunity as citizens to become genuinely involved. The bad side is that you get many more people who refuse to accept authority and this may lead to a breakdown of law and order, to violence, and even war.

The other great transformation is that people are living longer. When I joined my oil company many years ago the average life expectancy beyond retirement was eighteen months; nowadays it is already eighteen years and getting longer. Most people can expect to enjoy twenty to twenty-five years of healthy active life after they leave full-time work. The problem is that most people do not know what to do with this extension of life. It should be a blessing but it becomes a problem. Many people, for instance, are worried about how to finance their extra old age.

MANAGING OUR DESTINIES

These changes could be good for us. But, because they upset the way we live, many people think that they are bad. If we are to get the best out of this new situation, we have to unlearn – unlearn many of the old structures of society and certainties of organization, of who has authority and to whom we should listen. In their place, we have to take responsibility for our own destinies.

Taking responsibility for your own destiny may be exciting – and financially rewarding – for those who are used to it, like the professional classes, or those who are trained to do it, like the so-called 'symbolic analysts', those who deal with numbers and ideas, problems and words. But the majority, those who have been used to working for an organization, who have been happy to accept authority and to allow someone to arrange their lives, will find life very confusing. My worry is that we could end up with an even more divided society – the fortunate minority, the knowledge workers, the professionals and the managers, on the one hand; and, on the other hand, all the rest who will be increasingly impoverished and cut off from the opportunities of this new world.

The idea of taking more responsibility for your life is not a right-wing idea. In fact it is not a political ideology at all; it is something that is going to happen, whether we like it or not. But what we have to do is to ensure that everybody benefits. The market by itself will not – and cannot – provide all the answers. The market is fine if you are only worried with getting the best value for your buck. The market does not concern itself with ensuring that society as a whole is better off.

That is a task for government and other organizations. For example, there could be a new role for the unions. I no longer believe that the trade unions will be there in the future as the pay bargainers for large collections of workers around the country, because more and more employees, even in large companies, will be on individual contracts. What people want is help in taking charge of their destinies – help with education, with looking after money, with drawing up contracts. Those who are outside will need assistance even more than those inside organizations – unions ought to consider making them associate members. If they are to survive, unions will have to become like professional associations or agencies.

But it is government to whom most people will have to turn for help. The first duty of government is to tell the people the truth about what is happening. The second is to equip people to manage their own lives – which means a more effective education system.

RESHAPING EDUCATION

Education is crucial. If you accept the premise that we are increasingly going to have to look for a series of tasks or jobs rather than handing over our lives to some organization, what that implies is that firstly we will all have to have some skills that we can sell to our clients and secondly that we have to be equipped to cope with life. We need an educational system that actually prepares us for living in the real world – and then helps us to change ourselves when we have to change.

The task of education is to develop competences and capabilities as much as to impart knowledge. Education should be more about learning 'how' than about knowing 'things'. With the information revolution, all the information that you actually need to know is available to you, so why bother to learn it. The real educational questions are how to obtain access to that information, what to do with the information, how to turn that information into something that is useful to other people, and how to relate to other people so that the information can be sold or imparted to them.

Despite some improvements, our education system still needs major changes. I once asked a professor of English at Cambridge University how he helped prepare his highly qualified students to 'run the country'. The professor replied: 'But they come here to read English. And that is exactly what they do. The rest they pick up in the streets, I suppose.' Such a *laissez faire* attitude to the practical side of living will do us no good in the future. We also need to change the basis of examinations which are currently about testing how much you have acquired in terms of knowledge at certain stages. Instead there should be certificates of competences across a range of subjects which pupils sit when they are ready. Very few people fail a music exam. That does not mean the standard is low. It does mean that they only take it when they are ready to pass it. We have to understand that there are different types of intelligence – spatial, creative, interpersonal (or the ability to get on with people) as well as factual and analytical. The duty of every school should be to discover what each person's intelligences are, to provide help to develop them and then to ensure that every pupil leaves school with a portfolio of accredited competences.

Investing in education is the only effective way of ensuring that the majority are not excluded from the new information society. If people are going to shape their own destinies, then we shall have to spend money to help them do it. I would much rather invest in people rather than support them, though, of course, you have to support them while you are investing in their education, especially with the backlog of a lost generation, as well as providing a safety net. However, the priority for government is to put money into education conceived in the broadest possible way, to open opportunities for all. There should be extra resources going into inner-city schools, so that they are staffed by more and better paid teachers. Technology can help enormously – what a difference it would make if there really was a computer on the desk of every five-year-old.

As someone who was involved in the creation of the Open Business School (now the largest Business School in Europe), I am a passionate supporter of the idea of lifetime education. The 'information revolution' gives us a new opportunity to build on the success of the Open University. But the first thing we have to do is to create the sense that if you invest in yourself it is much better than investing in anything else, even in property. We should learn from other societies like Germany and Japan, and even more so from the catch-up economies of South Korea, Singapore and Taiwan where it is said that 50 per cent of the population are either teachers or students.

REFORMING CAPITALISM

We need to guard against triumphalist claims for Anglo-American capitalism. There is a hole in the heart of our capitalism. Communism had something we do not have. It had a cause. But Communism had a cause without an effective mechanism: Capitalism has an effective mechanism – the market – but no cause. It was Adam Smith in his *A Theory of Moral Sentiments* who argued that 'sympathy' was the basis of a civilized society. In my view markets only work well in the 1990s when they are balanced with a proper concern for others.

A big problem of Anglo-American capitalism is that the

organization is run primarily for the benefit of the shareholders or financiers. This means that the people who work
in these organizations are effectively the instruments of the
financiers. This may result in greater flexibility but the
downside is uncertainty and short-term thinking. Without
adopting all their practices (some of which are overindul-
gent), the British can learn something from the German
and Japanese models of capitalism where the financiers take
second place to the employees and the continuity of the
company. Financiers are entitled to get a fair return for their
money but they do not have the right to bleed the company
dry. In Britain we pay dividends twice as high as in Germany
and three times as high as in Japan.

There should be a middle way. We should think of a
business not as a piece of property owned by someone but
as a living community in which all the members have rights
and whose purpose is continued existence. Companies are
communities of people united by common aspirations rather
than a bundle of assets owned by shareholders. When I
worked for Shell in Borneo it was not the opportunity to
help the shareholders that motivated me; it was the prospect
of doing a reasonable job for the company's customers. In
the increasingly knowledge-based company, the company's
real assets lie in the brains of its employees. It is all the more
important that, as key members of the company community,
they should also have rights. Employees have very few
rights at the moment and financiers have a lot. The balance
should be adjusted. The case for the 'stakeholder' company,
in which all the players have formal rights, is a powerful
one.

There is much to be said for the German social-market
concept. German businessmen may be critical of the high
costs of their industry but they understand that the purpose
of the market should be to serve society as a whole. The
idea of a modified social capitalism should be reinforced by
an analysis of how the economy actually works. In Britain,

as in Germany, there are, in fact, three economies and different rules should apply to each. There is the internationally competitive economy, where prices have to be right, quality has to be high, and where the workforce is cut to the minimum; there is the local service economy which is usually too small for larger outside firms and which can therefore charge more and employ more people; and there is the insulated, basically public sector economy. In this third sector it is a great mistake to let the market forces run riot. In this sector, we should be more concerned with improving outputs – ensuring better quality students come out of our schools, treating more people more quickly in our hospitals, making sure that our roads are well maintained, having more efficient sewerage systems. Without investing in public services, there is an even greater danger of society becoming more unequal and whole chunks being excluded from civil society – with all that means in terms of poverty, crime and even riots.

A NEW SCORE CARD OF SUCCESS

If we are to make a balanced assessment of what defines a healthy society, we need a revised score card of what constitutes success. Economic growth is essential, of course, to spread wealth around but it does not necessarily spread happiness around. A country may have a very successful economy but everybody may be working too hard, the environment may be polluted and the streets may be jammed with traffic.

The United Nations has attempted to construct an international scorecard which goes beyond the conventional GDP and GNP numbers and includes comparative figures on health, safety, the environment, population figures, infant mortality, suicide rates, housing, the amount of holidays and so on. In the United Kingdom, we should publish a companion set of statistics to the national economic accounts which would give people a better understanding of the achievements of their country: Saying that we have a GDP of 3 per cent as opposed to 2 per cent or 1 per cent does not make much impression on people, especially as it appears to be only the top 20 per cent who are actually growing richer. But what they really want to know is whether the environment is improving, the streets safer and cleaner, transport more efficient and their children are getting a better education. These are things that matter to people and they need to be measured and compared with other countries' statistics. We may need economic growth to achieve them but we should be clear that this growth is the means and not the end in itself.

More fundamentally, there must be more to life than being a cog in some kind of machinery. In a sane society, there must be a point to life – a sense of continuity, a sense of contribution, a sense of connection.

At a time of great change, a sense of continuity is very important. People need to see themselves as part of a train of history: There was a before, there is a now and there will be a hereafter. I call it 'cathedral philosophy', the thinking behind the people who designed and built the great cathedrals, knowing that they would never live long enough to see them completed. We too must be able to build for the future. It is encouraging that RISC, the International Research Institute for Social Change, reports from its recent surveys that 'we can witness an increasing sense of responsibility towards the flux of history, lending a greater recognition of the importance of both past and future generally'.

A sense of contribution is also vital. If you ask people towards the end of their lives, of what they feel most proud, it is not so much the money they earned, it is the contribution which they were able to make – a contribution to something or somebody else which gave them a reason for their existence. People want to be able to feel the justified satisfaction that comes from work well done or constructive involvement in their communities.

Pascal once remarked that all the troubles in the world are down to the fact that a man cannot sit in a room alone. But it is natural that we should want to get out and belong to something – to a community. There are three main sorts of community, all of which are to more or less extent under threat – work, family and place. We need to take great care that the community of work does not disintegrate so far that more than half the people do not belong anywhere. Hence the argument for both work organizations and trade unions having a kind of associate membership, to provide some sense of belonging.

The family has changed: it is not necessarily the same nuclear family that it was fifteen to twenty years ago. But people must still have a community of 'kith and kin' to whom they can turn. In an increasingly contractual society, a mutual commitment which goes beyond the call of duty remains essential.

It was Disraeli who said that 'Modern society has no neighbours'. Loneliness may be the real disease of the next century, as we live alone, work alone and play alone. Knowing your neighbours is one way to break down this feeling of isolation. It also is more likely to lead to mutual respect and caring. So if people are to have a sense of belonging, they must be linked to their local communities and neighbourhoods. Without these three senses people feel lost and rudderless. It should be our particular care to restore and foster these senses whenever and wherever possible.

THE FEDERAL SOLUTION

An important reason why politicians have become unpopular is because the rulers have become too remote from the ruled. The answer is to make government more local. The British could learn from the idea of federalism. It is a tragedy that in Britain we talk about federalism as though it was designed to create a powerful, centralizing state. In fact, it is a total misunderstanding of what federalism is about. Federalism is basically a negotiated balance between big and small – small where things matter to be small and big when big counts. In a federal state, the smaller units, the regions or *Länder*, are not so much giving up sovereignty but allowing the centre to exercise certain powers on their behalf.

If you look at business, you find that it is going federal, because smaller units are more flexible, more responsive to local needs and people like working for them. On the other hand, there are also arguments for being big – the pharmaceutical companies, for example, are now merging in order to give their research more clout. In the same way, in defence, foreign policy and trade negotiations, size is also relevant. If you are going to compete with America, or Japan, or the Far East, then it has to be on the scale of Europe. Other powers are still best exercised at national level. It is all a matter of negotiation and balance.

A dose of federalism would revive democracy. Only by making government more local and giving local communities some power would respect for it be increased. People would be more prepared to pay taxes if they could actually see what the money raised is spent on and they would become more involved if more decisions were taken locally. There is a key role for the city. The city is an understandable focus of loyalty and enthusiasm. People will beaver away for Glasgow, for Birmingham, for Manchester in a way they will not for the nation state.

We should be realistic about the role of democratic politicians. We cannot expect them to be prophets or philosopher kings. If they get too far ahead, people will say that they are being unrealistic or talking idealistic nonsense. It is therefore difficult for politicians to strike a totally original note. Their task is to articulate, in the way Mrs Thatcher did and Tony Blair is now doing, the aspirations of the people. However, I think that independent or free-standing thinkers have their part to play. Their job is to come up with views of how the world is going or ought to go and put them in language that people can understand. If these views grab politicians' imagination, then the politicians should pick them up and run with them.

2 Family and Work

Patricia Hewitt

Director of Research for Andersen
Consultants, she has been a member
of the Social Justice Commission and
deputy director of the Institute for Public
Policy Research.

In the past, politicians on the Left have often felt uncomfortable talking about the family. In 1988 Deborah Mattinson and I carried out a major piece of research on women's political attitudes for the Labour Party (subsequently published by the Fabian Society as *Women's Votes: The key to winning*), which found that women of all ages were far more likely than men to view politics through the eyes of their family. The then Shadow Cabinet was devastated to discover that many women saw the Labour Party as 'macho' and male-dominated – even to the extent of believing that the Conservatives had more women MPs when the reverse was the case – and acted on our proposals, including increasing the number of women in the Shadow Cabinet. We also took the research to the Labour National Women's Committee and other party groups where a typical reaction was that it was patronizing to say that women were primarily interested in the family and politically inappropriate to talk about it. '"The family" is a right-wing concept,' we were told when we said that this was the term most women (and men) use to describe their nearest and dearest!

Superficially, Conservative politicians appear to be more at ease in talking about the family, though their espousal of so-called 'family values' has proved politically embarrassing to them. Their reference point, however, is the traditional nuclear family – married couple, two children, husband at work, wife at home. The Conservative MP, David Willetts, summed up this attitude when he wrote: 'The family, by definition, consists of a married couple and their children.' In reality, while today's typical family includes two parents, both have a job (usually the man full-time, the woman part-time), and a significant and growing minority of families involve children living with only one parent (or dividing their time between parents living apart) or with one parent and a step-parent. A modern family policy, therefore, has to be based not on some idealized and outdated model but on what is really happening to the family and at work.

WHAT THE FAMILY IS FOR

For most people, the commitment to children is central to what families are about. Children are seen as a crucial element in forming a relationship, getting married and keeping the marriage or partnership going.

Most people, however, think of their families not simply as their husband or wife and their children, but as a broader network of blood ties and relationships. Sociological research suggests that different people will put the boundary in different places. Some will say: 'I am responsible only for my husband or wife and my children', while most would probably go further, including their parents but not, perhaps, their brother-in-law or cousins. The common theme is that family are the people on whom you can count and who in turn can count on you.

Going back a century or more, family ties were often more precise and more compelling, with upper-class marriage and family ties defining rights of property, inheritance and succession. More recently, in the 'traditional' nuclear family, marriage involved an exchange between the man's paid and the woman's unpaid labour. It is not surprising that in the 1950s, women generally put 'the man being a good provider' at the top of their list of what made for a good marriage. Today, the exchange of *emotional* support seems to be central to what most people want from marriage or cohabitation; qualities such as 'being my closest friend', 'listening to me' and 'supporting me' have become correspondingly more important in a partner.

The changes taking place within families are real – but they are often exaggerated. Despite the growth in lone parenthood, the fact remains that seven out of ten children in this country are living with both their natural parents, while another one in ten is living with one natural parent and a step-parent. The remaining two in ten are living with only one parent. (These figures are a snapshot: a larger proportion of children will spend *part* of their childhood living with only one parent.)

Just as it is misleading to suggest that the two-parent family is vanishing, it is equally misleading to equate all lone parents with unmarried teenage mothers. They actually form a minority of lone mothers, most of whom had their child(ren) while they were married or cohabiting. It is, nonetheless, worrying that the birth rate amongst teenage women, after dropping steadily from the early 1960s, started to rise again around the mid 1980s. Although there may be several reasons, it is reasonable to assume that the rise in youth unemployment is an important contributory factor. (According to a senior civil servant, Peter Lilley, Secretary of State for Social Security, was once given a presentation in which a map showing the concentration of unmarried teenage mothers was superimposed upon one showing the concentration of youth unemployment. The fit was remarkable.) Young working-class women without a good education, like young working-class men in a similar position, have very little future in the economy bequeathed by Margaret Thatcher. For many of those young women, having a child is the only route to adulthood. Unlike the drug-dealing and crime to which many young men resort, motherhood is a creative role. The conditions in which most teenage mothers find themselves, however, are often damaging and depressing for the mothers and, above all, unlikely to give the children a good start in life. (Perinatal mortality rates and low birthweights are significantly higher amongst babies born to young never-married mothers.)

There is extensive evidence, too, about the impact upon children's educational, emotional and economic results of conflict between parents, and the loss, replacement or absence of a parent. The pattern is, however, far more complex than the simple 'two parents good, one parent bad' rhetoric of the Right. Children of widowed mothers do better, on some scores, than children of lasting two-parent families. The children most likely to end up involved in crime are the sons of fathers who are themselves convicted criminals. Children of never-married mothers seem to do better than those of separated or divorced parents. Conflict and violence within the marriage – often although not necessarily leading to a divorce – it also associated with lower educational and other outcomes in later life. And the worst outcomes are clearly linked with a series of transitions between different kinds of families, usually involving a succession of (married or cohabiting) step-fathers. Common sense as well as research suggests that much of the problem arises from the loss and rejection felt by the child in the parents' separation and divorce – feelings which (unlike those of bereavement) usually go unacknowledged and unsupported by the wider community – and by the added insecurity which is likely to follow from not one but a whole succession of new 'step' relationships.

If, therefore, changes within families present difficulties

for children – as they clearly do – what should government do? We need to start by recognizing that, in every industrialized country, women's economic emancipation (incomplete but significantly advanced compared with the 1950s) not only transforms the traditional family – from one earner to two earners – but is also associated with a rise in divorce (in Britain, the number of people divorcing per 1000 of the married population now stands at 13.9, 14 per cent higher than a decade ago), a postponement of marriage and childbearing, a growth in cohabitation, a growth in lone parenthood and a growth in the number of women who will never have children.

No government, however, could or should hope to turn back the clock on women claiming the rights of citizenship, the right to education, the right to employment, the right to economic independence. We can, therefore, expect to see changes in fertility and family forms continue, although not necessarily as fast as in the last twenty years. Indeed, there is a possibility that, as part of a new awareness of the values of community and social responsibility, there may be a greater concern about parents' responsibilities towards their children. That, in turn, could lead people to invest greater efforts to make the marriage or the relationship work at least until the children are grown up and, if it fails, to handle the separation or divorce in a way which is least distressing to the children. But government cannot *compel* such a change in attitudes and behaviours although, as I argue below, it can help to influence the climate of opinion about parents' responsibilities.

THE CHANGING DIVISION OF LABOUR

Beveridge built his vision of the welfare state upon the foundation of full-time, lifetime employment for men. He was able to assume that in most cases male employment would deliver a wage that was going to be adequate to maintain the family, providing there were also child allowances. He also assumed that women, once they got married and had children, would stay at home. In other words, the Beveridge system was built upon a division of labour with the man earning the 'family wage' from his employment and the woman looking after the child and the home.

The Beveridge view, which corresponded to the position of the majority of families in the 1950s, had a deep hold on Labour thinking. As late as the 1980s, it was obvious that, when many Labour politicians talked about full employment, it was full-time, lifetime work for men which they had in mind. They tended to dismiss increases in part-time work, failing to acknowledge that such work provided employment opportunities for women – usually women who did not wish to work full-time at that stage in their lives. Whether consciously or unconsciously, they appeared to believe either that a woman's place was in the home or that, if she did have a job, it should be full-time.

In the 1990s, these assumptions about the nature of employment and the division of labour within the family have broken down. Indeed, the notion of the 'family wage' was eroded by the equal pay legislation of the 1970s, since the idea that men should be paid more than women because it is their wage which supports the family is wholly incompatible with the principle of equal pay for work of equal value.

Even more important, market forces have been transforming the demand for labour. The globalization of the economy and technological change have drastically cut the demand for male labour, a phenomenon we can observe throughout the industrialized world but which has gone faster and further in this country. A whole generation of skilled working-class men in their forties and fifties have been thrown out of their jobs in such industries as mining, steel, shipbuilding and motor manufacturing. And these kind of jobs are no longer there to provide employment for their sons. The assumption of full-time, lifetime male employment supporting the family has been undermined by high levels of male unemployment and – for those in work – by wages which are generally inadequate to support the standards of living to which most families now aspire.

Despite the equal pay and sex discrimination laws, we still live in a 'gendered' labour market. While male employment has been declining, the expansion of the service sector has created new jobs, many of them part-time, which continue to be seen by employers and most employees alike as being better suited to women. (One should note, however, that a majority of cases to the Equal Opportunities Commission are now brought by men who, in their turn, are challenging sex stereotypes in the job market.) The growth of professional and white collar administrative jobs has also been to the advantage of women who now form half of the graduates in law, accounting and medicine. Current predictions are that the majority of new jobs created between now and the turn of the century, like the majority of jobs created over the last five to ten years, will be taken by women, mainly those with high educational qualifications. In the last thirty years, therefore, we have moved from a workforce that was largely industrial, male and full-time to one where most employment is in the service sector, nearly half of employees are women (a majority in some parts of the country), and a quarter of jobs are part-time.

It is inevitable that these profound economic changes should be reflected within families. The traditional one-earner family, which still underpins our social attitudes and many public policies, is being squeezed out between the two-job family on the one hand and the disturbing increase in the no-job family on the other. In the majority of families with children, both parents have jobs. At the top of the economic ladder are very well-off families with two full-time professionals, often living in London and the southeast. But they are a minority, whose prevalence is often exaggerated by professional journalists who often live in such households. Most two-job families are not at all affluent and may indeed be struggling to make ends meet; generally, the man has a full-time job while the woman works part-time.

At the bottom of the income scale is the 'no-job' family. Whereas a majority of women married to employed men are themselves in a job, the reverse is the case where the man is unemployed. Fifteen years ago, only one in twelve working-age families contained no adult in employment; today, it is one in five. There are three main reasons for this phenomenon. First, in many cases areas of high unemployment for men are also bad for women as well. Secondly, social and family pressures when the man is unemployed sometimes make it easier for the woman not to work. Thirdly, the social security system – with the present Government's heavy reliance upon means-tested benefits – has the perverse effect of penalizing the woman who keeps or takes a job while her partner is unemployed. If the woman takes a job for less than 16 hours a week, then (after once her earnings go over the disregarded amount) her husband's benefit is cut by £1 for every £1 she earns. If she works for sixteen hours or more, she could in theory move the family off income support and onto family credit. But family credit, unlike income support, offers no help with the mortgage and very few women earn enough to pay the mortgage on their own. Even where the family are tenants not home-buyers, the insecurity and administrative difficulties in moving onto family credit help to account for its relatively low take-up.

RENEGOTIATING THE FAMILY CONTRACT

In the traditional nuclear family, the division of labour between the partners was quite clear. Today, each family has to decide how to combine earning a living with bringing up children, a peculiarly difficult challenge when men and women often have very different ideas about how they contribute to the family; when there are no longer generally accepted conventions for what each partner should do; and when employment structures and the social security system generally restrict rather than expand people's choice. It is significant that one of the most common reasons women give for the breakdown of a marriage is that the man has not spent enough time at home. Men, however, often see the time they spend at work as the main contribution of a 'good father' and may increase their working hours when the first child is born, in order to earn more money and replace their partner's earnings. For women, on the other hand, being a good parent – a father as well as a mother – involves spending time at home, providing the practical and emotional care of children, helping to run as well as finance the household.

It is not the job of politicians to tell people how to renegotiate the family contract. But a new family policy could and should focus on the needs of children, and seek to create the conditions in which both men and women can fulfil their responsibilities towards their children. In practical terms, that involves enabling families to make the choices which best suit them about how they balance paid and unpaid work and how they allocate their time.

AGENDA FOR THE FUTURE

Children must be at the heart of a new family policy. Politicians have to tread very carefully indeed when it comes to adults' private lives and private morality, not least because they so often practise 'permissiveness' themselves. But the state, on behalf of society, has an overwhelming interest in the welfare of children: they are, after all, society's future. If we start by understanding children's dependency needs – for stable and committed parenting, a reasonable level of material provision, educational and other opportunities which will help them discover and fulfil their potential, and so on – then we can see the areas where government has a responsibility to act.

Traditionally government regulated relationships between parents and children by regulating marriage: we could assume that they amounted to the same thing. But as more children are born outside marriage, often to cohabiting couples, a gap has opened up between legal institutions and real family life. A century and a half ago in Britain, the legal rights over children were entirely vested in the father. Today, married parents share parental rights and responsibilities. Where the parents are not married, however, the Children Act places parental rights and responsibilities with the mother, even if the parents are cohabiting and the child is registered by both parents. The cohabiting or absent father has to obtain the agreement of the mother – or, in a dispute, the court – before he can share parental rights and duties. Where financial responsibilities are concerned, however, all fathers have been brought into the Child Support Act's net – not as part of any comprehensive redefinition of parental responsibilities, but in order to reduce the cost of lone parents to the Treasury.

The most useful way to make sense of this incoherent legal framework is to start by defining a new statement of parents' legal and moral responsibilities. Once that is done, we need to decide, as a society, whether those responsibilities belong to every parent or only to some. The new Right wants to reinstate marriage as the *only* legal framework for parental responsibilities and rights: the mother could only claim maintenance from the father, and the father could only claim access to the child, if they were married. From the child's point of view, however, every family is a two parent family. Even if the parents have never lived together, or have since separated, the child has a right to know who the other parent is and, where it is possible, to develop and sustain a relationship with him (it usually is 'him').

Recreating the social stigma of illegitimacy, and the material penalties which flowed from it, may persuade some parents to marry who would not otherwise have done so; but it can only deepen the disadvantages suffered by the children who will, inevitably, continue to be born outside marriage. Hence my view that parental responsibilities should be shared equally by all parents, regardless of whether or not they are married. It may be that a parent who has never lived with the child and the other parent should have fewer rights and responsibilities than others, although even that distinction would need very careful justification.

Once agreed, a new definition of parental responsibilities should become a focus for helping parents learn about parenting – one of the most difficult jobs in the world and the one for which we get the least training. Throughout preschool and school provision, we need to teach children generally how to share and cooperate with other people, deal with conflict, negotiate, express feelings and show anger without violence – what the psychotherapist, Susie Orbach, calls 'the curriculum of emotional literacy'. Involving children and their parents in drawing up school behaviour policies and antibullying policies is part of the same approach, based on a recognition that the more children learn to relate to each other, and to adults, in mutually respectful and successful ways, the better parents they will be later on.

In teenage years, preparenthood classes become appropriate, some of the most successful being run by teenage lone mothers themselves. There is also innovative work being done in some young offenders' institutions by probation officers with young men who have committed serious offences and who are already fathers, helping them to become better fathers than they generally had themselves. The statement of parental responsibilities could be used within antenatal classes (for expectant fathers as well as mothers). Practical support for new parents needs also to be expanded. Research in Cambridgeshire has demonstrated, for example, that a modestly expanded health visitor service (with health visitors trained in additional counselling skills) can substantially reduce levels of depression in new mothers. Given what we know about the link between maternal depression in the first weeks and months of the child's life and that child's later ability to learn and relate to others, early investment in supporting parents must be one of the most fruitful we could make.

Inevitably, some relationships will end in separation or divorce. Parenthood, however, is for life and the overriding aim of divorce law should be to minimize the damage and distress to the children's relationship with both their parents. The present Lord Chancellor is therefore right to reform the current law which has given couples a perverse incentive to seek divorce on the basis of adultery or other behaviour, with all the heightened conflict and argument that such divorces often entail, rather than wait for two years' separation to be complete. Lord Mackay's proposed twelve-month waiting period will make divorce more difficult to obtain where there are children, and should ensure (if properly backed up by resources) that divorcing couples can sort out disagreements less adversarially through mediation. Such services must, however, be available also to parents who split up after cohabiting without marriage; their children, just like the children of divorce, need support in ensuring that they keep relationships with both parents.

Since parents also have to earn a living, family policy needs to attend to what goes on in the workplace. The traditional male model of full-time, lifetime employment depended upon the presence of a wife and mother at home. In the 1970s, the implicit assumption of equal opportunities campaigners was that, in order to do the same jobs as men, women should be enabled to work the same hours as men. Enabling women to see as little of their children as men have traditionally done, however, is unlikely to be best for children (although high-quality substitute childcare may be positively beneficial for children, the poor-quality care, which is often all that parents can find or afford, is clearly damaging). In any case, most parents want to look after their children themselves.

Different parents, however, will want to arrange how they care for their children, and how they earn the family finances, in different ways. Greater choice requires, in turn, more flexible structures in the community, at school and at work. There is clearly an unmet demand from parents for under-fives' services, sometimes to enable the mother to take a job but also to extend the child's experience beyond the home. Those services need to be organized so that they can meet the different needs of children whose parents work part-time, or full-time, or not at all.

But the need for childcare support does not end when the child goes to school. In Australia, for example, most schools offer preschool clubs, including breakfast, from 8 a.m. or earlier because that is when many parents go to work. Similarly, after-school clubs provide a safe place for children whose parents cannot get back from work mid-afternoon. Extending the school day – not with longer lessons, but with other activities for children – does not mean that policy-makers are assuming that all parents should, or want to, work full-time, but is a way instead of extending the choices available to parents – while ensuring that children whose parents need to work full-time do not end up as latchkey kids.

For parents who have no earnings at all – the 'no-job' families – the first priority is employment. A jobs programme, particularly including measures for the long-term unemployed, will prove one of the most effective antipoverty and pro-family policies. But we also need a strategy for the reform of working hours. In most industrialized countries, especially in Scandinavia, childcare policy explicitly includes time off for parents – enhanced maternity leave, paternity leave, parental leave and time off when children are ill – as well as nurseries for children. A right to unpaid leave for parents of young children would recognize that many parents, especially women, do take unpaid time off but then have no automatic right to come back to their employment.

Radical reform of working time could seize the opportunity presented by economic changes which are, in any case, transforming the traditional model of full-time work. Trade unions have often led the way in bargaining about time as well as money. For example, over ten years ago the Inland Revenue Staff Federation negotiated a deal with the Inland Revenue whereby full-time revenue officers could opt for shorter working hours. Greater flexibility has not only helped meet the needs of employees with children, or elderly dependants, or a need for further education and training, but has enabled management to staff for 'peaks' and 'troughs' in the workload without resorting to casual and temporary staff.

Another example is offered by British Airways' response to the recession. The company wanted to reduce its work-force, but without resorting to redundancies. Instead, BA offered many of their full-time employees the option of reducing their hours, while keeping the same hourly pay, conditions, access to training, pension fund membership and so on. Employees in their fifties were guaranteed a pension based on full-time instead of part-time earnings, while all volunteers were offered a cash bonus. Both the company and workers gained. Not only did BA avoid the financial cost of redundancies, but the option proved so popular with employees that the cash bonus proved no longer necessary. Government could well take the BA model as best practice and change redundancy laws so that companies have to offer voluntary reductions in working hours before imposing redundancies. Reducing *over*-employment – by enabling people who want to work shorter hours to do so – will not solve the problem of *un*employment, but it is an essential part of an effective jobs programme.

Similarly the social security system needs to be reformed to remove the barriers which confront those without employment. The perverse effects of means-tested benefits cannot be removed within a system of means testing which inevitably depends upon a test of household income. Nonetheless, there are some immediate changes which could be made, for instance allowing an income support claimant who takes a job to keep their benefit until the wage is paid and family credit calculated. Following an Irish initiative, 'passported' benefits – such as free school meals – should continue to be paid for, say, the first year. Labour could also learn from the Australian benefits system, which combines a far more generous disregard for the partner's earnings with a much lower benefit withdrawal rate. (It is important to note, however, that for historical reasons, Australian benefits have always been means-tested, but at a far higher rate than in the UK and without the associated problems of stigma and low take-up.)

The longer-term solution, proposed by the Commission on Social Justice, is to modernize the national insurance system, ensuring that women as well as men earn individual benefits through their individual contributions. In striking contrast to means-tested benefits, national insurance benefits for one person have no effect at all on their partner's earnings. Under a modernized social insurance system, a man who becomes unemployed would receive unemployment insurance for himself and his children; meanwhile, his wife (in receipt of, ideally, a higher child benefit) would have every incentive to keep or take a job. The availability of part-time unemployment benefit for part-time employment would provide a further incentive to the man to take up a part-time job if no full-time job was immediately available. Instead of becoming wholly dependent on income support, the family would stay connected with the local labour market.

Pension schemes – developed to meet the needs of a standard working life (forty years' employment followed by a far shorter period of retirement) – could also be transformed in the light of modern working and family patterns. They could become 'time banks' which would enable people to take time off *before* they retire as well as after. Paid time off could be used to spend more time with children and family, or devoted to education, study and travel.

IN CONCLUSION . . .

A great deal of contemporary debate about 'the breakdown of the family' is acutely frustrating. Authoritarians seem to want to turn the clock back, to make marriage the only approved family form, and (in their more extreme moments) leave unmarried pregnant women with a choice only between abortion and adoption. But those of us who believe that we cannot reverse the social and economic forces which are transforming families – including the changed role and expectations of women – also have to grapple with the effects of family instability upon children, and with the new insecurities in the lives of men as the role of family breadwinner is changed. If we can engage with these new realities, in all their complexity, then I believe we can develop a new family policy which will speak to the needs of men, women and children alike.

3 The Creative Imagination

David Puttnam

An independent film producer, whose
work includes *Chariots of Fire*, *The
Killing Fields* and *The Mission*, he is
chairman of the National Film and
Television School.

'In the times when art was healthy and abundant,' wrote
William Morris, 'all men were more or less artists; that is
to say the instinct for beauty which is inborn in every complete man and woman had such force that the whole body
of craftsmen habitually and without conscious effort made
beautiful things, and the audience for art was nothing short
of the whole people.'

Like so much of Morris's writing I find that brief passage
thoroughly inspiring in its certainty and at the same time
as frustrating as any other glimpse of a utopia that, a hundred years later, seems as intangible as ever. But the absolute
confidence of his statement – the belief that daily life and
work should be, and could be, a source of pleasure and
fulfilment rather than drudgery – has continued to be a
powerful component in the energy of British socialism.

Two generations after Morris, J. M. Keynes, the newly
appointed Chairman of the newly created Arts Council of
a newly elected Labour Government, had this to say: 'We
look forward to a time when the theatre, the concert hall

and the art gallery will be a living element in *everybody's* upbringing, and regular attendance at the theatre and concerts a part of all organized education.'

And a generation on from Keynes, a director of the Gulbenkian Foundation restated that view, placing it emphatically in a larger context of public policy:

> The greatest resource possessed by any nation is the imagination of its people. Imagination nourishes invention, economic advantage, scientific discovery, technological advance, better administration, jobs, communities and a more secure society. The arts are the principal trainers of imagination. They can enrich, not replace the literacy, numeracy, science and technology we need for prosperity.

Why is it that we in Britain find it so *easy* to accord the creative imagination an honoured place in our vision of a prosperous and stable society, yet seem to find it almost impossible to summon up the determination to translate that vision into practical policies?

The policies of the present government are, if anything, heading off in the opposite direction. A recent report by the Royal Society of Arts drew attention to a devastating catalogue of failure in arts education, including the fact that infant pupils in British schools spend less than half the time on art, craft and construction than they did ten years ago; that the number of school-leavers unable to take up rather than turning down places on vocational dance and drama courses because they have been refused a grant has almost doubled over the same period, and that only a quarter of local education authorities have a full complement of advisors and inspectors for each of the four main arts subjects – art, music, drama and dance.

Yet never before has there been such a compelling case for the active engagement of the arts in tackling the economic, educational and social issues that are most pressing today, and are likely to hit us with ever increasing force over the next couple of decades.

There are perhaps three crucial areas of insecurity that confront us as a nation. The first is that we have no commonly agreed strategy in place for sustaining our relative prosperity in an increasingly open and global economy. The second is that we have an education system which is visibly failing; this could not be expressed more graphically than by the observation that the bottom third of British school-leavers would probably not be regarded as employable if the prevailing standards of Korean industry were applied. The third is that the basic fabric of our society appears to be under threat because of a disintegration of shared social values, a quality in the decline of our public life and ever deepening divisions between the haves, the have-nots, and what might be called the haven't-got-enough-to-feel-secure.

It seems to me that the arts or, more properly, that creative instinct which is best fed by the arts and in turn expresses itself most readily in the arts, has a crucial role to play in tackling each of these inextricably intertwined issues and that a combination of determined strategies and practical policies could help to transform both the prospects and the mood of our country over the next couple of decades.

It has become something of a truism to claim that we are now living in an 'information society' whose economic and social lifeblood will be electronic communication carried by means of digital technologies capable of handling ever larger amounts of information at ever-reducing cost. It would be more accurate to say that we find ourselves only at the 'threshold' of this new age because, although the technology already exists, we have scarcely begun to understand the economic and social consequences.

Terry Semel, the Chairman of Warner Bros, recently said of the audio-visual industries, 'We can only be sure of three things. First, everything we know to be true may change. Secondly, if and when it does change it will change rapidly.

Thirdly, he who controls the software – the product – will be the winner.'

That statement seems to me to contain a truth which goes much wider than the film and television industries. Professor Charles Handy has put it differently: 'Intelligence is the new form of property.' As someone who works in the film industry I am frequently treated to the assertion that the movie business is now America's second greatest export. That is not quite true. Intellectual property, in other words copyright, is the United States's second biggest export, and it is simply that American films, television programming and software are amongst the most successful earners and exporters of copyright value.

The information society demands that we redefine and revalue our 'natural resources'. Aneurin Bevan once explained Britain's wealth, self-confidence and power in the world as a function of its being 'an island of coal surrounded by fish'. Neither commodity has proved to be as durable as he supposed. At the end of the twentieth century the coal industry has all but disappeared and the fishing industry would seem to be following close behind. But suppose that today we could describe Britain as 'an island of creativity surrounded by a sea of understanding'? That may not have quite the poetry of Bevan's description but it sounds like a desirable place to be at the dawn of the multimedia age. More importantly, it offers an entirely realistic and achievable goal for Britain. Indeed, both parts of the proposition are already a reality. Without question we remain one of the world's most creative nations, and that 'sea of understanding' is of course our mother tongue. English *is* the language of the information society, the language in which 80 per cent of all electronic texts are stored, in which 80 per cent of the world's business correspondence is conducted; the language which, it is estimated, about a thousand million people either are learning, or *want* to learn as *their* second language. We enter the new millennium with a natural resource potentially every bit as valuable as coal and fish put together!

Whether we continue to live on 'an island of creativity' will, however, depend on how we choose to develop that resource. The key to future success can not simply be a function of the growth of communications technology itself but those multimedia products which can bring it to life. Only the individual and collective creative skills necessary to exploit the technology will give it *real* value.

What is already clear is that, even without the huge advantage of the English language, we possess many of the necessary skills for success. They are in evidence in our television industry, our animation industry, our advertising industry, our music industry. We tend to take these things somewhat for granted, but it is worth drawing attention to their significance. Our animators have won four of the last five Oscars. We are the second largest CD-ROM publishers in the world. Our rock musicians contribute more to the balance of payments than the steel industry. The world's largest electronic games company estimates that 40 per cent of its successful products have been developed by British programmers, (and the electronic games industry at around $10 billion a year is already significantly larger than the world's entire film industry). The audiovisual industries employ about 220,000 people in the UK – considerably more than the number of people making cars and vehicle components. And, unlike the car industry, we already account for 25 per cent of the total European Union audiovisual market, the largest developed market in the world and one which is expected to grow by 300 per cent over the next twenty years. The European Commission White Paper on *Jobs, Competitivity and Growth*, published in December 1993 forecast that information technology and the audiovisual industries were likely to be two of only three strategic economic sectors experiencing major growth in the coming decades.

All these industries are fundamentally dependent on the abilities of writers, designers, actors, musicians, artists, cinematographers, animators and other creative professionals. All of them seem destined to grow, some of them dramatically. All of them are high in added value; they are by nature labour- *and* skills-intensive. If our education and training system fails to nurture and develop those skills in the necessary numbers, the consequence will be wasted opportunities and lost markets on a truly devastating scale. The cultural consequences would be equally devastating, a point I want to return to in a moment.

On the other hand to develop them effectively will require forceful public policies, and financial institutions that are prepared to invest long-term and with relatively high risk. Neither prospect looks certain. There is, perhaps an unease amongst both public policy-makers and investment bankers that these industries, like tourism, are too ephemeral, too fast-moving, too high risk to be taken seriously as part of a stable and sustainable foundation for our national economy. The plain fact is, however, that the most distinguishing single feature that drives the present revolution in communications technologies is *entertainment*. Whatever the purpose or content of the software, whether it is for business, for retailing, for public information or, last but not least, for education and training, the most effective and therefore the most highly valued material is increasingly dependent on the graphic skills, the storytelling techniques, the effects, the music, the marketing strategies, in fact the whole compelling panoply of entertainment. Entertainment is not simply an adjunct of the 'information society'; it is rapidly becoming the dominant force, 'colonizing' the whole world of information to a quite remarkable degree. To the despair of some politicians, and the delight of others, that is as true of the prevailing values of the news media as it is of any other part of the present-day communications spectrum.

Although for some it may raise the haunting spectre of

the final years of the Roman Empire, I believe this driving force of entertainment is by and large to be welcomed. Storytelling, music, dance and drama are the oldest, most developed and effective forms of communication the human race has created. It is only in the relatively recent past that we have consigned them to the margins of public life. The technology of the information society is dependent on 'convergence' – the ability to integrate, by digitization, the previously incompatible media of television, film, computing and telephony. It is not unreasonable to assume that this electronic convergence is a harbinger of a more profound and far-reaching process of social and cultural convergence. We are already beginning to see an end to that seemingly complete divorce between home and work which has characterized our society since the industrial revolution; we are beginning to lose some of the more artificial distinctions between work and leisure; and, as I have been attempting to argue, the new systems of communication are themselves a revolutionary marriage between art and technology. But perhaps the most significant convergence for the information society is that between entertainment and education.

When resources that have traditionally been associated with the best in entertainment are applied to education and training, surprising results begin to flow. Anyone who has tried to learn a foreign language will know that to be able to see and hear people speak on an imaginatively constructed video tape is more effective than sitting alone with a textbook. There is already an abundance of evidence that creative software, matched with the appropriate technology, can radically transform the ability of children and adults to learn and, perhaps more importantly, to understand, to question and explore. This is particularly true in the scientific disciplines where audiovisual products can bring abstract concepts to life in a way that has simply never before been possible.

More than twenty years ago an early pioneer of virtual

reality in the United States wrote, 'A display connected to a digital computer gives us a chance to gain familiarity with concepts not realizable in the physical world. It provides us with a looking glass into a mathematical wonderland.'

As a child at school it never occurred to me for one moment that mathematics might be *any* kind of 'wonderland'. To me, and I suspect most of my classmates, it was not much more than a confusing nightmare. To end that dismal situation for the majority of schoolchildren would be of no small consequence to society, and the evidence is that good software, unlike many conventional textbooks, is an effective teaching tool right across the spectrum of individual ability. That is every bit as true for postschool education and adult training as it is for school-age pupils.

There are two keys to the successful application of this technology. The first, as I have suggested, is that we make available, as a society, the skills, financial resources and widespread awareness of our rich cultural and intellectual heritage to create high-quality content. The second is that the benefits are spread as widely as possible. The opportunity now exists, in a way Lord Keynes could not have foreseen, to make 'regular attendance at the theatre and concerts a part of all organized education'. Indeed, we can do even better than that. A single CD-ROM disk can, for example, make the National Gallery accessible to any school or individual in the country, and offer a commentary on each of the pictures by the foremost expert in the field, or even critical discussion on styles and technique.

Rather than thinking about ways in which this new technology can be absorbed into our education system we need to be thinking about ways in which our education system should adapt to embrace the new possibilities of the 'information society'. If children learn to work and explore on their own, whether at school or, just as likely, on some form of PC at home, the role of the teacher must change to become, in the words of the National Council for

Educational Technology 'the manager rather than the deliverer of learning'. That will become increasingly important as schools find themselves drawn into competition with material available on a screen at home, or purchased from a High Street shop. Education is becoming big business. And partly because of its increasing convergence with the world of entertainment, many of the most powerful global players in the entertainment business are recognizing its vast potential. Educational products can be sold to both institutional and individual consumers. Reversioned, they have access to expanding markets around the world. In the same way that educational publishers have been the steady, consistent profitable earners of the print-publishing world, there is every reason to suppose that the same will be true in this new world of multimedia publishing. One of Hollywood's most influential talent agents recently expressed the view that within ten years the highest paid performers in his industry would not be conventional movie stars at all, but an as yet undiscovered generation of educational presenters.

With their resources and experience, with their stars and their worldwide distribution systems, these giant entertainment corporations will become enormously influential players in the world of education. The consequences of all this are potentially momentous.

As information technology becomes more and more essential to the functioning of our education system, the need for software and support materials is going to grow at a prodigious rate. Suppose that in five years time, or perhaps even less, a school in Britain is confronted with two programme packages – one, untested and relatively expensive made in the UK, and one made in the United States or somewhere on the Pacific rim – tested and proven, cheaper, made to high and attractive production standards and with a full range of support materials and follow-on programmes to accompany it. Which is the hard-pressed 'fund holding' headteacher likely to go for? And what will happen ten years further on when a whole generation of schoolchildren have been through that school using entirely American software designed primarily for the needs and interests of American schoolchildren? This is not some distant prospect; it's already happening: 1995 is likely to be the first year on record in which Britain runs a trade deficit on learning materials, and I'll offer a prize to anyone who can locate a mass produced CD-ROM for children which *doesn't* have an American voice-over!

Before long what will it mean to call ourselves British or, for that matter, European? If we are to resist that future, we have to recognize that education is, in its own right, as big an industry as entertainment. The creative skills that have made Britain such a world leader in the wider field of software production must be brought to bear on the very specific demands of education. This won't happen by itself. It requires that we 'rig' the market, perhaps by using the combined consumer power of the entire school system in the same way that the NHS has provided a rigged market for our pharmaceuticals companies, to the immense benefit of both. Only in that way can we generate the economies of scale and the R&D production budgets that will allow our industry to create materials able to match the visual and dramatic skills of the giant US entertainment corporations while at the same time delivering high educational value.

If only we could become serious about developing this powerful new industry we would enjoy a double win. We can be leading players in one of the most important growth industries in the world, one that generates a demand for skilled creative people and one that, by its nature, is likely to remain highly labour intensive. At the same time we will be creating for our children and young people the best possible opportunities to fulfil their potential in the future. The more they are able to have that expectation of themselves at school the more likely they are to have that same expectation *after* school, with consequent positive demands on our national training structure, and equally positive benefits to our national work force.

Conversely, if we *fail* to take this opportunity, the images, ideas, styles, and attitudes that come to us through our screens, all those elements which are the source of this creative capital we enjoy as a nation, *all* of them will be created elsewhere. We will, in a very real sense be abandoning our future as an identifiable culture as well as that of our children.

It is relatively easy to make the argument that education and training in today's competitive world is straightforward common sense. But the application of common sense to tackle these issues presupposes a measure of common purpose and common values. It requires us to have confidence as a society – in each other, in our abilities and in our future. And despite all our manifest creative talents as a nation, despite the ingenuity of those new communications technologies to which we have access, we have conspicuously failed to sustain basic levels of social support and mutual solidarity which even the most primitive communities have, in the past, taken for granted. The seminal document on the 'information society' produced for the European Commission in 1994 by Commissioner Bangemann spoke of creating new ways of 'living as well as working together'. If this is truly to be an information *society* rather than simply a marketplace full of competing information *companies* then the process of steering its development and sketching out its possibilities must be conducted on the widest possible canvas.

I've already referred to the extent to which the distinctions between home and office, work and leisure, education and entertainment are being broken down. One view of the future has us all 'tele-working' from home; (those of us who *have* work, that is. The unemployed and the elderly will, presumably, be left much as they are today to get on with merely 'tele-watching'). I do not subscribe to that vision. It seems abundantly obvious to me that whether they realize it or not, people go out to work for social as much as economic reasons.

What does seem possible, and is indeed already happening, is that the need to separate living space and recreational space from working space in our cities – a logical and necessary consequence of a time when a great deal of work involved large-scale, noisy, polluting activities – is fast disappearing. The industries in which societies such as ours must excel if we are to prosper in the future are industries which, on the whole, will be comparatively small-scale and non-polluting. They will involve little raw material, relatively little energy, a very large application of human skill and ingenuity.

And because of that, we may find ourselves able to live in cities where working and living are as closely intermingled as in any guild town of the Middle Ages. High density urban living can once again become not just tolerable but even desirable. That is more than a vague and pleasant dream. It forms the central pivot for any long-term hope we have for our environment – rural as well as urban. If we do not once again make our cities attractive and vibrant places where people positively *want* to live, then we can forget any notion of conserving or sustaining a balanced rural environment. The idea that we might all live in the country, connected to each other by the electronic super-highway is, on a crowded island like ours, a certain recipe for environmental disaster.

If creative imagination is to become the core around which we might begin to build a new and profitable identity for ourselves and our country, is it not logical to assume that we should want that to be reflected in the way we plan and build our cities? The foremost quality of multimedia is that it is built on networks – it does not require a headquarters with a string of satellites. Here is an opportunity to re-invigorate our cities, and most especially London, as a network of functioning local communities. And through the cable television networks that are already substantially in place but still, with few exceptions, desperately short of quality content, there is the possibility of genuinely local news, information and entertainment services – able to promote a sense of identity and pride to neighbourhoods.

A leading computer consultant, writing in the 1995 *Public Policy Review*, described a pilot project developing a full-service information network, a kind of miniature Information Superhighway, in South Bristol. He wrote:

> We are constantly astonished by the real potential locked up in the three and a half thousand people who have been through our skills workshops. What is interesting is that our assumptions about age or any other barrier are constantly being rewritten through helping a community to help itself. Most notably, when exposed to the new technologies, we see individuals moving from being passive consumers of other people's material to creators of their own.

Is it too fanciful to suggest that we now have in our grasp the possibility of creating a society in which, in Morris's words, 'all men and women are more or less artists . . . and the audience for art is nothing short of the whole people'?

It has always been the role of the arts to inspire, to tell the stories which interpret the past, and by restating eternal truths, create confidence for the future. In a world in which the shared assumptions of religion, community, tradition and political ideology are disintegrating, the arts provide a means both of communication and identity. They provide a mirror in which we see our own lives and a window through which we can see the lives of others. Industrial societies have tended to divorce the arts from the central processes of production and wealth generation. We are now moving into an era in which the creative arts, and the imagination that feeds them, are fast becoming one of the central wealth-generating and employment-generating functions of the developed world. For democratic socialists that presents an opportunity to realize in practice opportunities about which previous generations have only been able to dream.

4 Community and the Left

David Marquand

Professor of Politics at Sheffield
University, Warden Elect of Mansfield
College, Oxford and former MP for
Ashfield, he is the author of *The
Unprincipled Society*.

To be on the Left is to espouse the values encapsulated in the immortal triad of the French Revolution – liberty, equality, fraternity. But these values do not always point in the same direction. More liberty may mean less equality or fraternity. Gains in equality may have to be purchased with losses in fraternity or liberty. The claims of fraternity – or, in non-sexist language, of solidarity or community – may run counter both to the claims of equality and to those of liberty. In this essay I shall be looking at the third term in the triad, but I do not suggest that it should always have primacy over the first two. I start from the double premise that community (which is a modern translation of fraternity) is an essential ingredient of a good society; and that that ingredient is sorely lacking in present-day Britain. But I accept that communities can be illiberal and inegalitarian; and I acknowledge that in certain places at certain times it may be therefore necessary for the left to give a lower priority to community than to liberty or equality.

Britain, however, is not such a place; and the final decade

of the twentieth century is not such a time. In the 1960s and 1970s, British governments sacrificed community to equality; in the 1980s and 1990s they have sacrificed it, far more brutally, to liberty. Partly because of this, but much more because of the impact of a worldwide transformation of economies and cultures, present-day Britain is threatened by progressive atomization and growing alienation. The social glue of shared obligations and mutual trust is visibly cracking; swelling numbers are effectively excluded from the common life of the society; public space is increasingly degraded and the public domain impoverished. In Britain today, the chief priority for the Left must be to strengthen – perhaps even to recreate – the community ties which are so manifestly fraying. In the rest of this essay, I shall explore the implications of this priority, the tensions it will encounter, the obstacles to its pursuit and the ways in which these obstacles may be overcome.

DISTINCTIONS

My approach is based, like all political approaches, on a mixture of description and prescription – on a view of human nature, allied to a set of values. The two are, of course, logically distinct. 'Ought' cannot be derived from 'is': community as value cannot be derived from community as fact. I believe that, as a matter of fact, John Donne was right in saying that no man is an island, and that, by the same token, William Morris was right when he said that lack of fellowship was death. In less elevated language, I believe that, like dogs or wolves, human beings need to belong to a group, and to feel loyalty to a group; that it is through group membership that our lives gain dignity and meaning; and that our psychic wellbeing will suffer if that fundamental need is denied. I also believe that it is morally right to make sure that it is not denied: that it is right to create spaces in which people can come together, learn to interact with each other and absorb the loyalties that group membership implies; and that a good society is one in which there are plenty of such spaces. But the first of those statements does not logically entail the last. Still less does it entail approval of any particular set of spaces. The Mafia, Hezbollah and the National Front all foster and depend upon group loyalty; no doubt, they all help to satisfy their members' needs to belong. But it does not follow that they should be approved of.

This leads on to another important distinction. Community values are often said to be altruistic as opposed to egoistic. I think this is a misunderstanding. In the language of altruism, the key words are 'compassion', 'generosity' and 'sympathy'; in that of community they are 'duty', 'loyalty' and 'obligation'. These words have different connotations, and the actions that correspond to them spring from different moral and emotional roots. The Good Samaritan – surely, the paradigmatic altruist – was not *obliged* to act as he did. Nor was he bound to the beneficiary of his actions by the ties of community loyalty. The whole point of the story is that they came from different communities; that they were *not* bound together by ties of mutual obligation; that all they shared was their common humanity. The Good Samaritan was loyal, if at all, to the entire human race; and the entire human race is hardly a community. By contrast, a soldier who gives his life for his country exhibits community loyalty, but it would be odd to call him an altruist. Altruism is wide, but shallow: community, deep but narrow. If the paradigmatic example of altruism is the Good Samaritan, that of community is ancient Athens or Renaissance Florence.

A third distinction should be explored as well. For much of the twentieth century (though not in the nineteenth century, when they first appeared on the scene) socialists and social democrats have tended to equate the community with the state. The results have been almost uniformly disastrous. The state can, of course, be a friend of community. It can promote community values and pursue collective purposes. But it is, at best, an unreliable friend; and it can sometimes be a dangerous enemy. An overweening state, even if well-intentioned, can crush the smaller communities that stand in its way; it can disrupt the delicate web of mutual obligation on which community depends; it can erode the loyalties that hold communities together. In the twentieth century, it frequently has.

Community values are embodied in what I shall call the public domain, not in the state. This public domain is distinct from the private domain of family and friendship on the one hand, and from the market domain of buying and selling on the other. In it people are motivated, not by the hope of gain or the love of friends, but by an ethic of public service and a commitment to the public interest. But this public domain should not be confused with the public sector as conventionally defined. It is not a separate space, consisting of a set of institutions. It is rather a set of practices, animated by a principle. And that principle can be realized as fully by a business firm, a trade union or a group of animal rights protesters as by a government department or a local authority.

DILEMMAS

It follows that a politics of community will encounter painful tensions and difficult dilemmas. Central to such a politics is the notion of civil society – of a web of intermediate institutions lying between the individual on the one hand and both state and market on the other, much as the ozone layer lies between the earth and the pitiless rays of the sun. For a big community can flourish only if it is made up of a mosaic of smaller ones; civil society – which I take to be another name for that mosaic – is an indispensable ingredient both of political vitality and of social wellbeing. The intermediate institutions which make it up include a vast range of organizations and groups: trade unions, business associations, cooperatives, universities, cricket clubs, churches, Rotary Clubs, the Women's Institute, local councils and the BBC are only some of them. Each is a kind of mini-polis whose members absorb the practices and learn the skills of self-government, mutual adjustment and co-operation, and in which they assume the obligations that go with mutual loyalty and trust. When Edmund Burke famously declared that the 'germ of public affections' was love of 'the little platoon', he meant that it was in and through these intermediate institutions that people learned how to become – and how to behave as – full members of the wider society. His insight applies even more forcefully to the puzzled and fragmented societies of the late twentieth century than to those of his own time.

The trouble is that the little platoons, like all constructs of human hands, are Janus-faced. They have a potential both for good and evil. They are the indispensable foundation stones of civility and sociability, but they can and do collide, sometimes savagely – neighbourhood against neighbourhood, work group against work group and, as in Northern Ireland and the former Yugoslavia, 'community' against 'community'. There is also a tension between small groups on the one hand and the wider society on the other. Neoliberal thinkers have warned that, in the economic domain in particular, smaller communities may become antisocial mini-Mafias, extracting monopoly rents from those who do not belong to them; and there is something in the warning.

There is also a potential conflict between community membership and individual rights. By definition, communities constrain the freedom of action of their members; a community whose members are completely unconstrained, totally free to behave as they please, is not a community at all. To join a cricket team is to be bound by the rules of cricket; to belong to a church is, at the minimum, to pay lip service to its values and to participate in its rituals. But there is an important distinction between communities of fate and communities of choice. It is easy to escape the constraints imposed by a community of choice, like a cricket team or a Women's Institute. All the would-be escaper has to do is to leave the community. There may be a cost in other satisfactions (playing cricket, for example, or swapping recipes for plum jam) but it is not an inordinate cost. Communities of fate – communities like nations, into which the members are born and through which their identities are shaped – are much harder to leave; and some communities of fate make it virtually impossible to do so. It follows that the more closely a given community resembles a community of fate, the more essential it is that the constraints which it imposes on its members should be tempered by respect for individual dignity and autonomy. That is why civilized nation-states – of which the United Kingdom, in this respect, is not one – entrench adherence to fundamental human rights in their constitutions.

Most little platoons are communities of choice, but some have at least some of the characteristics of a community of fate. Leaving a professional association may be tantamount to giving up one's livelihood. In certain religious groups, one of the obligations of membership is to bring up one's children in the faith. For the children, at least, membership of such groups may, for all practical purposes, be as involuntary as membership of a nation; and escape from the constraints of membership as difficult. Some such groups reject the whole notion of individual autonomy, and understand individual dignity as subjection to the will of God. Suppose such a group possesses many of the communal virtues: a strong sense of loyalty, a high level of mutual trust, a low level of antisocial behaviour. But suppose too that it holds that women should not be entitled to education or to participate in the labour market, and that they should be prohibited from showing their legs in public. How should a pluralist democracy approach it?

The answer, of course, is that there is no single, all-embracing answer, universally valid at all times and in all places. We can set out certain broad principles. A politics of community need not, and should not, be a politics of moral relativism. Diversity, pluralism and tolerance are part and parcel of a politics of community; there must be a presumption against imposing majority values on a little platoon that dissents from them. But tolerance is a two-way street. There can be no moral obligation to tolerate the intolerant; it is a matter of expediency, not of principle, to decide whether more good than harm is done by tolerating them in any particular case. Equally, cruelty is always evil; and the deliberate stunting of human potential is a form of cruelty. A little platoon that denies its members the right to develop their human potential to the full is behaving cruelly, and the wider society is entitled to stop it from doing so. If the values and practices of the platoon in question tell it that girls have a different potential from boys, it is entitled to argue its case before the wider society of which it is part. But in the end, it must accept the judgment of the majority.

The real point, however, goes deeper. It is that this and similar dilemmas are inescapable. A politics of community must be a politics of negotiation, discussion and what I have elsewhere called 'mutual education'. Such a politics is bound to be tentative, exploratory, uncertain. It will be bottom-up, not top-down; it will shy away from universal solutions and all-embracing formulae; it will run with the grain of human ignorance and recognize that, although it is possible to design institutions that foster mutual adjustment, it is not possible to foresee the course that mutual adjustment will take. For these reasons, it will be an extraordinarily difficult and demanding politics, requiring levels of humility and openness from which the political class of today falls abysmally short.

Yet these inevitable difficulties are the price of societal health and personal fulfilment. A society without the little platoons of civil society may perhaps be easier to govern than a society in which they proliferate. But it will not flourish, because its members will not have learned the practices and disciplines of self-government and mutual adjustment. They will lack mutual trust and therefore mutual respect. The countries of the former Soviet Union offer the most poignant contemporary example. Partly for ideological reasons and partly because they were terrified of organizations that they could not control, the Communists systematically destroyed or colonized the (mostly feeble) intermediate institutions left over from the previous regime, and allowed new ones to come into existence only if they were so firmly under the thumb of the party-state that they were not truly intermediate at all. Small groups made up of families and close friends sustained extraordinarily high levels of trust; outside the fortress walls of friendship and kinship lay a Hobbesian desert in which no one dared drop his guard. Then Communism collapsed and its totalitarian controls withered. The result was a kind of vacuum of community, which the Mafia, on the one hand, and a miscellany of ethnic fundamentalists on the other, have rushed in to fill.

British civil society is still incomparably richer than that of the former Soviet Union. The forces that threaten it are much weaker than those that devastated Russian civil society after 1917. But we ignore the Russian example at our peril.

EROSIONS

For most of the last 300 years, Britain has had an exceptionally vibrant civil society. The doctrine of absolute parliamentary sovereignty fostered and legitimized an awesome concentration of executive power at the heart of the state. But – except in Ireland – that power was, for the most part, employed cautiously, tentatively even diffidently. In its formative period, the central state had virtually no local agents. The landed elite was never absorbed by the royal Court, as in prerevolutionary France, or transmuted into a state bureaucracy, as in Prussia. There were no Intendants, Prefects or Governors to subject the localities to the will of the central power. Ancient colleges, hospitals, municipalities and inns of court effectively governed themselves. In most of the country, what we would now call local government was conducted by unpaid justices of the peace. State power was turned outwards, to the race for empire, not inwards. Partly because of this, industrialization and urbanization grew slowly, higgledy-piggledy, piecemeal, from the bottom up.

This pattern continued in the nineteenth and early twentieth centuries. The raw, new, atomistic industrial settlements of the early nineteenth century that astonished and horrified foreign (and for that matter southern English) visitors – the Manchester of Engels, the Coketown of Dickens – became proud, confident cities, with city halls mimicking Gothic cathedrals or Renaissance palazzi, and boasting art galleries, orchestras, universities, parks, grammar schools endowed by the grandees of local capital. It was in these cities that the welfare state began, the product of local initiative – 'gas and water socialism' – rather than central direction. The same was true of the labour movement. Cooperatives and trade unions also grew from the bottom up, piecemeal and unplanned. The national unions that emerged in the late nineteenth and early twentieth centuries were loose, octopoid federations of local bodies, fiercely independent and suspicious of central control or even central coordination.

In the last fifty years, however, the intermediate institution of civil society have steadily lost autonomy. The process began in the two world wars, but it continued apace after 1945. The postwar Labour Government nationalized the public utilities, significant proportions of which had previously been municipally owned; despite a stubborn rearguard action by Herbert Morrison, the greatest municipal socialist in Labour history, Aneurin Bevan also nationalized the municipal hospitals. Under the Labour governments of the 1960s and 1970s, the central state proceeded to force unwilling local authorities to reorganize secondary education, irrespective of the wishes of local electorates. Under the Conservative governments of the 1980s and 1990s, centralization speeded up. One reason, no doubt, was that left-Labour local councils sometimes sought to negate central government's economic policies in order to protect their constituents from its local consequences, provoking central government to clip their wings in retaliation. But whatever the reason, the consequences are plain. Local authorities are now hamstrung at every turn. They cannot raise and spend local taxes as they wish; they have lost a huge range of functions to nominated bodies outside their (or their electorates') control; a whole tier of local government has been abolished altogether. As a result, British local government is probably the weakest in the democratic world.

That is only the beginning of the story. There is an eerie parallel between the radical Left in Bolshevik Russia and the radical Right in Thatcherite Britain. The Bolsheviks looked forward to the withering away of the state; the Thatcherites to a drastic attenuation of its scope and role. But both soon grasped that their utopias could be realized only through a far-reaching cultural revolution; and both discovered that the only agency capable of prosecuting such a revolution was the state they theoretically disdained. In Britain, the result was the now familiar paradox of a state-imposed free market. The Thatcherites' economic ideology told them that, in the economic domain, intermediate institutions other than the business firm were, by their very nature, monopolistic, market-distorting cabals of rent seekers, out to exploit the consumer. Their political ideology told them that intermediate institutions that embodied and transmitted non-market values and codes of behaviour were, also by their very nature, enemies of their project. Accordingly, they set out to tame, to curb, or to reconstruct, not just local authorities, but all such institutions – trade unions, universities, the professions, the school system, even the system for public support of the arts. Through privatization, marketization and deregulation, they drastically curtailed the public domain, undermined the ethic of public service and let loose a wave of market imperialism whose effects can be detected in every corner of the public culture.

But even this is only part of the story. The left does itself no service when it attributes the contemporary erosion of community solely to governments of the right. The lesson of the Thatcher counter-revolution goes much deeper than that. The Thatcherites sought cultural and intellectual domination – in a word, hegemony – as well as political power; and they largely achieved it. They did not, of course, return to the entrepreneurial ideal of the early nineteenth century: that was an impossibility, since the entrepreneur of the early nineteenth century no longer exists. But, as Labour's nervousness over taxation and public expenditure vividly demonstrates, they did redraw the map of politics, much as the Attlee Government redrew it after the Second World War. And they were able to do this because they were running with the grain of global capitalism.

For the real enemy of community in our time is not New Right ideology. It is the worldwide gale of economic change and social disruption let loose by the capitalist renaissance of the last twenty years. That renaissance has no single cause. The information revolution, the transformation of the labour market, the virtual disappearance of the 'old' working class, the collapse of the delicate social and political balance of the postwar period, the associated delegitimation of the Keynesian welfare state, the deregulation of financial markets and the fall of Communism have all played a part in it. For our purposes, however, the causes matter less than the results. Community loyalties depend on stability, commitment, security. They grow slowly, and they demand continuity. But the hallmarks of the restless, voracious gobal capitalism of today, with its down-sizing, delayering and casualization, its repeated restructurings and its spreading atomization, are discontinuity, instability and insecurity. It is an illusion to imagine that societies with New Right regimes are alone in experiencing the hollowing out of community which is the most obvious feature of contemporary Britain. Thatcher's and Major's Britain has embraced the resurgent capitalism of the late twentieth century with a special enthusiasm. But, to take only three poignant examples, Mitterrand's France, Keating's Australia and Clinton's United States have not been far behind, despite quite different ideological preferences.

IMPLICATIONS

The implications are daunting. To be sure, the fashionable notion that we are in the grip of a mysterious force known as 'globalization', thanks to which national boundaries are economically irrelevant and from which there is no hiding place, is a dangerous oversimplification. Some markets are global; some are not. A few firms are global; most are not. Competitive advantage within the global marketplace, moreover, does not necessarily go to those with low labour costs, low levels of taxation, correspondingly low levels of public expenditure, deregulated labour markets and atomized societies. In the European Union, all of whose member states are capitalist market economies, open to the global market place and subject to the same worldwide economic pressures, there are very striking differences in the quality of public goods, the tax take of public authorities, the strength of the trade unions and the resilience of community values. Britain and Denmark are at opposite ends of this spectrum; but the notion that Britain is more competitive in world markets than Denmark is a patent absurdity. The same is true at the municipal level. Bologna has been governed for many years by the Communist Party, now the PDS. It has a vibrant, prosperous, successful economy, with skilful and adventurous small firms that dominate many specialist markets. Yet, as any casual visitor can see, the quality of its public goods would be the envy of almost any British city of comparable size.

The fact is that different countries – for that matter, different regions or even different cities in the same country – can pursue competitive advantage in the global marketplace in different ways. Cost-cutting, tax-cutting, deregulation and the rest of the Thatcherite armoury may lead to success in markets for the cheap and the shoddy. In high-value-added markets, the social capital that comes from strong community ties – motivation, commitment, loyalty and trust – is a competitive asset. By the same token, low real wages paid to badly trained workers are not the only attraction for inward investors. It is also possible to attract them with crime-free streets, with high quality education and training and with a clean environment.

When all the qualifications have been made, however, there is no doubt that the nation-state has much less freedom of action in the economic sphere than it used to have. No single nation-state, certainly no medium-sized nation-state, can insulate itself against the gales of intensifying competition and accelerating change now sweeping across the globe; it follows that national policies alone cannot halt the erosion of community which seems to be their inevitable by-product. One response – the response of the American communitarian movement associated with Amitai Etzioni – is to vacate the political sphere altogether, and to rely instead on a mixture of moral exhortation and voluntary action on the local level. That is a counsel of despair. Voluntary action on the local level has an indispensable part to play in the restoration of community ties, but if it is to be effective it must be buttressed by the appropriate use of public power. And public power can be deployed on the local and supranational levels as well as, in many spheres better than, on the level of the central state.

The right response to the gathering crisis of community is to adopt the old Christian Democratic principle of subsidiarity – the principle that decisions should be taken at the lowest level of government appropriate to the issue concerned. Many of the policies needed to restore social capital and protect community ties in the new economic era are best carried out by localities and regions. Some should be left to the institutions of the European Union. Economic and social regeneration of the sort pursued by a number of old industrial cities, Glasgow and Manchester conspicuous among them, are examples of the former. Policies to curb social dumping, to prevent exchange-rate instability and to bring the world's financial markets to heel – all crucial to a politics of community – are examples of the latter.

Subsidiarity alone is not, however, enough. Two more fundamental changes of direction and purpose, affecting all levels of government, are equally crucial to a politics of community. The first has to do with the public domain: with the dimension of social life where an ethic of public service and civic duty takes precedence both over the market ethic of free exchange and over the private ethic of loyalty to kin and friends. The public domain nourishes and, in turn, draws nourishment from the little platoons of civil society; almost by definition, community ties will wither if the public domain is undermined. But, as I tried to show a moment ago, that is precisely what has happened in the last fifteen years.

Undoing the damage will be a slow and difficult business. The public-service ethic is about trust; and trust, once lost, is notoriously hard to restore. Detailed policies are scarcely to the point. What matters is consistent adherence to a different governing principle. The public domain must be separate from the market domain. In the public domain, goods should not be treated as commodities or proxy commodities. Performance indictors designed to mimic the indicators of the market domain are not appropriate, and frequently do more harm than good. The language of buyer and seller, producer and customer, does not belong in the public domain and nor do the relationships which that language implies. Doctors and nurses do not 'sell' medical services; students are not 'customers' of their teachers; policemen and policewomen do not 'produce' public order. The attempt to force these relationships into a market mould merely undermines the service ethic which is the true guarantor of quality in the public domain, and in doing so impoverishes us all.

The second change of direction is more radical. It challenges a crucial element in the conventional wisdom of the entire postwar period – an element as common on the Left as on the Right. Left and Right alike have taken it for granted that the central objective of economic policy is to promote wealth creation; that wealth is to be equated with GDP per head; and that the rate of growth of GDP per head is therefore the litmus test of economic, perhaps even of national, success. They have disagreed about the way in which growth should be pursued, and even more about the way in which the proceeds should be distributed. But for both, a high rate of growth has been the paramount goal.

It is time to abandon that assumption. Etymologically, wealth is closely connected to welfare; and welfare is a far more complex matter than GDP per head. A country may be rich in terms of GDP per head, but impoverished in terms of other indices of welfare. A country at the top of the range in terms of welfare may be in the middle of the range in terms of GDP per head. And maximum welfare should be the goal of public policy. Once this approach is accepted, the familiar notion that we have to choose between the creation of wealth and the pursuit of community values no longer makes sense. Community and the ties of community cease to be luxuries to be postponed until economic success has been achieved. They are part and parcel of welfare and therefore of wealth in the true sense of the word. To pursue wealth creation without at the same time pursuing community values becomes a contradiction in terms. A nation wracked by crime, unemployment, decrepit public services and social exclusion is, by definition, unsuccessful – no matter how high its GDP per head. By the same token, policies that protect the nation from social dislocation make it more successful, even if they lower the rate of GDP growth.

IDENTITIES

Community goes with identity. To belong to a community is to identify with it; communities, in turn, help to shape the identities of their members. A politics of community must therefore be, in some sense, a politics of identity. And in present-day Britain, one of the chief obstacles to a successful politics of community is that the identity once conveyed by the terms 'Britain' and 'British' has become increasingly problematic, contested and confused.

For most of the time since the Act of Union of 1707 – and it is important to remember that it was the Act of Union which created the British state and made it necessary for its rulers to forge a British identity in the first place – that state has been quintessentially, inescapably imperial. To be British was to be part of a political community which was, by definition, oceanic, global and, as such, extra-European, if not quite non-European. The British saw themselves as inhabitants of the world. Their cousins, their kith and kin, were to be found right across the globe as far as the Antipodes. They were part, moreover, of an 'English-speaking world' which also included the United States. For, although the American colonies had broken away from the British Empire, politically speaking, in the eighteenth century the colonists' descendants were still, in some almost mystical sense, part of the oceanic community whose heart lay in the British Isles.

This vision of Britain's identity – the vision which inspired such varied luminaries as William Pitt, Winston Churchill, Ernest Bevin and Hugh Gaitskell – has obviously unravelled. The disappearance of the British Empire in the years since World War II, the application to join the European Community at the beginning of the 1960s, the belated accession of the United Kingdom to the European Community in the early 1970s – all of these have made nonsense of the oceanic, extra-European and imperial identity which the British state had claimed to embody ever since it came into existence at the beginning of the eighteenth century. But no alternative vision has replaced it. For twenty years now, Britain has been a member-state of a proto-federal European Community, the governing principle of which is that all member-states have more in common with each other than they do with non-members. But no one has managed to invent a new British identity, centred upon her new European destiny.

That is only the beginning of the story. The British loyalties and language on which the governments of the postwar period could draw ceased to be available to subsequent governments. At the same time, Scottish, Welsh and English identities and loyalties began to revive. In Scotland, and to a lesser extent in Wales, the result was an exciting, outward-looking pluralism. The Scots and Welsh are both used to multiple identities. They are, in a profound sense, quintessentially British. Britain is Britain only because Scotland and Wales are part of it. But at the same time, they cherish their own particular national identities. Perhaps because of this, they have had little difficulty in constructing a further, European identity to add to the other two. Scotland, the Scots can truthfully say, is a historic European nation, and Edinburgh a great European capital. The Welsh say much the same. So far, however, this has been conspicuously untrue of the English. No one has succeeded in constructing a simi-

larly plural and similarly European English identity. Not
the least of the reasons for the New Right's political success
is that it was able to mobilize the strangulated, inward-
looking English nationalism which increasingly held the field
in Britain's largest national community after the end of
empire.

It would be wrong to end on a despairing note. Identities
are not set in concrete. National traditions are always con-
testable, and therefore malleable. The imagined community
of the nation can be re-imagined. Open, generous, outward-
looking nationalisms, congruent with the politics of community I have been trying to sketch out, have existed and
still exist. Verdi was the hymnodist of the Italian Risorgi-
mento, and also of European liberalism. Vaclav Havel is a
Czech patriot, and a citizen of the world. George Orwell was
both an English nationalist and a socialist internationalist.
Winston Churchill – significantly, a bogey to New Right
revisionist historians – embodied, in his own person, a
defiant British nationalism that ran in double harness with
the cosmopolitan whiggery of his ancestors. As that implies,
there are resources in the English and British traditions to
support a nationalism that runs with the grain of subsidiarity and Europeanism. But fire can only be fought with
fire: emotion with emotion. One of the central questions
in present-day British politics is whether the Left has the
imagination and courage to trump the passionate xenophobia of the Right with an equally passionate alternative. On
that, the jury is still out.

5 National Identity

Neal Ascherson

A columnist of the *Independent on
Sunday*, his latest book, *Black Sea*, won
the 1995 Saltire Society Award for
Scottish Literature.

'Jim Bloggs, 101 Inkerman Terrace, Scratfield, Staffordshire,
England, Great Britain, Europe, the World, the Galaxy, the
Universe . . .'

When schoolchildren used to write things like that in the
front of their books, they were producing a classic old model
of identities. It was a concentric model. It was seen from
the central dot of all those concentric rings – the individual.
The house was the nearest ring; the Universe the most
remote. The model was a statement about the self: 'I am
the centre of creation'. But it was also a list of overlapping
memberships – identities, if you like. You 'came from' the
Potteries, but you were also English. You were British, but
also European, Terran, Inner-Galactic, Universal.

The question which the model does not answer is this:
which of these identities, if any, has priority? By which ring
does the central dot wish to be identified by others? Pope
John Paul II, who derives some of his theology from Polish
nineteenth-century patriotic mysticism, also leaves this
question open. In his view, God created humanity in three
concentric categories, all of which are sacred: individual,

family – and nation. But which is the defining identity, and which might you be entitled to betray in order to save one or both of the others? There the faithful receive no clear guidance.

The schoolchild's site of identity could be the house. It could be the Continent: 'I feel that I am a European, really'. It could, when the schoolchild becomes a self-obsessed first-year student, be the dot itself: 'I am myself, and nothing else'. It could be several different rings at once.

Once, they used to ask a stranger: 'Where do you come from?' But these days people are more often asked who they are – a very different, more loaded matter – and to answer with a single word. Mostly, the answer is the name of a state or a nation. This is a learned response; ordinary people did not always think like that. In parts of Belarus – once the Soviet republic of Byelorussia – language, religion and custom vary from village to village, and the only common cultural experience is of brutality at the hands of invaders. There, peasants who are confronted with that 'Who are you?' question will often reply: 'We are *tutejszy* – we are "from-here" people'. But the world will not allow them to go on getting away with that answer for much longer.

Identity has now become a problem in Britain as well. To talk about an 'identity crisis' would be exaggerated. But there is an enormous identity muddle.

Many people in this state have difficulty finding a satisfactory answer to the question of who they are. And this muddle has developed with quite astonishing speed. The suggestion that the British were not sure who they were would have seemed absurd even fifteen years ago. No people in the whole world, it might then have been retorted, were more placidly certain about their identity and suffered less *angst* about it.

I believe that this new muddle is healthy. It pains and exasperates some, and gives others a sense of vertigo. But it is part of Britain's adaptation to the new world and its disorder, of which the European Union is the leading edge. This adaptation, after the end of the Cold War, does not just mean institutional change or a less 'sceptred isle' approach to national sovereignty. All that is necessary. But with it comes a change in the way that the British understand themselves as a political community, an ethnicity, a nation, a people . . . however you name it. In other words, we have to transform not only ourselves and the way we do things, but also the names we give ourselves.

Like almost all British problems of modernization, the identity muddle relates to the archaic nature of Britain's constitutional system, now a unique survival in Europe. This system was set up by a limited and primitive reform: the principle of absolutism was not abolished but simply transferred from the English Crown to Parliament. This was a process which had begun with the high democratic hopes of the English Revolution but ended in the cautious compromise settlement of 1688–9. This settlement enabled the future British state to escape almost entirely the political influence of the Enlightenment – to say nothing of the French Revolution. This has not only deprived Britain of institutional reforms like a written Constitution, a code of administrative law, or a citizenship based on a 'culture of rights'. It has kept out of British usage the very language used by all European states and the Union itself to describe their political societies.

Take the distinction between 'state' and 'nation'. Although in the past these definitions were more pliable, they are now reasonably standardized on the Continent and beyond. 'Nation' describes an extensive community which feels united by common experience and culture. A state is the set of institutions which a nation (or group of nations) may set up as the structure of government and administration. Of course, not all nations do decide that they must have an independent nation-state of their own. Some (like the Catalans) are for the moment satisfied with powerful self-government, with Home Rule within a larger multi-national state. In other words, a nation can express itself politically as a 'region'. But in the last two or three centuries, most communities which have defined themselves as 'nations' have at least tried to establish their own states. The difference between nation and state was quite clear to them. It was expressed with brutal clarity in the old Soviet passports: 'Nationality: Ukrainian (or Kazakh or Jewish). Statehood: Soviet.'

But in Britain that difference has never been fully understood. England or Britain are sometimes referred to as nations, sometimes as states. Most seriously – because this is a misunderstanding which gets in the way of comparing like with like in Europe – the phrase 'multinational state' is almost never applied to the United Kingdom.

And yet that is what the UK is. It is not tidy or symmetrical in its diversity. The UK consists of two ancient king-doms united by treaty, one conquered Celtic nation, the rump of another and a scatter of islands. One component – England – is ten times as populous as all the others put together. In spite of this diversity, the state governing these nations is tightly centralized and unitary. This central-ism, which grew far more painful and constricting with the huge growth of centralized state bureaucracy after 1945, arises from the absolutist doctrine of parliamentary sover-eignty whose roots stretch back to 1688, and beyond. Under this doctrine, sovereignty – undiluted by Enlightenment doctrines of constitutional federalism – cannot be shared or distributed.

It is not surprising that confusion has arisen in the United Kingdom over identity and terminology to describe identity. Mostly, it is English confusion. For the past few decades, at least, Welsh and Scottish subjects of the UK have found it fairly easy to define themselves as Welsh or Scottish by nation, but British by citizenship (or statehood).

The word 'English' has been through many vicissitudes,

especially in England. Until fairly recently, English people used the word 'England' to describe the main island of the archipelago, and in my youth London politicians visiting Scotland almost invariably referred to 'England's victory over Hitler' or 'England's special relationship with America'. The Scots silently resented this, although there had been a time in the late eighteenth and early nineteenth centuries when middle-class Scots travelling on the Continent were proud to name their culture 'English'.

Then, some twenty-five years ago, a change set in. I believe it was the huge expansion of higher education in the 1960s, rather than the Nationalist surges in Scotland and Wales during the 1970s, which encouraged it. The English began to use the term 'British' to describe not only the other inhabitants of the multinational state – but themselves. It was not just that the political and media classes grew aware – led to a great extent by the BBC – of how irritated Scottish and Welsh audiences and viewers became when they were called English. The change went further, until the term 'English' began to acquire a vaguely improper, even negative flavour to English ears. It seemed to imply not simply obtuseness to the sensibilities of others, but a right-wing nationalist self-assertion ('There'll always be an England!') which was best left to football hooligans or Prom audiences. Before the gospel of political correctness was even heard of, Englishness became politically incorrect.

Some, like Enoch Powell on the Right and the late A. J. P. Taylor on the Left, continued to say England when they meant England. Others ducked out. Absurdities appeared, like travel-mag references to 'Britain, land of hedgerows, cream teas and thatched cottages'. Here, plainly, a frontier was being crossed. 'British' was being used to describe a national vernacular culture – in this case, the appearance and tourist menu of the English countryside – rather than to describe aspects of the United Kingdom state or of politics. It looked as if a new nation called Britain was being invented.

In fact, closer inspection showed that the word 'British' was merely being substituted for the word 'English'.

Was there, then, never a *nation* called Britain? Can we ask, as Professor Gwyn Williams memorably asked about Wales: 'When was Britain?' The answer is that a common culture did come to exist in certain areas of life, after the Anglo-Scottish Union of 1707. 'Britishness' existed with particular intensity during wartime and on the frontiers or in the trading houses of the Empire, both as a set of standards and as a commitment to defend the particularly British way of doing things. 'Britishness' also described a battery of political conventions, involving aspirations to fair, impartial, non-corrupt government. As time passed, a *homo britannicus* was actually bred up, although never in sufficient numbers to compose a nation rather than to lead it. This was the British upper class as it existed by the mid nineteenth century, which wore the same tweeds, remembered the same public schools, spoke with the same accent, subscribed to the same code of manners and owned almost all the land between Land's End and John O'Groats. The social and political eclipse of this class is an important factor in the decline of this short-lived 'British' cultural identity. To take a small example, boys and girls emerging from the public schools now mostly speak with versions of the 'Estuary' accent of southeast England. It is significant that the voice of the ruling class is no longer 'above locality' but has become the voice of one particular geographical region. More importantly, Mrs Thatcher was the first Conservative prime minister to be instantly identifiable as English rather than 'British'.

There are parallels in history for British confusions about identity. None is more haunting than the experience of the Austro-Hungarian Empire, the multinational state which collapsed in 1918. The novelist Robert Musil, whose theme was the empire's decline, nicknamed the state 'Kakania' – from the German abbreviation 'K.u.K', short for 'Imperial

& Royal'. This has tempted the political philosopher Tom Nairn to nickname the British state 'Ukania', another royal and multinational state beset by external weakness, internal decay and nationalism at is margins.

Musil wrote that Kakania 'did not consist of an Austrian and a Hungarian part that . . . combined to form a unity, but of a whole and a part; namely, of a Hungarian and an Austro-Hungarian sense of nationhood, and the latter was at home in Austria, whereby the Austrian sense of nation-hood actually became homeless.'

The other day I attended a meeting of broadcasters and historians to debate a project for a grand millennium TV series on 'British history'. Inevitably, this discussion soon acquired a Musil flavour. When was Britain? Many of those present thought the series should start with the Roman con-quest – as if the Roman province of Britannia, which did not extend to Ireland or beyond southern Scotland, had developed in some 'natural' linear way into the United King-dom. Others acknowledged that in effect Britain as a single 'experience' could not have existed before 1603 (Union of Crowns) or 1707 (Union of Parliaments), but they proposed to bolt on extra programmes which would rush through the separate histories of Scotland, Wales or Ireland before their respective incorporations by England.

This seemed to beg the question. But my own sugges-tion – that the series should be called something like 'From England to Great Britain: the Story of English Imperial Expansion' – was greeted rather coldly. It might be an accu-rate title. A generation ago, it would have probably seemed acceptable to a similar London gathering. But in 1995 it reeked of incorrectness. The broadcasters professed to fear that such an approach might give offence at the Celtic per-ipheries. In reality – as I diagnosed – they were not prepared to accept that there is no such animal as a British history two thousand years long. To put it another way, they were reluctant to come out as English.

Coming out, all the same, has always been an English option. Since the confusion between England and Britain descended, there have been many in Scotland and Wales who have wanted the English national identity to reassert itself. At least, runs the argument, we would know where and who we were. Great Britain would be revealed as the multi-ethnic state it is. And then a rational future for that state could be worked out.

The fearsome 'West Lothian Question', for instance, rests on this confusion of British-English identity. The 'WLQ' complains that if there were a Scottish parliament with power over internal affairs, then Scottish Westminster MPs would be able to vote on bills concerning English education, while English Westminster MPs would not be able to vote on Scottish education. Conversely, if the Scots MPs were deprived of the right to vote on purely English legislation, then Parliament might find itself with two conflicting majorities: a Labour majority on British matters, but a Tory one on English matters. Government would become impossible.

The logical remedy would be to establish an English parliament as well as a British one. The United Kingdom should be reformed into a quasi-federal structure with three (or four, counting Northern Ireland) national parliaments and a central legislature dealing with foreign affairs, defence, shared services and perhaps macro-economic policy. Logical – but in the state of political awareness south of the Border at present, unthinkable. The House of Commons in the Palace of Westminster is perceived by the English as England's ancient parliament, the ark of the covenant honoured and fought over between Crown and people through the centuries, the chalice of national liberty and sovereignty. The notion that this sacred place should be diminished to a sort of underused federal chamber, with, say, hot, living debate on the laws of England evicted to the Queen Elizabeth Conference Centre across Parliament

Square, would seem to most English people like a monstrous, senseless act of vandalism.

But what if the English did come out of the closet, and embraced their own national identity? This is beginning to happen. Here and there, Englishness is being displayed without the fig leaf of Britishness. During the 1992 election campaign, John Major told his Scottish audience candidly that he was English, and therefore not entirely qualified to understand their feelings. This was significant. Mrs Thatcher, similarly, had made no pretence to the old upper-class 'British' culture and was widely identified in Scotland (in a pejorative sense) as 'English'. But she none the less felt entitled to instruct the Scots about their true national character, and did so in her notorious 'Sermon on the Mound' before the General Assembly of the Church of Scotland. Major's humility was not only a contrast. It marked a slight but perceptible change in the relationship of ethnicity to authority in Britain. To govern, it is no longer necessary to deny one's Englishness.

And, if we learn to read them, there are other signs of a reviving English identity. Newspapers like the *Independent*, founded only ten years ago, or the even younger *Independent on Sunday*, are content to be perceived as essentially 'English' papers for the English reader – even the southeast English reader. The *Guardian* and the *Observer*, in contrast, still strain dutifully to be 'British' in their emphasis – although their proportion of readers outside the M25 ring or north of Watford is not much greater than those of their *Independent* rivals. In scholarship, English nationalism is clearly on the move. Thus we have work claiming that the Anglo-Saxon peasantry – Thatcherites *avant la lettre* – developed an individualistic entrepreneurial culture long before the rest of Europe escaped from primitive collectivism. Or that the post-Roman Saxon 'invaders' were in fact a tiny elite minority who so dazzled the Romano-British population that they persuaded them to change their language, religion and material culture to that of the new-comers. This theory tries to demonstrate that England really 'is' Britain in an ethnic, genetic sense. England therefore would have a continuity which did not start merely at the Dark Ages but reached back for many more millennia: perhaps into the early Iron Age, perhaps even further. It was in this spirit that the archaeologist Lord Renfrew has spoken of ancestral territories which 'we' have possessed for many thousands of years.

But if it is true that the English are beginning once again to claim English national identity, is that an entirely healthy development? Some Welsh and Scottish nationalist politicians may feel that it is, because it brings with it the admission that Britain is no more than a multinational state. Clearly, there is a gain in lucidity when British identity is under discussion. But beyond that is a much larger, murkier question. What is modern English nationalism going to be like? Could it turn out to be a great deal less biddable and 'civic' than peripheral Celtic nationalisms? Could it, in fact, adopt a vengeful and irrational form which would set itself against any reform which seemed to diminish this English-dominated Britain?

This is a question which nobody asks. But they should. So far, English opinion (according to polling) has been strikingly tolerant of Scottish and Welsh aspirations to self-government. Mr Major apparently believes that his appeals in 1992 to 'defend the Union' against Labour's devolution plans went down well with English voters. There is little hard evidence to support him, but the point is that he has begun to 'play the English card'. At a certain moment, English nationalism may begin to rise and come to meet him or his successor.

English nationalism has been mobilized by a variety of (mostly tiny) political groups for brief periods in the first half of this century. Putting their experience together, a disconcerting picture emerges. In his book *Blood and*

Belonging, Michael Ignatieff made the rough contrast between 'ethnic' and 'civic' nationalism, between the atavistic wish to plunge back into the mire of an imaginary past and the modernizing impulse to construct a new, responsible society which joins the world on its own terms. Surprisingly, English nationalism registers at a point towards the ethnic end of this scale. It has been xenophobic (anti-French, anti-Irish and anti-Semitic), ruralist rather than urban, deeply suspicious of industrial society and the 'uprooting' influence of modern life. As Patrick Wright suggests in his *The Village that Died for England*, this blood and soil emphasis left English nationalism open to fascist infection, above all from Germany, in the 1920s and 1930s. Compared to the ultra-respectable, small-town reformism of mainstream Welsh or Scottish nationalism, the English version is not a pretty sight.

And here the idea of 'Britishness' acquires an extra, unexpected function. It may be that feeling British has protected the English nation against its own worst instincts. We all know, if we know the history of the 1930s, what happened when post-Habsburg Austrians decided to feel German. The fiction of a British 'nation' has kept English nationalism in check. It has channelled its passions into Empire-building, into defensive wars against Continental powers, into pride in British social achievements – whether as the old 'workshop of the world', or as the site of a National Health Service envied by most of the world.

Britain survived the loss of colonial empire surprisingly well. Colonies and Dominions became independent, and yet Britain itself did not seem to change dramatically. The United Kingdom certainly did not lose its identity by losing its empire. The question now is whether the next transition can be so successful.

Britain is multinational, but it no longer consists of the English, the Scots, the Welsh and the Irish – plus 'a few refugees and foreigners'. There are now some five million British subjects and residents whose ethnic origins are outside Europe: principally in the Indian subcontinent or the Caribbean. Very few of them want to remain in foreign enclaves, living exclusively within the culture of their roots. Almost all of them are happy to venture out and inhabit overlapping rings of identity. There is the ring which has to do with their daily life and schooling in these islands. There is the ring which contains the cultural traditions of their family and milieu which relate to lands far from Britain. And, in most cases, there is the 'political' ring with the designation of British citizenship in passport and other official documents.

These inhabitants of Britain raise several questions about identity. First of all, who do they *think* they are? A few years back, there was a hopeful anticipation that these immigrant communities would emerge as the last true Britons – that they would define themselves as proudly 'British' above any petty local ethnicities. They would, in short, replace the gentry as the authentic British class.

This would have been a piquant outcome. The 'true Brit' would turn out to be a child of the Empire – not only son or daughter of those who created it, but also of the black and brown millions whom it ruled. The reality is more complex. Yes, they do see themselves as British but usually with the qualification – 'Black British' or 'British Moslem'. To add to the complexity, in Glasgow or Cardiff, locally born children may even say that they feel 'Scottish' or 'Welsh' as well as British. Maybe they are becoming like the Jewish community in Scotland which, with its roots mostly in Poland or Lithuania, has regarded itself for a hundred years as Scottish as well as Jewish, with 'British' honoured as citizenship rather than culture.

There is, then, no living heir to British cultural identity. This fact makes the rise of English nationalism, freed of its 'British' restraint, all the more dangerous. At one level, it leaves the non-European communities ideologically defenceless; the Britain which 'built the Empire' and brought them to London, Bradford, Liverpool and Cardiff no longer exists to justify their presence. And at the wider political level, we can begin to see ahead a deadly confluence. The river of Eurosceptic xenophobia is beginning to converge with the river of intolerant English nationalism. If they become one torrent, England may rapidly cease to be a country where men and women with ideals would care to live – and not only men and women whose skin is black or brown.

Time may be short. The remedy is not merely a change of government, although that is indispensable and urgent. It is a new government which will keep the British state on course towards further European integration – and which will have the courage to argue that case for European Union up and down the land.

Europhobia, as a party-political disease, can be rooted out by fresh air, intellectual exercise and new parliamentary majorities. But intolerant English nationalism cannot be rooted out. Instead, it must be confronted, educated and slowly tamed.

Sooner or later, England will have to come to terms with being English. I leave aside intricate questions like whether Scottish independence – if that ever came to pass – would produce two successor states, one called Scotland and the other, presumably consisting of England, Wales and Northern Ireland, no longer entitled to call itself Britain or the 'United Kingdom'. The immediate problem is whether English national identity can be managed in a much looser version of the British state, without allowing the unregenerate aspects of English nationalism to break through. That identity has to be inclusive and 'civic', turning away from old-fashioned ethnic definitions to a wider identity in which the cultural traditions of England's Asian and Afro-Caribbean populations can find a home.

And here I am optimistic. It would be a cruel irony if the long-prophesied, long-delayed 'post-imperial hangover' arrived because of the decentralization of Britain itself. But that does not have to happen. As I have argued, the path to safety and sanity lies through the European Union. If the Union can continue into further integration and enlargement, both 'widening' and 'deepening', then a new notion of identity will emerge. In Northern Ireland, there has already been profound and hopeful discussion of how different 'cultural traditions' can co-exist by separating cultural identity from traditional political allegiances to London or to Dublin. This can be the future for Britain.

It is a long path. But at the end, the Union of Europe can replace the unions, forcible or contractual, around which the United Kingdom was built. The pressure will be taken out of identity. To be Welsh and British, or simply Welsh and European, will no longer imply an unresolved tension with England. To be English in Europe will no longer imply an unresolved nostalgia for 'Great Britain'. But children will continue to imagine their concentric, spreading rings of identity reaching out to all humanity and beyond, and in this archipelago of ours, one of them will be called 'Britain'. The difference will be that no single ring will have sovereignty over the others. Those children, our grandchildren, will be Lords of all the Rings, the heirs to an infinity of identity.

6 The New World Disorder

Denis Healey

One of Britain's leading authorities on
international affairs, he is a Labour Peer
and former Chancellor of the Exchequer,
Secretary of State for Defence and
deputy leader of the Labour Party. He is
author of *The Time of My Life*.

Nearly half a century ago Jim Griffiths, a Welsh miner and
leading figure in the Attlee government, summed up the
problems of the postwar world in the words: 'Science has
turned the world into a parish, but its peoples have not yet
learned how to be neigbours'. That is even more true as we
approach the twenty-first century, with the future of the
United Nations itself at risk.

The world in the 1990s is entering a period of fundamental transformation. There is no sign of a 'new world order'
or of 'the end of history', predicted by some optimists a few
years ago. Instead we face a new world disorder – and
history has come back with a bang.

During the period of the Cold War, partly because both
sides had nuclear weapons, there was no major war between
the two camps. Although over twenty million people lost
their lives in armed conflicts in the Third World, the Cold
War created stability over two-thirds of the globe.

Today there are eighty-two armed conflicts of which

seventy-nine are taking place inside national frontiers. In addition to the chaos created by the collapse of the old Soviet empire, Africa south of the Sahara is a disaster area, with the shining exception of Mandela's South Africa, and there is fighting in parts of the Middle East and Asia. Global instability is increased by the spread of weapons of mass destruction, the rapid growth of population in much of the Third World, and, above all, by the forces, both internal and external, which are undermining the sovereignty of all nation-states.

THE COLLAPSE OF THE SOVIET EMPIRE

One reason for the failure to establish a new world order after the end of the Cold War is that the West did not win the Cold War. The Soviet empire collapsed because of its own internal contradictions. When Lenin said that the victory of Communism would lead to the 'withering away' of the state, he was right – though not in the sense he intended. The fact that the Cold War ended not with a bang but with a whimper means that the West was never in a position to impose a new international system, as the victorious powers did at the Congress of Vienna after the defeat of Napoleon, at Versailles after the defeat of imperial Germany, and at Yalta and Potsdam after the defeat of the Axis powers.

The end of the Cold War was due to the disintegration of a Communist empire which stretched from Berlin to Vladivostok, from the Arctic Circle to Central Asia, and covered roughly a quarter of the globe. The disintegration of empires has almost always led to horrific conflicts. The collapse of the Roman Empire was followed by the Dark Ages which lasted for at least five hundred years; the collapse of the Ottoman empire produced over a century of wars in the Balkans and the Middle East; and the collapse of the European empires after 1945 led to a series of conflicts in Asia, the Middle East and Africa which are not yet over.

The same phenomenon is now being repeated in the Balkans and in what used to be Soviet Central Asia, from the Caucasus to the Chinese frontier.

Since President Wilson first insisted on the right of national self-determination, almost any ethnic or religious group has been liable to believe that it is entitled to a separate state. However understandable, such a demand is a recipe for conflict on a catastrophic scale. There are more than 3800 ethnic groups in the world. The old Soviet Union contained at least a hundred nationalities. Even the present Russian Federal Republic contains twenty million people who belong to non-Russian ethnic groups, while in the other republics which once belonged to the Soviet Union there are twenty-five million Russians – some of whom, most obviously in the Crimea, are trying to create a new state for themselves.

The moment a dominant group establishes a separate state, there is a danger that it will seek unity by expelling minorities – in Yugoslavia this is nowadays called ethnic cleansing. In the nineteenth century the Americans employed ethnic cleansing to confine the native Indians in small reservations. The First World War led to an exchange of populations between the Greeks and the Turks: the Greeks who lived in Turkey were expelled to Greece and the Turks living in Greece were expelled to Turkey. And following the defeat of Hitler, eight million Germans were expelled from Eastern Europe to Germany. There are no grounds for believing that ethnic cleansing can provide permanent stability; the creation of Israel out of the Jewish diaspora and the behaviour of Palestinians and Kurds suggest otherwise. We certainly do not want to see a world in which 3800 states are expelling people who do not belong to the dominant ethnic or religious group.

THE INTERNAL CHALLENGE TO THE
NATION-STATE

The ethnic problem is most obvious in the post imperial countries, because the colonial powers drew their boundaries without concern for the ethnic identity of the peoples they ruled. But the nation-states in the so-called victorious West are themselves being threatened by similar forces.

Internally, there is a growing demand by minorities for more autonomy inside existing states. In the United Kingdom, the Scots are pressing for more self-government and they threaten to secede if they do not get it. The Catholics in Northern Ireland exert similar pressure. In Canada, Quebec came within a hair's-breadth of achieving independence, while the French face a similar situation in Corsica. In Italy, there is a danger that the country will break apart because the Italians in the north do not want to pay taxes to the centre if some of it is going into the pockets of the Mafia and the Camorra in the south. Indeed the demand for separatism may not depend on ethnic or religious differences alone. Many Russians in Siberia now complain of paying taxes to Moscow in much the same way as the English colonists in Boston complained of paying taxes to London two centuries ago.

Some way must be found of satisfying such pressure for more autonomy without creating separate states. The lesson of history – not least of the American Revolution – is that a government faced by such demands must go some way to meet them or lose everything. Devolution, or greater local autonomy, is a better answer. The subsidiarity rule that issues should be dealt with at the lowest possible level should be applied inside individual states no less than inside groupings of states. In Britain the castration of local government and its replacement by unaccountable quangos poses a major threat to democracy itself.

THE GLOBAL CHALLENGE

The nation-state is being undermined not only by such internal factors but also by external forces largely created by information technology which has allowed globalization to take place in many areas of national life. Finance is now globalized. About $1300 billion dollars a day now cross the exchanges in search of profit with no sort of control. These flows, 99 per cent of which are speculative, largely determine exchange and interest rates and through them the flow of trade and levels of investment and growth. This greatly reduces the ability of governments to manage their economies; at present all the central banks in the world together have reserves only half as great as the daily flow in the foreign exchange markets. I find it odd that some British politicians have been so concerned over the risk that Jacques Delors or Jacques Santer might destroy British sovereignty; yet when in September 1992 George Soros did in fact remove it in twenty-four hours by forcing Britain out of the European Exchange Rate Mechanism, they did not appear to notice – and they have done nothing to prevent it happening again.

Investment is also being globalized. Companies now tend to put a new factory wherever the relevant skills are cheapest and where it is closest to the ultimate market. So there is now a great flood of capital investment from Europe and North America to the Far East. Similarly Japan is putting new factories not only in mainland Asia but also in Britain where the relevant skills are cheaper than elsewhere in the European Single Market.

Business is being globalized as well. Forty-seven of the 100 biggest economies in the world belong to transnational companies, not nation-states. A third of all trade is not between countries but between factories owned by transnational companies in different parts of the world. Many of Japan's imports from the United States are from Japanese subsidiaries there, while the United States' sales from its subsidiaries abroad are two and a half times its exports from within its own frontiers.

Crime is now globalized. Drugs, made from raw materials grown in Central Asia or in Latin America, are now distributed through international networks to schoolchildren on both sides of the Atlantic. It has been estimated that up to $1500 billion a year are being laundered by criminal gangs in countries outside their own frontiers; over a third of this money comes from drugs. The Sicilian Mafia is forging dollars for the Russian Mafia, which is using some of its money to buy property in Chelsea, Hampstead, and Kensington. Such criminal gangs are cooperating more successfully with one another than the police forces of the nation-states which are supposed to control them.

Pollution is now increasingly a global problem. Sheep are still being slaughtered in Cumbria because of a nuclear accident 1000 miles away at Chernobyl in 1986. The European Commission calculates that there are 100 Chernobyls waiting to happen in Russia's Kola peninsula; the recent black farce over the nuclear submarines in Murmansk is a warning. The British government blamed the appalling level of atmospheric pollution in London during the summer of 1995 on a breeze which was moving foul air from the Low Countries to Britain, while the Germans and Norwegians blame us for killing their forests by exporting our acid rain to them. The erosion of the ozone layer and global warming may have disastrous consequences throughout the world in the next century.

Meanwhile the globalization of communications, which made possible many of these other forms of globalization, is accelerating at explosive speed. Governments as far apart as Nigeria, Saudi Arabia, Iran and China are increasingly worried about the impact of satellite television and the fax machine on the stability of their regimes. The fax is now being overtaken by E-mail and soon, we are told, the

Internet may become the main means of communication throughout the world.

It is difficult to guess the full scale and nature of the problems with which the communications revolution is going to present us. A student in St Petersburg recently removed millions of dollars from a bank in New York by computer. In Britain a big computer retail firm has refused to allow its staff to use the Internet for fear of importing viruses into their own systems. The Internet is already spreading worldwide not only pornography but also instructions on how to make bombs and blow up buildings. Yet it is not clear that governments have any idea how to control the Internet.

Some financial experts believe that a viable international electronic currency will be available before a European single currency could be introduced. It would then be possible for anyone in the world to hold an appreciating foreign currency for transaction at home and abroad. This would make EMU irrelevant and open direct competition between currencies throughout the world – including the dollar and the yen. This would present the weaker currencies with the threat of continuing depreciation.

GLOBAL REGULATION

The problems created by these new global developments in finance, business, investment, crime, pollution and communications cannot be left to market forces. They must be the concern of governments working together at a global level. Controls which are limited to individual states or even to regional groupings would simply invite those affected to move elsewhere. Thirty years ago it was Washington's attempt to control the dollar by legislation inside its own frontiers which led to the creation of the Eurodollar market.

The main areas which require global regulation and control have been well described in the 1995 report of the

Commission on Global Governance. This Commission was chaired by the Prime Minister of Sweden and drawn from governments and other organizations from all parts of the world. The United Nations Secretary-General gave it his support.

Though this report has already had a significant influence on governments in the smaller countries, it has been largely ignored by politicians in the larger countries. There are two reasons for this neglect. First, the scale of the domestic problems faced by national governments is particularly daunting at a time when national policies can so easily be frustrated by international factors. Yet governments are too obsessed by these problems to devote sufficient time and energy to the international developments which make them so intractable. Second, the political parties through which choices are presented to electorates in the Western countries do not reflect adequately the real issues or the concerns of people today. Thus the search for strong men to solve problems is noticeable not only in the former Soviet Union but in the United States and Western Europe too.

The governments which won the Second World War established the United Nations and the Bretton Woods institutions, such as the IMF (International Monetary Fund), the IBRD (International Bank for Reconstruction and Development), and the GATT (General Agreement on Tariffs and Trade), to create a new world order. These are still the only tools available to deal with the new global problems which face us half a century later. Unfortunately most governments in 1995 are reluctant to support them either politically or financially – still less to embark on the daunting task of reforming them as necessary. Serious commentators are already wondering whether these institutions will survive at all into the next century. In the United States some politicians openly talk of abolishing them altogether.

Yet the disappearance of these institutions would turn the new world disorder into a catastrophic anarchy. The central problems they now face are formidable indeed. If we are to survive them and to have a chance of creating a new world order, we shall have to determine our priorities for the existing international institutions in order of urgency.

STRENGTHENING THE UNITED NATIONS

The most urgent single need is to develop the ability of the United Nations to deal with the new threats to peace which arise from conflicts within nation-states. The temptation is to leave these problems to the great powers which happen to believe their national interests are threatened, and to allow them to act either directly, like the United States in Grenada and Panama or Russia in the Caucasus and Moldova, or under United Nations auspices but without effective United Nations control, as with the United States in Haiti, Somalia and Bosnia and Russia in Tajikstan.

Such intervention by the great powers is liable to cause more problems than it solves. Some disputes, like the civil wars in Sub-Saharan Africa (such as Rwanda and Liberia), will be largely ignored by the great powers since they do not sufficiently appear to involve their interests. In other cases, like Somalia and Chechenya, the great power concerned may have little understanding of the political realities on the spot. In Bosnia, the United States' use of NATO for its intervention is seen by Russia as a threat to its own national interests and raises the spectre of a return to the Cold War or even of a war between the great powers themselves. In any case, great power intervention may appear to some of the parties to the conflict as an unacceptable new form of imperialism.

However, it is not easy to devise acceptable forms of intervention by the United Nations in a conflict inside national frontiers. Indeed the United Nations charter specifically forbids such intervention, except for humanitarian purposes. However, international action designed purely for humanitarian purposes may drift inevitably into international intervention in a civil war, as in Somalia and Yugoslavia. In general, external intervention in civil wars has rarely succeeded, from the French and Russian Revolutions, the American Civil War, Vietnam and the Lebanon; at best it can lead to a form of colonial occupation from which the external powers then find it difficult to extricate themselves. So it is highly dangerous to cross what has been called 'the Mogadishu line'.

One clear lesson can be drawn from past experience. Rather than intervening when a conflict has already started, it is far better for the United Nations to concentrate on preventing conflict, either by conciliation or by positioning deterrent forces in the area at risk. For conciliation the United Nations needs better intelligence of developing threats, and a more active machinery for diplomatic intervention. For deterrence it needs forces capable of rapid introduction to the threatened area. The presence of a small UN force in Macedonia has so far succeeded in preventing the Yugoslav civil wars from spilling over into an international war, which might involve Albania, Bulgaria, Greece and Turkey.

If such deterrent intervention is to be effective, the United Nations will require a small international force on permanent standby which can be moved to the area concerned in days. Brian Urquhart, who has exceptional experience in UN peacekeeping, has suggested that such a force be composed of volunteers from all over the world – a kind of UN foreign legion. However, such a small permanent force of volunteers might require reinforcement preferably by standby forces earmarked for that purpose by national governments, which could be moved to the area in weeks. The UN Military Staffs' committee should be given direct responsibility for command and control of such forces and should have adequate transport and intelligence resources of its own at its disposal.

These reforms would also help the UN in another vital task – to help in restoring political and economic order and protecting human rights after a conflict in which the social structure has been destroyed. Such improvements in the ability of the United Nations to pursue its peacekeeping role has been recommended for many years by the Secretary-General but have been vetoed by the permanent members of the Security Council, although supported by governments of many smaller countries. Yet by now the great powers themselves should have learned that improvements in the machinery of the Security Council would be politically and economically far less expensive for them than the type of intervention which they have so far preferred.

It is equally desirable, but perhaps less urgent, to revise the United Nations Charter itself to make the Security Council and General Assembly more representative of the realities of the twenty-first century. Germany and Japan now have at least as good a claim to permanent membership of the Security Council as the United Kingdom and France; but if their case was accepted, Southern Asia, Latin America and Africa would certainly demand a similar representation but are unlikely to agree quickly on a single representative.

The General Assembly will never be more than a talking shop if the role of India, which has 846 million inhabitants, counts for no more than that of the Vatican with under 10,000 citizens. Indeed the recent United Nations conferences in Cairo on population growth and in Peking on women's rights found it odd that their procedures could be held up – in Cairo for weeks – by representatives of a state with fewer inhabitants than a small town, none of whom are mothers or children.

Arguments about voting rights under a new constitution, however, might well take years – as would the equally desirable revision of the Charter to allow United Nations intervention inside national frontiers to go beyond peacekeeping to peace enforcement. So it makes sense to concentrate immediately on the peacekeeping role of the UN under its existing constitution.

PAYING FOR THE UNITED NATIONS

New methods of financing United Nations activities are urgently required even for its present roles. The UN regular budget has grown ten times since 1945, to $1181 billion. Its estimated total expenditure worldwide, including peace-keeping and its specialized agencies, was $10.5 billion in 1992. By comparison, the annual expenditure of United Kingdom citizens on alcoholic drink alone is three and a half times greater. Spending worldwide on national military forces is seventy-five times greater – about $800 billion.

But at present the UN is unable to raise even the money which its members have contracted to pay. In 1993 only eighteen governments, accounting for only 16 per cent of the UN budget, had paid in full by the 31 January deadline. At the end of August 1995 governments owed the UN a total of $3.7 billion, and the Secretary had to borrow from the peacekeeping budget to pay its regular costs. The USA owed the most, $1580 million, followed by Russia, $590 million.

Thus, it is not now possible to raise the money needed for the UN's current responsibilities, let alone for the tasks it should undertake to deal with global poverty, pollution, crime, and population growth. The IMF and IBRD have similar financial problems, which could soon destroy their ability to deal with the financial issues and development problems they were set up to tackle.

I do not believe it is realistic to aim at raising the money required by the UN and its sister bodies to deal with the new global problems simply by redistributing contributions among national governments. However, there is a strong case for a rapid redistribution of obligations which cut the US share, say to 10 per cent, and substantially increase the contribution of the wealthy Gulf states, and some of the newly rich Asian states. This would at least gain time for a more fundamental change. I believe the medium-term objective should be to raise the money by taxing internationally activities which currently escape tax altogether and in many cases contribute to the problems which require solution.

Speculative cross-border financial activities are the most obvious target. At present they escape taxation altogether at a time when almost all other activities attract tax. Professor James Tobin, the American Nobel laureate economist, first proposed such a tax over twenty years ago, primarily to dampen such transactions and thereby reduce the volatility of exchange rates to which they contribute.

This proposal has attracted increasing support from other economists, and from prominent bankers such as Felix Rohatyn, who rescued New York City from bankruptcy in the 1960s. In 1992 Nicholas Brady, the US Treasury Secretary under President Bush, persuaded the IMF to set up an official group to study it. Nothing more was heard of his proposal after Bush lost the election later that year. However, in 1995 such a tax was endorsed by the Commission on Global Governance, by the late President Mitterand, and by Lionel Jospin as Socialist candidate for the French Presidency in 1995. Later that year it was recommended by the Independent Working Group on the future of the UN, with Paul Kennedy as its Secretary. The Canadian Prime Minister's proposal that the 1995 G7 Summit should discuss it was vetoed by Britain and the USA.

The most thorough exploration of this approach was published in 1995 by two outstanding international civil servants, Dragoljab Najman and Hans d'Orville. Their paper points out that in 1992 the total global turnover in the foreign exchange markets was equivalent to ten times aggregate world GDP. Since then it has increased at least 50 per cent, largely because of the explosion in derivatives trading. A charge of only 0.1 per cent on such transactions would now raise some $80 billion. A similar charge on trading in government securities would raise about $54 billion. Other potential sources of revenue which would also help in themselves to reduce the new global problems I have described would be an international tax on arms transfers, on polluting fuels, and on transnational corporations.

No one should underestimate the difficulty of reaching global agreements on such new forms of international taxation, and of creating a watertight machinery for collecting it – though information technology would make this infinitely easier than it would have been even ten years ago. But I believe it would be even more difficult to raise the sums required from national governments. It is hard to see any other way of dealing with the new global problems, which are certain to grow in scale and to pose an increasing threat to national governments as well as to global security in its widest sense. It might be wise to entrust the collection and control of such new taxes to a neutral international body such as the Bank for International Settlements, until the world agreed how they should be distributed, and to what agencies.

CONCLUSION

I believe that the end of the Cold War will prove to have ended two centuries of history dominated by the idea of the nation-state, which grew out of the French Revolution in 1789. It is as impossible in 1995 to foresee the world of 2020 as it was in 1795 to foresee the rise and fall of Napoleon and the Congress of Vienna. But it is possible to see that any new world order will depend on the will of national governments to surrender some of their power upwards to global institutions and other powers downwards to regional and local authorities. Subsidiarity will need to be the guiding principle in this redistribution of national power.

The United Kingdom is well placed to take an initiative

in this field since it is a member of the G7, the Commonwealth, the European Union, the IMF, the IBRD, the BIS (Bank for International Settlements), and of course the UN. It seems most unlikely that the United States would take such initiative in the near future given its current tussle between isolationism and unilateralism. The countries of the European Union, under British influence, however, could provide effective leadership as long as they acted together.

In any case the European Union needs to redirect its attention away from arguments about its internal constitution which are costing it a serious loss of public support. If it was seen to be dealing with urgent problems of direct importance to the security and prosperity of its members, I believe it could establish a new importance in the minds of its peoples.

If the next Labour government makes this one of its priorities, it will find the door at least half open.

PART TWO

Issues and Themes

7 A Competitive Economy

David Sainsbury

Chairman of J Sainsbury plc, he is also
a member of the IPPR Commission on
Public Policy & British Business and
Chairman of the Governing Body of the
London Business School.

In looking at economic and industrial policy, I start from
two strong beliefs. Firstly, it is companies that create wealth.
It is they that have to build and sustain a competitive advantage over their rivals in foreign countries, and any attempt
at shadow decision making by government should be
avoided at all costs. Given the complexity and speed of most
product markets today, there is no way that even the most
able civil servants can make decisions about the strategies
that companies should pursue.

Government should not get directly involved in corporate
decision making, but should seek to create an environment
in which companies can build competitive advantage. As
Michael Porter wrote in *The Competitive Advantage of
Nations*, 'Government is indeed an actor in international
competition, but rarely does it have a starring role'.

Secondly, building and maintaining competitive advantage in world markets today is a tough and demanding task.
It requires constant improvement and sustained commitment. It means endless change. Most companies would

prefer to have a protected or controlled market. If government seeks to put a break on economic change by protecting companies or giving them assistance, they will not make the necessary changes.

Subsidies have almost never been associated with the building of competitive advantage. Usually, they simply delay adjustment and innovation. Protection is equally undesirable. It is usually justified on the grounds that it gives industry a breathing space in which to adjust itself, but it is difficult to think of any mature industry anywhere which has made itself into a world-class competitor after a period of protection. To achieve productivity growth a nation's economy must constantly change and upgrade itself, and the role of government must be to help it do so, not provide it with easier options.

THE GOALS OF NATIONAL ECONOMIC POLICY

In considering how government can help companies create wealth, it is necessary to define our economic goals. It is almost universally agreed that we need to be a 'competitive' nation, but competitiveness can have two very different meanings. In the first sense it is used to mean simply the relative prices at which a nation's goods exchange in world markets. Those prices may be low only because the rewards to the capital and the labour employed to make them are low as a result of, for example, devaluation, poor profits or a declining standard of living relative to competing nations. Competitiveness in that sense cannot be seen as a desirable goal for a nation.

In the second sense, competitiveness is used to mean the ability of companies to expand and to produce high and rising levels of productivity, and therefore a high and rising standard of living for a nation's citizens. Productivity in this context is defined as the value of the goods produced by a unit of labour or capital. It is a function of both the quality and features of the goods sold, and, therefore, their desirability to customers, and the efficiency with which they are made. Productivity defined in this way is what in the long term produces the standard of living of a country, as it determines national per capita income, and should be seen as the goal of national economic policy.

To produce increasing levels of productivity over time a nation's companies must continuously upgrade themselves. In existing industries they must raise their level of quality, introduce new products and increase production efficiency. They must also develop the capability to compete in new and more sophisticated industries. This will involve the movement of less productive jobs to developing countries either through foreign investment or foreign sourcing. If less productive jobs are being transferred overseas this is an entirely healthy process, but if high productivity jobs are being lost this will clearly damage long-term prosperity.

THE STATE OF BRITISH INDUSTRY

The main criticism of recent government economic policy is that it has failed to sustain a stable environment so vital to industry. Industrialists have experienced a 'boom and bust' cycle – recession, followed by an upsurge, followed again by recession. Although over the last two years macroeconomic conditions have been relatively stable, the danger is that, as the election approaches, there will be another boom which will lead to another recession. Such instability has a very harmful impact on industry.

Economic instability not only creates unnecessary business failures; it also creates 'short-termism' and demands for short pay-back periods. It is sometimes argued that the best way to stimulate investment is to reduce the cost of capital. But there is no better stimulus to investment than a steady and growing level of demand. And the worst environment for investment is undoubtedly a short-term boom which industrialists do not believe will last.

Over the last ten or fifteen years there has been an improvement in the flexibility of UK industry, and resources have moved more easily out of declining industries. It is, however, difficult to see any significant progress in any of the underlying factors which make for long-term growth and efficiency, such as capital investment, training or product development. In the last recession there were major cutbacks, leaving us, as always, in a poor position to take advantage of the upturn. Unfortunately, the capacity lost during recent recessions, and especially the recession of the early 1980s, was not replaced by new, technologically advanced firms. As a result, while what remains is more efficient, we desperately need to see more growth coming from new world-class companies and products.

Despite what Conservative ministers used to say in the 1980s, manufacturing is still vital to the future of the British economy. This is not to argue that manufacturing should be seen as an inherently more virtuous activity than services. The UK, for example, exports more than £500 million a year of legal services, and Britain has had a trade surplus in legal services for every year since at least 1970. If we could earn our living by selling services to the world, there would be nothing wrong with that. The facts, however, are that 80 per cent of world trade is in manufacturing and 20 per cent is in services, so there is no realistic way that we can earn our living just by selling services. Any serious analysis has to conclude that, to achieve sustained growth, we need a growing and dynamic manufacturing sector as much as a successful services sector.

THE INDUSTRIAL CHALLENGE

Looking ahead, British industry will face a number of formidable challenges. One is that there are going to be many more economies in the world where moderately complicated manufacturing activities can be undertaken. Because of the explosion of literacy, labour in the developing countries is now starting to reach productivity levels which make it competitive. According to the 1991 World Development report, between 1965 and 1988, secondary school enrolment increased from about 26 per cent to 55 per cent of the school-age population in the fifty-eight middle income developing countries, and tertiary enrolment jumped from 7 per cent to 17 per cent. Though there are no more than 600 million literate workers in the world today, it has been calculated that in the next twenty years the figure could rise to three billion. If our only weapon in competing for work is low labour costs, we will always be outbid by countries whose workers have comparable productivity levels and are paid less.

The second pressure is from technological change which is an opportunity as well as a challenge. The new technologies such as electronics, advanced materials and biotechnology, will have applications in many industries, and industrialized countries should not regard a few high technology sectors as the only refuge from low-wage developing countries. This is the place where they have the greatest advantage, but these sectors will be able to provide only a small part of total added-value and employment. Companies should seek to operate in all those segments of industry where high technological and management skills can create advantage. The creation of economic value is a coupling process which brings together technology and customer needs, and requires managers who have enough knowledge of an industry and its technologies to engage in a real appraisal of technological developments, competitors' strategies and product opportunities. An appropriate combination of managerial know-how and technological advance is necessary if we are to compete successfully in world markets.

The implications for British industry are clear. A highly trained and educated labour force is key to economic and industrial success. The most striking thing about Asian development today is the importance that is given to education. For example, it is common ground in Japan or Taiwan or Singapore that the way to be successful is by becoming more technologically competent as an individual, as a company, or as a country. Five years ago I visited an Apple factory in Singapore which originally was engaged only in assembling Apple computers. Now some of the production engineering for Apple computers is being done there. I was told a third of the employees in the factory were spending some part of their evenings studying to get higher qualifications – the company paid for the fees for them to do this but they did it in their own time. Of how many British factories would that be true? In most of these Asian countries, education is seen as an investment which will help the individual become more prosperous.

I do not believe that British teachers give enough priority to the acquisition of the knowledge and skills essential to industrial success. As a result many young people enter the labour market condemned to a life of poorly paid, unskilled work, interspersed with long periods of unemployment. Similarly, British employers cut back on training in difficult times instead of seeing it as vital to the survival of their companies.

LONG-TERM COMMITMENT

Management needs to make long-term commitments, and not only to education and training, but also to investment, to product development or to positions in export markets. Competitive advantage is not something that can be built up over a couple of years. The export drive of Japanese car manufacturers started in the 1950s, but it was not until the 1970s that they began to achieve strong market shares abroad. Economists tend always to think in terms of the mobility of resources, and the mobility of resources is essential to the upgrading of an economy if resources are not to remain locked into situations where a company cannot become competitive. But often when a new product is being produced or a new business developed, or an export position built up in a new country, losses will arise. In these circumstances a manager has to take a decision either to continue because he believes that he can improve the productivity of resource utilization or to reallocate the resources. It is essential that such decisions are taken on the basis of a long-term view of a company's prospects, and it is therefore vitally important that the goals of managers are long-term ones.

Closely linked to taking a long-term view is the idea of a company as an organization of 'stakeholders'. There are two main stakeholders – those that provide the capital and those that provide the labour. From a company's point of view there are strong arguments for trying to secure a close relationship with the providers of capital, while it is obviously advantageous to have a committed and involved workforce. However, our institutions and legislative framework do not encourage such long-term commitment.

A revolution in work organizations is taking place in the world, with the world's best companies replacing the methods of mass production with high-performance work organizations which use the intelligence and skills of their workers. As a result they are unleashing major advances in productivity, quality, variety and speed of product introductions.

This revolution in work organization means that the success of companies depends increasingly on the skills and initiative of the whole workforce. And that is why it is necessary to align the interests of the individuals who make up an organization with that organization's interests. This is not just a question of becoming impassioned about excellence or staging celebrations, as some American authors would have one believe. It is about getting a company's policies right in areas such as job security, involvement and profit sharing.

THE ROLE OF GOVERNMENT

I am a firm believer in a market economy. But companies work in markets which are very much affected by the framework within which they operate. Here government has a vital role to play. Its task is to shape regulations, institutions, infrastructures and policies in such a way that these help companies improve their performance.

It is crucial that government helps industry upgrade the factors of production. Increasingly, those which are most essential to productivity growth are created rather than inherited. Whereas in the past natural resources, climate, location and unskilled and semiskilled labour were important, today it is the supply of skilled employees, such as graduate engineers and computer scientists, specialized research institutes and modern digital data communications which are the key to success.

Top quality education and training is vital. In my judgment we will not find it easy to produce the number of world-class companies we need unless we make some basic changes to our educational system. There must be a big improvement in basic literacy and numeracy skills. It is not good enough to provide a reasonable education to the top 60 per cent of children. The goal of educational policy must be to bring the vast majority of children up to reasonable standards. It is absurd that companies are having to upgrade the basic numerary and literary skills of their workers.

We must also create a high prestige and effective technical stream in our schools which will capture the enthusiasm of pupils who excel in practical subjects, impart some basic knowledge, and win the full support of employers. And we must replace A levels with examinations which require all students to take a wider range of courses up to the age of eighteen. Our system of specializing at the age of sixteen is ludicrous both in human terms and in terms of producing people for industry. We need far more students who feel comfortable in a number of disciplines, especially mathematics, English and science.

Government has an important part to play in helping industry improve its technology. There are two main aspects to this; one is the role of the science base, especially the universities; the other is the receptivity of companies to inflows of technological knowledge. In the past there was always a tendency to say that, if the science base was supported, that in itself was sufficient. But it is quite clear that a country can have an extremely successful science base and very poor economic performance. So, while it is very important that government backs the science base, that strategy has to be linked with trying to make companies more receptive. We can learn from German institutions which assist in the transfer of technology from universities. Government could also give financial incentives to universities to help industry by providing extra funds which match the amount of money which universities themselves earn from industry.

Another way that government can encourage the upgrading of industry is by affecting the demand conditions of industry. It can achieve this both through its role as a buyer of goods and services and through regulations that affect product standards and the processes by which they are made. In both cases, government policies can either encourage or hinder competitive advantage. For example, there can be no doubt that when British Telecommunications was a state monopoly, it had a disastrous effect on the telecommunications supply industry in this country because it was not allowed to have foreign suppliers and laid down idiosyncratic standards for the industry which made it very difficult for the supply industry to sell its products to the rest of the world. By contrast, Japan established tough quality standards for export goods in the 1950s and 1960s, and these were a stimulus to improving quality in Japanese industry. Strict regulations are particularly helpful if they anticipate standards that other countries eventually adopt. Sweden's tough standards for product safety and environmental protection have led to a number of Swedish companies achieving competitive advantage in a number of different industries. Atlas Copco, for example, has been successful internationally with quiet central heating compressors that can be used in urban areas without disturbing nearby residents.

Just as important is for government to make certain that underlying policies – competition policy, trade policy, our relationship with Europe – help to make the economy more dynamic. A strong anti-trust policy is essential to the upgrading of an economy. We should also make mergers and acquisitions more difficult as a way of encouraging companies to expand through organic growth. Mergers and acquisitions have not led to a commensurate improvement in industrial efficiency, and they have helped to shorten the time horizons of management, because managers are reluctant to undertake long-term investment which may temporarily depress profits and make them vulnerable to a takeover. A policy of encouraging rivalry between domestic companies needs to be matched by a commitment to free trade. Companies will not become world-class ones if they are protected from world-class competition by restricted public purchasing or 'voluntary export restraint agreements'. In particular we need, as John Kay has pointed out, to focus our efforts on achieving trade liberalization in those areas where we have a competitive advantage. Trade liberalization in recent years has concentrated on semisophisticated manufactured goods such as cameras, cars and industrial machinery, where the UK has relatively few competitive advantages. We need to put more effort into trade liberalization in areas such as airlines and retail financial services where we are successful.

We also need to achieve stability in our relationship with Europe. Europe is now effectively our home market and we need for straightforward commercial reasons, if no other, to play a central role in its development. There is no way we can disengage without damaging the long-term interests of the country.

Finally, government can help industry improve its performance by providing the right tax and legislative framework. This includes laws relating to corporate governance, tax incentives, and employment. For example, if a government wants to encourage companies to take a long-term view of investment, it can give favourable tax treatment to capital gains on long-term equity investments in companies. In this country we have equalized tax rates on income and capital gains. This is a policy which I believe attaches too much importance to financial market efficiency and too little to encouraging companies to take a long-term view. In the same way, if it is desirable that employees make a long-term commitment to their organizations, then there is a case for laws safeguarding employee rights and guaranteeing involvement.

The main goal of government policy should be to create an environment in which all companies can upgrade their competitive advantages, and in this way produce a rising standard of living for the country. A high level of productivity allows a high level of income and the resources to pay for public services. It also enables a nation's companies to meet high standards in such areas as the environment and health and safety without compromising their international competitiveness.

8 Taxing and Spending

David Lipsey

Political Editor of the *Economist*, he
was special adviser to Anthony
Crosland from 1972–77 and worked
for James Callaghan at No 10 from
1977–79.

'Labour is no longer the party of tax-and-spend.' Since his
election, that has been Tony Blair's repeated claim. It may
even be that voters are starting to believe him.

Pedants old enough to remember Labour governments
might cavil. But Mr Blair is not addressing Labour's record,
which is now ancient history. He is addressing Labour
attitudes.

At any rate until recently, Labour activists were invariably, and Labour voters were often by instinct in favour of
'tax-and-spend'. It was, for Labour, an important means
towards its goal of a fairer, more equal society.

Labour activists were for tax because they thought it was
something paid by the rich. In the minds of activists, the
words 'rich' and 'undeserving' were indissolubly linked. The
more tax, the fewer rich; the fewer rich, the fewer undeserving; and the fewer undeserving the better.

Activists were for spend because they thought it benefited
what they called the 'working classes'. There was a certain
vagueness about the term to be sure. It was sometimes used

to embrace white-collar workers and sometimes not. But whatever the working class was, it was assumed to be the chief gainer from cheap health care and state pensions and universal free education.

Activists were strongly reinforced in the 1960s by the arguments put forward by the great American liberal, J. K. Galbraith, of which Dick Crossman, a Labour intellectual, became the leading British exponent. Advanced societies, they thought, suffered from 'private affluence and public squalor'. Though this argument was transparently more true of the United States than of Britain, the state of Britain's Victorian schools and hospitals gave it credibility even here.

Behind this argument lay a less creditable one. 'Tax-and-spend' took resources away from individuals and gave them to the state. For a party like Old Labour, still committed to Clause Four and the public ownership of everything, that seemed a good thing.

WHAT THE VOTERS THINK

The more recent debates on tax-and-spend have focussed on the electoral arguments for and against it. Some Labour modernizers are convinced that it was John Smith's shadow budget of 1992, proposing higher taxes on the rich, that lost Labour the election – a proposition to which opinion research for the Tories lends support. Labour cannot win as a high-spend party, it is said.

In fact, the evidence here is mixed. No one has convincingly proved that the shadow budget cost Labour votes. According to the authoritative British Election Study, Labour was lost even before it was unveiled. Moreover, there is some evidence of growing public support for *more* tax-and-spend. Successive British Social Attitudes surveys have asked 'If the government had to choose, should it reduce taxes and spend less on health, education and social benefits; keep taxes and spending at the same levels as now;

or increase taxes and spend more on health education and social benefits?' The results have been:

	1983	1986	1990	1993
Reduce taxes	9%	5%	3%	4%
Keep taxes as now	54%	44%	37%	29%
Increase taxes	32%	46%	54%	63%

Taking such results at their face value, you might think that tax-and-spend is just the vote-winning policy which Labour needs.

This argument should be taken with a big pinch of salt. First, the question is a loaded one, identifying only those objects of public spending which are most popular with voters. If, for example, voters were asked to choose between reduced taxes and increased spending on, say, overseas aid, scroungers and government offices, the results might be very different.

Secondly, the Social Attitudes Survey answers may not mean quite what they seem to mean. When respondents say that taxes should go up to pay for more spending, the assumption is often that they are willing to pay those taxes themselves. But the assumption may be wrong. Many people want more spending, particularly or only on services they use themselves. They may favour new taxes to pay for them, particularly or only if those taxes fall on other people. 'Don't tax you, don't tax me; tax the man behind that tree.' If told that, in reality, there is no painless way of taxing others, and they would have to pay themselves, voters' answers might change.

Thirdly, it may be that sentiment is shifting away from higher spending. A recent MORI poll for the *Economist*, for example, asked whether people supported or opposed reducing government spending in order to reduce levels of taxation. Forty per cent said they didn't but 50 per cent said they did.

Despite these reservations, public attitudes continue to be broadly in favour of public spending. The Tories have lost support by squeezing spend too hard.

True, spending has been held roughly constant as a proportion of GDP since they came to power. In 1995 it amounted to 41.6 per cent of GDP according to the Organization for Economic Cooperation and Development, compared with 41.4 per cent in 1978.

But these numbers understate the severity of the squeeze. For one thing there are more unemployed to pay for. For another, spending, particularly on health, tends to rise faster than GDP, since health care is something which people want more of as they get richer. And this has led to the public perception, clear from the survey evidence, that the Tories are not to be trusted to maintain crucial public services such as health, education and welfare.

This argument must not be pushed too far. There is no evidence of public enthusiasm for much higher taxes. Indeed, the Tories have also been punished for their cavalier attitude towards tax cuts, promised in the election and ditched once the votes harvest was safely garnered in. It would be an act of political unwisdom, to put it no higher, for Labour to think for a minute that it could run and win as a high-spend, high-tax party – which is one reason why Mr Blair will do no such thing.

SORTING OUT THE ARGUMENTS

What it thinks, however, is another matter. Labour's policy towards tax-and-spend should not be determined by electoral considerations alone. After a generation of Tory rule, expectations of New Labour will inevitably be high. They will be highest amongst those pressure groups for particular deserving groups in society who will think that, at last, they have a sympathetic ear and loose purse strings in Whitehall. They may go along with the argument from expediency before an election. They will not abide by it after an election. Unless Labour has its case on tax-and-spend really sorted out, it will only too readily be overwhelmed by the complaints of such groups.

So the party must think through the arguments on tax-and-spend. It should retain those bits of its traditional philosophy that are still relevant and ditch the rest. It should understand why some arguments for spending are now weak. But babies should not be chucked out with bathwater; and it should be prepared to argue seriously the case for a proper level of expenditure, and a proper distribution of the taxes through which it is to be paid.

As with Clause Four, tax-and-spend exemplifies a cast of mind which has outlived its day. Certainly, taxing and spending remains a powerful instrument which a Labour government can use in its pursuit of a fairer and more secure society. But it is no longer the sole means of pursuing that aim. It needs revision not just because people will not vote for it (though they won't). It needs revision because it can no longer do what Labour originally hoped it could do.

Why not? Because, first, public spending has risen so greatly as a share of national income. At the end of the nineteenth century it amounted to only about 10 per cent of GDP. Even immediately before the Second World War it amounted only to a quarter. But with the advent of the welfare state it rose to around 40 per cent by 1950, often threatening to rise much higher. If more spending was enough to bring about socialism, Britain would long since have been a socialist country.

Public spending at these levels cannot, as Old Labour thought, be supported simply by taxing the rich. Denis Healey put the point well in his memoirs. *The Time of my Life*: 'Any substantial attempt to improve the lot of the poorest section of the community must now be at the expense of the average man and woman since the very rich do not collectively earn enough to make much difference and the average man does not nowadays want to punish those who earn a little more than he, since he hopes ultimately to join them.'

If public spending now stands above 40 per cent of GDP, so something close to 40 per cent of GDP has to be raised in taxes because international capital markets will not allow such borrowing. Even after what can be extracted from the better off has been extracted, a lot will have to be extracted from everyone else. Moreover, we live in a world of international mobility of labour and capital. If we tax the rich too much, they will simply emigrate. Capital and jobs will emigrate with them.

Labour must live with these facts of life. But this does not mean that it should bow supine before them. The period 1979–95 has seen a big increase in income inequalities. Indeed by some measures, the bottom 10 per cent of the population actually saw its income fall during that period. Changes in the tax system are by no means the only cause of rising inequality; and the plight of the poor certainly owes more to the rise in unemployment in the period. But it remains the case that the Tories have run a tax system that is exceptionally generous towards the better off. Labour need not follow their example.

The Party says that it believes in 'fair' taxation. Even in a world of international mobility, there is no reason why the heaviest burden should not fall on the broadest shoulders and why the richest should not be asked to pay most in taxation. Even modest and gradual increases in taxes on the very well off would produce useful sums of additional revenue, while making the distribution of income less unequal.

But the way the money to pay for public spending is raised is only one side of the equation. On the other side, the old Labour certainty that public spending is intrinsically more desirable than private spending is now more problematical.

It is not obvious that the public sector has suffered more from a shortage of cash during the recession than private enterprises. Private living standards are squeezed by high mortgages and high borrowing, and the need to try to preserve a cushion against uncertain employment prospects.

Moreover, the rise in living standards over the past fifty years has not in any way diminished the popular appetite for more private spending. Nor should it. The belief that Joe Soap has less right to aspire to decent homes, to private savings, to adventurous holidays and exciting leisure activities than those who already enjoy them is profoundly undemocratic, illiberal and elitist. Labour exists to raise people up. And if it doesn't, the people will opt for parties which do – especially as, with membership of the European Union, more and more people are conscious that there are other countries similar to our own, such as Germany, France and even Italy, where the mass of the population enjoys higher living standards than our own, as well as superior social services.

New Labour too must be conscious that time has thrown up ways in which public spending may become perverted in practice. One is by inefficiency in spending, or even corruption. Bureaucracies sometimes divert resources which are meant to be devoted to the public weal to their own selfish purposes. We do not need to turn to what has happened in ex-Communist Eastern Europe for the proof of that, for there is evidence for it aplenty in the liberal Western democracies too.

It must also be remembered that state spending is not automatically redistributive. Broadly speaking, it still has some redistributive effect, mostly through the impact of cash benefits. Before taxes and benefits, the bottom 20 per cent of households receive only 2.3 per cent of income; after tax and benefits they receive 7.0 per cent. Before taxes and benefits, the top 20 per cent of households receive 52 per cent of income; taxes and benefits reduce that to 44 per cent.

But public money has often not, in practice, gone to the less well off. The more affluent sections of the middle class, for example, have been adept at getting health service resources channelled into the leafy suburban areas where they live. The government-funded Arts Council lavishes resources on its beloved Opera House, while community arts projects languish. The lucky opera-goer enjoys his cut-price night out at the expense of the taxes paid by the poor.

Public spending *per se* does not redistribute income. Public spending *per se* does not make life chances more equal. Its effect on these depends on where the money is actually spent, as well as on who actually pays for it.

None of this is to buy the argument of the Tory Right that public spending is a bad thing. Even Kenneth Clarke, the chancellor, has argued strongly for the importance of properly funded welfare. Only with a welfare safety net, he says, will people be willing to live with the insecurities implicit in a dynamic market economy. This argument was also convincingly developed in the report of the IPPR's Labour-sponsored Commission on Social Justice. In general a Labour government that did not believe in a proper level of collective provision of benefits and services would not be worth having.

Nor should Labour accept the Thatcherite argument that public spending and a prosperous economy are in conflict. Rather, the truth is the reverse. Without a prosperous economy, the country will not be able to afford a proper level of public spending. To maintain high quality services in a stagnant economy would require rising levels of taxation and falling levels of personal disposable income, and voters will not stomach that. However, without a proper level of public spending, the economy will not prosper. Prosperity requires government investment in roads and rail. Perhaps above all, it requires investment in education and training. The secret of success is not to favour public spending or private spending *per se*. The trick is to achieve the right balance between the two.

BEYOND TAX-AND-SPEND

Crude tax-and-spend is (or ought to be) dead. But what should be put in its place? How can Labour construct a robust strategy for expenditure and taxation that will survive both the economic and the political pressures upon it? Obviously, it will not be easy.

Labour will inherit from the Conservatives an imbalance between taxes and spending. From where they are in the opinion polls, the Tories will have no choice but to cut taxes between now and polling day, and hope for the best. But from where they are in the opinion polls, they will certainly not choose to pay for these cuts by chopping spending. In 1991–2, Norman Lamont unleashed the mother-and-father of a short-term public spending spree in an attempt to buy votes. Unfortunately, it worked. Having no other trick to play this time, no one familiar with the Tory Party will expect it not to try it again.

Some devices which the Tories have used to balance taxing and spending will not be available to Labour. The Tories to their credit have been ingenious in creating new devices to increase the efficiency of public spending: market testing, contracting out, cuts in bureaucracy and so on. But the savings produced are by their nature one-off. They must be persevered with, but they cannot be repeated. Nor will there be any more opportunities to raise money by privatization.

Another difficulty lies in the device used by the Tories to keep spending down. That is restraint over public sector pay. The Tories have held back public sector wage increases by a policy which says that the pay bill must not go up. Meanwhile the private sector is allowed to do what it will. But by the time of the next election, the clamour from public sector workers demanding to be allowed to catch up will be mounting. Labour will naturally be reluctant to sustain public services at the expense of public servants.

There is, moreover, the effect of Labour's policy on the minimum wage to consider. If it is set high, as the unions have demanded, many low-paid workers in the public sector will benefit. So, some will say, they should – but if they do, it will add to the pressure on spending and on taxes. Hence, the importance of ensuring that a minimum wage is introduced cautiously, and at a level that does not bust the Exchequer.

Then there is the risk of a recession. Unless the business cycle has for ever been eliminated, the upturn will by 1997, the probable election year, be six years old. A slowdown will be overdue. True, in time, Labour will hope that its economic policies for investment and training will increase the potential growth rate of the economy. But there is bound to be a lag before such policies have their effect.

In the meantime, the likelihood is that the economy will slow, and that unemployment will in consequence edge up. This will increase spending on social security benefits, adding to the pressure on the rest of the government's budget.

Labour Party members must avoid thinking that that is an easy way off the spending hook. The Party is committed to allowing local authorities to spend unused receipts from council house sales and to using private capital for public sector projects. There are doubtless arguments for and against, but they do not negate the fact that money spent by the public sector cannot be spent by the private sector. And they will certainly not serve to hoodwink international finance into allowing Labour to borrow and spend more than Britain's economy can sustain without inflation.

These are good reasons for an extreme caution by Labour in making commitments to new spending. But is there a more important reason still for restraint? Is there a danger that the resources of the welfare state will be overwhelmed by a demographic crisis which makes it impossible to fund proper pensions and decent health care?

Fortunately, Britain is not badly placed in this regard. According to calculations by the government actuary, the support ratio, the proportion of those of pensionable age to the working population, currently around 30 per cent, will actually fall slightly in the years 1991–2010. According to the OECD, it will almost double in Japan, and rise by between 5 and 10 percentage points in other European countries. More broadly, according to John Hills and his colleagues at the London School of Economics, if the economy grew from 1993–2000 at 2.5 per cent a year, and unemployment fell by a quarter, social security would take only the same share of GDP as it does now. Even on the extreme assumption that benefit levels were to keep up with overall living standards, which is not current policy, the effect on the public finances of demographic changes would add up to 5 per cent of GDP – no more than the increase over three years during the recent recession.

Of course, Labour must keep an eye on making commitment now, which will cease to be affordable in the next century. Moving into the second decade of the new millennium, strong pressures will emerge. Pensioner numbers will rise quite rapidly. And, because state pensions are based on an implied contract whereby you get back later what you pay now, they cannot just be cut back at will at the last minute. A strategy for pensions soon would help avoid the risk of a crisis in pensions later.

But the party should not get too het up about them now. For one thing, they may never happen. History records many predicted demographic changes which went away, and many forecast economic downturns that were averted. Some of those who cast their arguments in terms of demographics are in fact using them to justify an ideological crusade against the welfare state.

There is no need to panic. Nor is it sensible to draw up blueprints for public spending, which are only too often overtaken by events. The sensible way forward is for Labour to formulate a set of principles now which will inform its decision making in office.

The first is that Labour should not get hung up on the quantum of public spending. Politicians like to think that this is a decision under their control. But this is, to a large extent, an illusion. The level of spending will depend on short-term economic performance, long-term demographics, the ebb and flow of democratic debate on spending and the tolerance of international markets. A Labour government will be able to influence these only at the margin.

More important, how much more Labour is able to spend depends on how well the economy performs. It is one thing to look at an increment in the nation's wealth, and to seek to make sure public spending gets its share of it. It is quite another to try to take more from a national product which does not grow. If it were possible to increase growth beyond the trend rate of (say) 2 per cent, spending might rightly lay claim to much of the excess. If however growth falls below that rate, what the state can spend will be more limited; for popular pressure for most of that growth to be devoted to people's personal incomes will be hard to resist.

Certainly, public spending should be higher at the end of a Labour government than if a Tory government was in office in the same economic circumstances for the same period. How much higher will depend on the economy. Public spending will have a high claim on the product of growth; and the higher the growth rate, the faster the rate of spending increase that the economy will be able to support. But money not made cannot be spent.

This leads to the next point. Labour claims that it will increase the rate of economic growth. Its weapon for doing so is not Keynesian demand management, but, primarily, a radical upgrading of the skills and education of the workforce.

That means more spending. If the Labour government

really believes that the key to economic growth is more state investment in education and training, it must make it. Of course it may well be possible, as some argue, to reallocate existing education budgets in order to ensure that spending is more effective. But, in the end, more money will have to be invested in education. No one should delude themselves that small increases in expenditure will change economic performance. On the other hand, the more that is spent on education and training, the less there will be for other programmes.

There is no painless way of paying for that by raising taxes. Gordon Brown has been ingenious in finding tax loopholes and promising to close them. But the political reaction to the chancellor's attempt to close the loophole on the taxation of share options shows that closing tax loopholes is not a soft option.

Britain's tax system has manifest inadequacies. Expenditure taxes are too narrowly based. Income taxes are too easily avoided. The taxation of wealth is a standing joke. Reform in all these areas is desirable. But it will not provide a Labour chancellor with a pot of gold with which to satisfy the desires of all the supplicants for his largesse.

So Labour must get the most out of every pound it is able to spend. That means, first, an unremitting drive against waste and for efficiency. It must be a matter for decision in each individual case whether provision should be directly undertaken by the public sector, or whether the state should purchase services from private providers. *Pace* the Tories, the latter is not always more efficient; as in the National Health Service it can involve horrendous paperwork, wasteful expenditure on consultants, and a burgeoning bureaucracy. But *pace* Old Labour it can often cut costs, sometimes dramatically. Labour dare not let up on the reforms that go under the head of the 'New Public Management' designed to reduce costs and improve service standards.

For detailed Treasury control must increasingly be substituted a devolution of budgets, which gives individual public managers an opportunity to get the most out of the available cash. And, whatever Whitehall says, devolution of budgets to local level, to local authorities, regional authorities and sometimes even quangos, may often lead to greater efficiency.

Then there is the question of priorities. One such, training and education, has already been mentioned. The other should be a serious drive to do something about long-term unemployment.

Short-term unemployment exacts a high price, but it is an unfortunate necessity in a thriving, mobile market economy. Long-term unemployment is very different. It is a social evil. It is also an economic evil, turning people from potential wealth-generators into wealth-consumers. What is needed is a radical policy combining job subsidies for those who take on long-term unemployed people and direct state provision of useful work for them to do, with a determination that long-term unemployed people who refuse proper offers of work are no longer subsidized by the taxpayer.

Generally the answer for the unemployed is jobs, not dole. If more people get jobs, then fewer people will need state help – which could even, eventually, save the state money. The Social Justice Commission estimated that every unemployed person costs the state £9000 in benefits and lost taxes directly – without counting the indirect costs of increased crime and ill health.

However, if more is to be spent on these things, less has to be spent elsewhere. Some, no doubt, can be cut from defence once the Tories' absurd post-imperial ambitions are abandoned. And there are still some public programmes which should be pruned. A Labour government should look again at spending on the rural areas, asking how much of it helps deprived country people and how much goes to rich Tory farmers; and at how spending on the arts is allocated; and at a legal aid budget which is apparently able to find limitless sums to provide Rolls Royce defences to Rolls Royce defendants.

But even these programmes will not yield big savings easily. Defence has already been cut. There is only one programme of a sufficient size to yield real savings: social security, which accounts for nearly one pound in three the state spends.

Here the dilemma is easily stated. The Tories have already cut what can be relatively easily cut. Indeed, in many regards they have cut too hard. Incomes support has been uprated only in line with prices. So the poor have been denied any share in rising national prosperity. And anyone looking at the lives of most poor people must conclude that they need higher benefits, not lower.

But if they are to get them, and the budget is to be restricted, savings have to come from elsewhere. That must mean savings in spending on large universal benefits, most particularly on the state pension. The trouble is not that pensions on current policies cannot be afforded. As we have seen above, they probably can. It is that, since the basic state pension now rises in line with prices and not earnings, it does not give pensioners who rely on it alone any share in rising prosperity. So we need a system that does.

In the long-term it is hard to resist the conclusion that the bulk of pensions should be paid through personal provision, whether through compulsory state savings schemes (as proposed by Frank Field, MP) or through voluntary private schemes. This is not because such schemes are ideologically preferable; it is because, pragmatically, decent provision for old age will not otherwise be fundable.

CONCLUSION: 'AN INCH WORTH LIVING IN'

To summarize the argument, how much it taxes and spends is no longer the important test of how successful a Labour government is. Certainly spending will have a high priority in the allocation of any increment from economic growth. Equally certainly, the growth must come first. In the early days, that means giving priority to spending designed, such as education and training, to increase growth over spending which is desirable in its own right. In general, whatever the amount of spending, it is vital, first, that every penny be well used, and, secondly, that spending priorities reflect social priorities.

Many New Labour minds will accept all this. It is their Old Labour hearts which will rebel. If New Labourism is so like Toryism, is it worth having at all?

One answer is that Labour will be different in many ways that lie outside the economic area altogether – in, for example, constitutional and libertarian reform. Another lies in the wise words of Richard Neville, an Australian liberal who has lived since 1983 under an unbroken Labour government: 'There is perhaps an inch of difference between an Australia governed by the Labour Party and an Australia governed by the Right. But, believe me, it is an inch worth living in.'

The gap between Mr Major's Toryism and Mr Blair's modernized New Labour is not as wide as (say) the gap between Mrs Thatcher's Toryism and Michael Foot's old-style Labourism. But there is a gap nevertheless. It will no longer be that Labour spends and the Tories don't. It will lie in fairer taxes on the rich; in a willingness to invest public money in training and education; in a determination to concentrate benefits on those most in need rather than on middle-class benefits; and in a determination to give a high priority, in the distribution of the eventual fruits of growth, to better public services. By these criteria should the performance of a Labour government that has rejected crude tax-and-spend be judged.

9 Reforming the Welfare State

Frank Field

Labour MP for Birkenhead and
Chairman of the Commons Social
Security Select Committee, he is the
author of *Losing Out, Beyond
Punishment* and *Making Welfare Work*.

Our welfare system badly needs to change. The social security budget already takes by far the biggest slice of government spending and it will go on rising. At the same time, a third of all households claim means-tested benefits, a proportion which has doubled under the Tories. Means testing on this scale is undermining the original purpose of welfare because it acts as a disincentive to work and strengthens the dependency culture. In this essay, I propose a long-term package of reforms to encourage self-improvement, to strengthen individual commitment to the welfare state, and to provide a framework for the new millennium.

ESCALATING COSTS

The welfare bill has reached almost £90 billion. In 1949–50, we spent £597 million on welfare. Translated into today's money, that figure rises to £10 billion in terms of prices or to £20 billion in terms of earnings. Even so, it is less than a quarter of what we are actually spending on welfare today.

Put another way, in 1949–50 the social security budget was only one-sixth of total spending. Today it has gone up to a third.

The reasons for this dramatic increase are that benefits have risen in real terms; new groups, for example the disabled, have been brought into the benefit system; and, since 1979, unemployment has risen sharply. The big increase in those receiving means-tested benefits is also a significant factor in rising costs because it creates dependency.

The Conservatives have tried their hardest to cut back on costs by abolishing some benefits and cutting back on others; the breaking of the link between pensions and earnings was the most drastic of their measures. The present Social Security Secretary, Peter Lilley, has attempted to control spending by cutting down on the numbers of new claimants and by throwing as many existing claimants as he can off the rolls. Even so, the Tories have had to shift from the policy of cutting the actual size of the budget to one of reducing the rate of its increase.

The increasing size of the social services budget will present a Labour government with very grave difficulties. If it allows the budget to continue to grow, it would derail the government's whole programme. But if a Labour Social Security Secretary adopts the Lilley strategy of cuts, it would demoralize the party. The only other scenario is one which tries to take people off the present system and into an alternative one.

THE CANCER OF MEANS TESTING

The Beveridge plan was to create an insurance system which over time would guarantee that nobody would suffer from want – which was Beveridge's word for poverty. However, national insurance benefits were never paid at a level above national insurance levels, so throughout the postwar period people were continuing to claim means-tested benefits.

Today, so far from playing the residual role envisaged in the Beveridge report, means testing has become the main prop of the welfare state. Whereas, in 1949, only one-tenth of households were on means-tested benefits, now it is a third. They have been massively expanded under the Tories, rising from one-sixth in 1979. Insurance costs have risen by less than 30 per cent since 1979, while the costs of means tests have gone up by 300 per cent.

I now see means testing as the cancer in the system, because it is operating in a way which goes against the grain of human nature. It also acts as a disincentive. Means tests tax effort in that as you increase your income, you lose benefit; they put a penalty against savings because by saving you can make yourself ineligible; and they also tax honesty in that if you answer questions dishonestly, you can actually gain benefit.

Means testing has become the main recruiting sergeant of the dependency culture. It induces, cultivates and spreads dependency. Once a person is on means-tested benefits, all the effort is devoted to working the system rather than working to get off it.

Take the example of unemployment benefit. The revealing thing about this benefit is not so much that the government has been deliberately cutting back on it and plans further cuts; it is that, of those who are actually claiming this inadequate benefit, very few are also claiming means-tested assistance to top it up. The reason for this is that their partners are in work. Note the advantage of an insurance over a means-tested benefit. If a person has an insurance benefit, it does not stop anybody else in the household working because their income is not taken into account. But when unemployment benefit runs out, and a person becomes eligible for a means-tested benefit, it does not pay a partner to work. And indeed the advice that is given in benefits offices is for the partner to give up work.

But once a person is off unemployment benefit, it is not

only that the partner gives up employment but the mechanics of getting back into the labour market are drastically changed. If a person is on unemployment benefit (and his partner is working), it is worthwhile getting a modestly paid job. But once the person is on means-tested benefit, his partner has left employment and the household is getting housing benefit and the rest, there is likely to be an income of £200 a week plus coming in benefit – considerably more than most of the entry jobs which are below 75 per cent of medium wages. In other words, once in the means-tested system there are very limited opportunities to escape.

So what happens? Either you just give up or you start to do jobs on the side or your wife or partner continues to work and you lie – and once you have told one lie, it is easier to tell the next one. So what we now have is a welfare system which is destructive to society as a whole – and it is in this sense that I see means testing as the cancer within.

RESHAPING THE BENEFITS AGENCY

I argue for a plan of reform which will, over time, transform means testing into an insurance system which links contributions to benefits and is comprehensive in coverage.

We need to begin by changing the Benefits Agency from a passive into a pro-active agency. The current income support system exemplifies some of the worst aspects of the Old Poor Law. Benefit is paid only on condition that claimants remain idle. It does nothing but pay out benefit and occasionally check on fraud – and it is not very good at either task. Indeed the Comptroller and Auditor General has qualified his audit every year since income support started.

Income Support must be reshaped into a body which acts as a life raft for taking people back into work. The change would be that every able-bodied person on income support would be expected to draw up their career or job plans, so that we would be expecting people to use their period on income support to acquire the skills and gain the openings to further their own job prospects. Instead of saying, as at present 'Do not spend more than sixteen hours a week doing a course or you will make yourself ineligible for benefit', we would be asking 'Why are you not going on a course? Remember you can keep your benefit while you are studying'. And we would expect single mothers, for example, while their children were at school, to think seriously about their careers, to acquire the skills, and to get back into work.

To pay for the child-care cover we should have a universal system of student loans run by the private sector, the repayment of which is made through the national insurance or tax system. There will be almost no defaults, so that the interest charges that will need to be made will be quite low. We will then gain a very substantial new tranche of money for the education budget (which ought to go to nursery education and other forms of child care) without necessarily increasing the total amount of money publicly spent on education.

So though turning income support from a passive into a pro-active agency will involve costs, in that more people will be going on courses, and there will need to be child-care facilities while parents are on courses or going to work, the money for this would come from a redistribution within the budget. There will also be the cost of some people staying on benefit somewhat longer because they were completing their course. But in the longer run they will be making fewer claims, thus reducing part of the welfare budget. So the basis of this reform will be to block the supply routes to the culture of dependency.

A NEW SOCIAL INSURANCE SYSTEM

In an age when many people want to cut expenditure, someone has to pay for spending on welfare. The first reason is the change in the labour market. While some of us will be able to keep our employment, many of us will have a large number of different jobs. The labour force survey shows that of those who are in work, 52 per cent did not have the same jobs for three years. We have to have an unemployment insurance that reflects this enormous turnover. And if we work less during our working lives but live longer, we will have to transfer more of our current income to our retirement income. So unless, like ostriches, we put our heads in the sand, individuals do have to save more.

But I do not believe that the voters will be prepared to pay more if they are to pay through taxes. I used to think, like Anthony Crosland, that if we could get growth, people would not object to paying tax increases out of increased income. But as we have seen over the last sixteen years, taxes are contracts with the government that people will tear up if they want to.

What has clearly happened is that, once the level of income gives real choice, people want a genuine say in how the additional income is spent and delivered. If we are going to persuade people to pay more for their welfare, then they have to feel both that their contributions are clearly linked to their benefits and that they have a say in the running of the welfare state – what I call a 'stakeholder' welfare system. The scheme which I propose is based primarily on self-interest. You not only save for your own pension and pay into your own unemployment benefit but you also have a stake in how the system is run.

But within this new framework, a balance has to be struck between self-interest and the need to ensure that those who are at the bottom of the heap are protected. That is done not by setting poverty targets but by making the system comprehensive. It has to cover those who are outside the labour market – the unemployed, the sick, the carers, as well as all those on low pay. These groups will have their contributions paid or subsidized by the taxpayer.

The difference from now would be that this redistribution would be open and above board. So there will be this altruistic element in the scheme, though even the altruism may have some self-interest in it because it might be your son or daughter that is having real difficulty getting into the labour market and holding down a job.

I propose the setting up of a new national insurance corporation, run, as in France, by employers and employees. The government's input will be only to the extent to which they make contributions on behalf of all of us taxpayers. The rates will be set by a process of bargaining between these three groups. In other words, the public will have a much greater say over the level of contribution than before.

The representation of employees will give a new opportunity to trade unions if they are prepared to seize it. One of the features of this century has been the way that the trade unions have lost functions. Now that even the deciding of money wages is under challenge, the unions need to promote a new slate of activities. Providing people with a cheap and safe means of saving for their pensions could help trade unions attract many new members.

This is a long-term project. It would be a disaster to adopt a 'big bang' approach – the Child Support Agency is a warning of the likely consequences. There are, however, two real pressure points: first, there is an unemployment benefit system which, as I have argued, actually encourages dependency; second, there is a community care system which penalizes savings and the acquiring of assets. We should entrust the new corporation with the introduction of a new employment insurance benefit and a new insurance-based care pension, triggered on medical grounds.

SECOND PENSIONS FOR ALL

By 2020, the basic pension will only amount to about 8 or 9 per cent of average earnings. If we are to ensure a reasonable standard of living in old age, then a major reform will be needed.

My solution is to rely on a compulsory private pension to provide a second pension for all – which would become the main pension. Private pension contributions already amount to a larger sum than that paid to cover the cost of the national insurance retirement pension, so the universalization of private pensions would be building on an existing success story. A second body, a pensions corporation, established on the stakeholder model, would be set up to oversee the reform.

The case for compulsion is that otherwise those of us who are paying for our pensions will also end up paying the cost of those who have not paid because they will be on welfare. Those on low pay or who are outside the system will have their contributions paid or subsidized by the Exchequer. Many people will stay in their company scheme, some may wish to stay in their own personal scheme but the real problem may be to stop everybody transferring to the national private pension scheme when they see what they are currently being charged for their own personal pension arrangements.

Part of this reform is the idea of establishing National Pension Savings Schemes. When I asked my constituents to explain how they thought their personal pension worked, they all said that it was like a building society savings account. So why not make it like a simple savings account, which could even be marketed through the Post Office and against which under certain circumstances people could borrow?

CONCLUSION

My reform package involves a number of fundamental changes in the way which we look at welfare. It is not about creating an anti-poverty programme: it is about appealing to the majority but trying to set the rules for the majority in a way in which we can protect those at the bottom as well. It is not about setting a new poverty line: It is about creating a comprehensive insurance coverage which does not stop people adding to that level by their own and their families' efforts.

It also involves a reappraisal of the role of the state. The job is too big for the state alone and there is, in any case, no longer the support for a state being involved as it was in the 1945–60 period. The state's role should be as a rule setter and umpire rather than invading every little nook and cranny of our private lives.

The introduction of the insurance principle and the creating of stakeholder organizations on the basis of my proposals will, hopefully, provide a new popular commitment to welfare and protect the welfare state from a taxpayer's backlash against the size of the current social security budget.

10 Educating our Children

Tim Brighouse

Now Chief Education Officer of
Birmingham, he was Chief Education
Officer for Oxfordshire for ten years
and Professor of Education at Keele
University from 1989–93.

Imagine a society where *all* children, when they emerge from
nursery education, are confident in language, able to play
together and have all the social and motor skills needed to
take advantage of their early days in primary school. They
are happy, know some nursery rhymes and are soon successful early readers who learn more easily and avidly than they
ever will again. They estimate, exercise their memories, and
have a range of sporting skills. If they are not naturally
bi-lingual, they have the chance to learn another language.
They are also tasting the success which comes from a range
of artistic experiences.

The schools in this society are not cramped or dilapidated:
they are handsome and full of the new technology which
extends the pupils' learning opportunities and connects the
school to the local community.

The children naturally go on to their local secondary
school: it is an inalienable right of their parents or carers
that their children can attend the school nearest their home
if they wish. If they are misfortunate enough to be in care,

a visiting tutor or an elder of the community supplements the work of the staff of the carer's home so that their education is assured as the key priority.

The youngsters in this society navigate adolescence more confidently because they belong not merely to their local secondary school, but also to a University of the First Age where intensive interest-led vocation courses are held at Easter and the summer offering a model of accelerated learning not possible in the ordinary school, and where first-class distance learning courses straddle the last year of primary and the first year of secondary school.

In a schooling system like this if children have severe learning difficulties, whether of a sensory, physical or mental kind, they will attend sanctuaries built into the local community school – 'a school within a school'.

At sixteen or thereabouts – earlier or later according to need – the youngsters pass on to courses at colleges, which are the junior arm of a network of universities which offer a range of diploma and graduate courses across all the scholastic and occupational fields.

Parents in this society are encouraged to take their own learning seriously as well as that of their children. Child benefit from birth to eleven includes personal vouchers for their own learning, and at sixteen the allowance goes up to encourage participation in further and higher education. From eighteen onwards courses are charged for, but loans are only repaid by the richest 10 per cent in society who, if they are graduates, pay a 2 per cent surcharge on their income tax. On retirement from full-time employment, the older citizens enjoy an entitlement to a pension which includes both the right to further individual learning opportunities and the responsibility to give back some time in one-to-one tutoring among the children in schools.

Is this an impossible dream for *all* our children? It is the contention of this chapter that we must discover the political will to transform our society's record from one that gives the glittering prizes of a successful education to the few on the backs of the failure of the many, to one that expects success for all. Unless we do that, we shall be carrying within our ranks a fifth column – the educational and economic have nots.

THE ELECTRONIC REVOLUTION

One overriding cause for educational optimism today is the teaching and learning breakthrough which is represented by the 'electronic revolution'.

First, there is the use of the computer as a tool, including applications such as data analysis and retrieval, spread sheets, spell checks, calculators, word processing and desktop publishing. These free effective learning from the daunting, debilitating and frustrating delay that can be experienced without the help of information technology.

Secondly, the telecommunication revolution epitomized by Internet has the potential to liberate teachers from their dangerous propensity to be intellectually diminished through isolation. The application of instant communications to the creation of 'conferencing' among subject enthusiasts, moderated by leaders drawn from circles of teachers in schools, advisers in LEAs and researchers in universities, offers the means of transforming the staffroom and the subject work room.

The third application, that of the CD-ROM in the context of an expanded library, is also linked to the communication revolution. It will shortly be possible for any school library to have access to the best library facilities in the world.

The fourth application – that of the computer as a tutor – has already spawned promising programmes, especially for helping young pupils who are starting to develop a skill or gaining conceptual understanding whether in English, maths or a foreign language. Too often in the past learning difficulties encountered in the basics of acquiring an essential skill have proved an insuperable barrier to progress and a debilitating drain on vital confidence.

The challenge for the next fifty years is how we shall harness this technological breakthrough for education in order to build on the progress which has been made since the middle of the twentieth century.

I now turn to each of the four ages of learning in turn – pre-five, primary, secondary and further. In each there is a need for simple but far-reaching change in order to help us move towards the ideal society described earlier.

FROM PREGNANCY TO AGE FIVE

At the preschool level, our future society will have moved beyond the present debate, which is about the value of nursery education. By then we will accept that nursery education is a natural entitlement for all from the age of three, at least on a part-time basis (though full-time for those in particular need). The key issue will be the appropriate focus for developmental programmes for those children below the age of three whose parents need support to give them the best start in life.

What is needed is a shift of focus of the health visitor's role, so that there is an explicit educational as well as health brief. Priority should be given to first-time mothers and the fourth and fifth siblings in large families. They would provide a structured child development which would lead to voluntary playgroups and, on the child's third birthday, access to full-time nursery education. The whole 'pregnancy to age five' programme should be framed within an 'Early Years Guarantee', and it will need to be managed by a single agency charged with its delivery and accountable for the outcome.

Unless something along these lines is introduced and targeted within specific identified urban areas to the children in need, we shall continue to see the stunted growth of children starting school with what professionals chillingly call 'language delay' and 'deficits in social skills'. These disadvantages increase the likelihood of an impoverished life, costly both to the individual concerned and society as a whole.

THE PRIMARY YEARS

Most educational and medical researchers and theorists accept that it is during the first seven, eight or nine years of a child's life that most cognitive development takes place. During the same period some say that children are capable of learning with greater ease than is possible later in their lives. It is not simply the Jesuits who confidently assert that 'give me the child till he or she is seven . . .'

Currently there is a complex range of primary school provision which is sharply contrasted according to social and geographical location. It is important to draw a distinction between rural and suburban primary schools on the one hand, and their counterparts in the inner-city or outer-ring estates on the other.

Rural and suburban primary schools make up 70 per cent of total primary schools, but are attended by only 30 per cent of our children. Meanwhile, 60–70 per cent of children attend much larger inner-city and outer-ring estate schools.

To put it simply, the children of the former group will be well cared for members of a secure community. They go to school with all their peer group, which is usually well supported at home and eager to learn. Many of their parents will be in employment.

The parents of the children of the other group are likely to have suffered disproportionately from the recessions. Their teachers tend to drive to their schools while living elsewhere. They park their cars in safely guarded corners of the playground, working behind doors closed with security locks.

The children may come from different cultures with different languages in the home and have different faiths. Teachers struggle to implement language policies conscious of the strong family and community ties, and the high expectations buried beneath an unpromising social and environmental context.

It is against these realities of our society – secure rural areas and deprived urban areas – that we must create a vision for primary education. So what is to be done? How can we ensure that the few examples of really outstanding primary schools can become the norm and, equally importantly, sustained at ever higher levels of performance? How can we increase literacy standards by 100 per cent?

Some local education authorities are now trying to establish a way of sharing good practice from school to school. What is now needed is a national framework. The next step is to establish a kitemark or standard which represents a school making a commitment to try to provide 'success for everyone'.

What would a 'success for everyone' primary school do?

It would give a guarantee to parents of one-to-one intensive tutoring outside school hours. As part of a more explicit home/school partnership of learning in two critical years – the first two junior years at age seven and eight – the autumn term of the school year would begin with a teacher/parent/pupil consultation at which mutual commitments would be registered with clear targets for the child's learning experiences and skill acquisition. A subsequent mid-year parents' evening would then have a better focus.

The school as a whole would set targets of new and ever higher standards for children at the end of each of the first two key stages – at age seven and age eleven – especially in literacy and numeracy.

Each school would commit itself to monitoring outcomes of their practices for pupils so that analysis by gender and ethnicity in order to modify policy and practice would become the norm rather than the rare exception. The local education authority would be charged with producing families of schools of like characteristics. The schools themselves would use this information for monitoring purposes in a drive for ever higher standards.

In the 'success for everyone' school, teaching staff would talk about teaching rather than social matters, observe each other, plan teaching courses and activities together, and even teach each other new skills.

Accreditation of progress being made towards 'success for everyone' standards could be incorporated in a revised inspection process for schools. At the moment we spend more in externally assessing our schools and their pupils' achievements than any other country. Most foreign visitors are bemused at the preoccupation we display for external examinations, tests and school inspection. Each year all children sit externally marked tests at the ages of seven, eleven, fourteen, sixteen and eighteen, besides being pupils in schools which are subjected to an elaborate inspection system which requires them to be fully inspected every four years. The annual extra cost of this, without taking into account the hidden costs of teacher assessments and recordings and school preparation, is just over half a billion pounds.

A far cheaper but more rigorous and integrated system would be achieved by linking the inspection cycle with the accreditation and validation of the school and the teachers' own assessment capability. Using the framework for inspection established by the Office for Standards in Education (OFSTED), schools could write their own reports after a process of self-review. This would be followed by a two or three day visit from external HMI Inspectors who would write a critical commentary on the report. During the visit, teachers' assessments of pupils' achievements both in course work and in tests drawn from a national bank would also be inspected and validated. Each teacher in this process would be licensed (or not as the case may be) as a bona fide assessor of children's work and confirmed as capable of doing their job. In the course of these HMI visits the school's progress towards 'success for everyone' would also be the subject of official comment.

Besides the substantial annual savings such a scheme promises – probably in the region of £250 million per year – its virtue lies in the connection it makes between school effectiveness, school improvement, and inspection and assessment.

Progress towards every school being a 'success for everyone' school would inevitably be gradual. A ten-year programme with that as a goal should be declared a national priority. An early start in the inner city and the outer-ring estate is critical.

A NEW DEAL FOR SECONDARY EDUCATION

The contrast between urban, suburban and rural systems is nowhere more marked than at secondary level. Most rural communities have a local comprehensive secondary school which all but a few attend. Such is the sense of community amongst families and businesses at village and small town level, that there is often a strong sense of continuity and shared values in these secondary schools.

Most importantly, the teachers and support staff in such schools send their own children to the school: in doing so they speak volumes to their fellow citizens. In some suburban and affluent settings where housing is expensive, very similar circumstances apply. These schools too are sought after by the whole community.

In urban settings, on the other hand, there is a marked contrast. Many teachers do not send their children to the schools they teach in or nearby schools, nor do they live in the inner city. Often their talk is of children in the impersonal third person: 'If you saw some of their homes, poor things, you would be amazed they survive.' Mostly such schools are in large urban areas where there are concentrations of 250,000 people or more, although there are smaller areas where a combination of housing policies and unemployment has created similar school environments.

In these schools the pressure against achievement is so great that there is a nearly insurmountable barrier to the levels of success that are taken for granted in their suburban and rural counterparts. It is only in exceptional circumstances that a group of teachers, either within a department or more rarely in a school as a whole, create the confidence that transforms achievement standards by youngsters. It is usually down to outstanding leadership and a high proportion of energy creators among the staff.

It is against this reality of two educational worlds and opportunities that the debate about the systems of secondary schooling has taken place since 1944. The debate has been mostly concerned about whether there should or should not be some form of selection according to ability for one sort or another. Whether the system has been selective or comprehensive, however, there is little evidence of educational success for those living in certain areas in the inner city or the outer-ring estates.

There is scope at the secondary level to copy the 'success for everyone' kitemark proposed earlier for the primary sector. Schools would similarly set targets for 'improvement against previous best'. Self-selected start targets for improved attendance, fewer exclusions, academic achievements by the end of the third year of secondary schooling, and increased percentages at sixteen or earlier of those achieving five or more grades A–C would be features of the 'success for everyone' mark.

But for the future we need to consider a radical alternative. We should consider a system where at the age of eleven the pupil would attend both their local secondary school and, in an attempt to extend choice and diversity, another institution which I shall call the University of the First Age. How would this transform choice and diversity?

The University of the First Age could offer two types of courses. The first sort of course would be offered in concentrated periods – perhaps a week or a fortnight at the end of, or as an extension of, the spring and summer terms. It would be intensive, whether in the Arts, in Language, in Science, in Mathematics, in Technology or in Sport.

We know enough about children's motivation, or rather the increasing lack of it, between the first and the third year of secondary school to be confident that there is an increased prospect of success if we give them an individually tailored learning opportunity which fits with their own particular preference. The prospect which opens up is of a youngster taking a fortnight of Languages (or whatever is their preference) in Year 7, followed by a top-up course in Year 8 and accredited examination success that summer. There is a real possibility that success could be achieved by those with very undistinguished records in other aspects of their school work.

The second principal course variant for youngsters in the first three years of secondary schooling would be to take part in a choice of distance-learning units. Again, the youngster would choose from a menu. Here the model is more familiar. The Open University has long experience of creating distance-learning packages distinguished by their high quality design and content. Their impact on the quality of other university courses has gone largely unremarked. Similar benefits could accrue to the quality of secondary courses (especially in teaching and learning, as well as in assessment), through the enlistment of groups of the best urban teachers in the design of a similar set of packages to be made available to youngsters through the University of the First Age. Now that the benefits of the new technologies beckon through the use of the computer, we can motivate youngsters in ways which have baffled traditional supported self-study development in schools previously.

A personal tutor would link the local school attended by the young secondary pupils and the University of the First Age to which they also belong. The tutor's responsibility would include providing guidance to youngsters in the choice both of distance-learning units and of intensive vocation-courses, and offering continuing tutorial support for the former. The school sites in urban areas along with local colleges and sports campuses would be the network for the intensive vocation courses in the spring and summer.

It has been estimated that the annual cost of the University of the First Age incorporating both these new course features in the heavily urbanized areas is £120 million, which happens to be almost the same as the cost of the Assisted Places Scheme – an initiative which researchers suggest has failed to address the problem of urban education.

There is of course no reason why the network of distance-learning courses should not be a feature of rural and sub-urban schools, nor why variants on the intensive spring and summer vacation units should not be available there too. But the worst problems which need to be addressed are to be found exclusively in urban areas.

FURTHER AND HIGHER EDUCATION FOR ALL AGES

The last and most important systemic change affects the phase of further and higher education, usually taken by young citizens after the age of sixteen, and by others later in life. At present the application of market principles is producing something akin to chaos, as schools are allowed to continue with, or even to recreate, post-sixteen units which are often too small in number and therefore offer a restricted range of courses. Meanwhile in the further education funding sector, colleges compete one with another, to no great advantage for young and old alike.

It is clear that there needs to be a minimum size of student

body to offer the range of courses across the academic vocational divide which may be appropriate to the various individual needs of young people, especially when it is so
important to combine academic and vocational needs. That
figure may be 300 full-time students. That is not to say that
smaller units might not exist, but where they are allowed,
they should be under clear franchising/accreditation
arrangements laid down by a linked parent college of further
education.

Colleges themselves should be an integral part of the university system, at least in urban areas. The great educational
advantage of the heavily urbanized environments is that the
metropolitan areas happen to be the locations both of the
great civic universities which were founded in the Victorian
era and just after, as well as of the newer universities which
originated with the polytechnics. There are, moreover, many
colleges of higher education which were founded because
of the need to create a steady supply of teachers for the
large populations of the industrialized cities.

We now have to look to the more formal planning of our
further and higher education system rather than continue
to leave it to the chance operation of market forces. The
ultimate pattern would include at least some of the following
characteristics. Each university would be linked as a leading
teaching university to a network of between, normally, ten
and twenty junior colleges in its hinterland. Each university/
college would be required to provide a hub of lifelong education for the metropolitan catchment area. The whole
system would be linked to the Open University.

The funding of such a comprehensive further and higher
education system could not depend on existing structures.
Benefits would be linked at advantageous levels to further
and higher education participation whether in child allowances, family income support, pension, etc. Pay deals would
receive favourable tax breaks if they were to include education opportunities/vouchers for accumulated sabbaticals.

The Lottery would have an element geared to support sponsored groups in further education. Finally, it is inevitable that some sort of loan or grant is required for any late adolescent or early adult who is participating full-time in a degree course, even if they support their activity with part-time work. Therefore the privileged graduates would carry an obligation when they reach a certain salary level to more than pay back their loan/grant, by an extra 1 or 2 per cent on their income tax.

FINANCING AND ORGANIZING THE SYSTEM

The cost of independent schooling is roughly twice that in the state sector, and it shows: almost all the 100 leading A-level schools are in the independent sector, which also disproportionately dominates university undergraduate courses. How therefore can we increase funding to the state sector?

First, we could switch funding progressively from the failed Assisted Places Scheme to the University of the First Age. Secondly, we could use the savings from reforming an expensive external testing and inspection system to pay for other priorities such as pre-five services. Thirdly, the Rate Support Grant should be ring-fenced (for housing, health and education) and targeted to the urban areas. Fourthly, there should be tax inducements to the corporate sector to back local partnerships, for example for the expansion of pre-five facilities.

To oversee these changes, we will need a national task force, perhaps overseen by a House of Commons select committee. It would be charged with overseeing existing and dispersing some new funds targeted to raise standards in named local education authorities.

Each LEA would be matched with two others displaying broadly similar characteristics whether of ethnicity, poverty or other socio-economic indicators and all three would be charged with promoting in-depth mutual exchanges of information, research, professional development and practice with the express purpose of learning from each other's achievements.

Within such a system each LEA would be required to give an account of itself and of its route and rate of progress against its previous best performance. To ensure this is a focused comprehensive account, the national task force or commission would hold a three-day review session every couple of years with each LEA. The task force's meeting would be informed by a whole range of statistical and other information such as OFSTED inspection reports, HMI and LEA-wide reviews, attendance rates, post-sixteen profile of destinations, exam performances, sports and artistic activity and health and housing information. There would be a supplementary session involving the two other matched LEAs in order to establish agreed most promising practices.

Unless something like this is established, along with other systemic reforms, such as those affecting admissions to schools, the provision for special educational need, and the establishment of priorities and funding for buildings, we shall continue to see a ramshackle set of educational arrangements which serve the needs of a few rather than us all. That requires planning, for left to market forces alone the outcome will be unplanned and unpredictable. Our collective future's wellbeing demands more than that.

11 The Nation's Health

Helene Hayman

Chairman of the Whittington Hospital
NHS Trust in North London, she was
recently made a Labour Life Peer and
from 1974–79 was the Member of
Parliament for Welwyn & Hatfield.

All over the world, governments, economists, and health
professionals are debating the future organization and
funding of their national health services. The pressures of
demographic changes, improvements in technology and
rising public expectations are common to developed and
developing nations alike, whether their health services are
state funded or predominantly free market. Similarly the
affordability of health care and the most effective split
between public and private finance are matters of international concern; whether it is the United States spending
$2500 per person per year or Bangladesh spending $10,
cost remains key.

The original principles of the National Health Service still
stand – universal care, free at the point of use and funding
by the taxpayer. For nearly half a century, the quality, effectiveness and low administrative costs of the UK system have
been the envy of the world. But the NHS needed to respond
to the pressures and dissatisfactions which built up in the
1980s. However, the Thatcher and Major governments

imposed untested new structures, based on a doctrinaire belief in market solutions. As a result, they have seriously damaged morale and confidence in the service, while failing to address the real problems.

The case against the Health Service 'reforms' is threefold. First, they have exposed the National Health Service to years of exhausting organizational change and to an escalation of bureaucracy. Secondly, despite evidence to the contrary from all over the world, policies have been based on blind ideological faith that a market would be more efficient in delivering value for money in health. Thirdly, the language of the reforms – competition, business cases, purchasers and marketing – has convinced many patients and staff that the real agenda was the commercialization, even the privatization, of a much-valued public service. The public response, not unreasonably, has been a profound distrust of decision making at all levels of the service, a distrust which has been strengthened by suspicions of ministerial influence in appointment procedures, particularly in the early days of the reforms. Today, there is huge cynicism about the motives for *any* proposed change to the health service. A Conservative government has created a conservative opposition that immediately says 'Save our ——' when change is proposed, almost regardless of its intrinsic merits. As a result, we are not able to conduct an honest, constructive debate about the present, let alone the future.

The re-creation of public confidence in a government commitment to a publicly funded, free-at-point-of-use health service, with proper public accountability, is a prerequisite to progress. We will never be able to have an open discussion about funding and priorities, the balance between local interests and national standards, until the basic principles upon which we are operating are clear to and agreed by public and professionals alike.

A CONSENSUS ON PRINCIPLES

Different models of health-care funding are in operation throughout the world. These range from those which are mainly public and funded by tax or social insurance (e.g. Scandinavia and the UK) to those which are predominantly private and individually funded (e.g. the United States). It was not a romantic attachment to the creation of the 1945 Labour government but a hard-headed economic analysis of competitive expenditure and effectiveness that led Anatole Kaletsky writing in *The Times* in September 1995 to conclude that 'world-wide experience over the decades has shown clearly that a centralized state-financed health system tends to be cheaper than one based on private spending or insurance'.

Private systems have other disadvantages; they tend to leave vulnerable groups unprotected against the potentially ruinous costs of treatment. In the US, despite the spending of double the UK proportion of GDP on health, some 25 million people remain uncovered by either public or private health schemes. Administrative costs (as we have seen in our own 'internal market system') tend to spiral, and governments and insurance companies are struggling to hold down expenditure on unnecessary medical treatments. The notion of a 'managed care' system – where appropriate treatment guidelines are agreed and funding limited accordingly – is now being promoted in the US. In a national, publicly funded service where value for money and high national professional standards are paramount these disciplines are already inbuilt. A comparison of treatment rates between the United States and the UK in areas as diverse as tonsillectomy and forceps delivery at birth illustrates very well the dangers of the combination of a privately funded system and a litigious society and the advantages of the NHS.

Money is not the only scarce resource in the National Health Service: people and skills are crucial. A publicly funded, nationally organized service can minimize unnecessary duplication of expensive facilities, maintain high standards of practice and training, help plan investment and assist equitable access to limited resources. In health, a culture of collaboration and common commitment to a national service produces research, training and service development that is cost-effective and avoids duplication and waste.

So we are on firm economic ground in arguing for a tax-based universal system. Since 1948 we have also had a broad national consensus on the principle that access to health care should be determined by medical need rather than wealth. It is firmly in the public interest for us to continue to provide a comprehensive service, with the private sector operating only at the margins.

Although it would be fatal to repeat the Tories' mistake of focusing on organizational rather than substantive issues, some aspects of the new structure have to be addressed. So as well as the reaffirmation of the universal, taxation-funded basis of the NHS to re-create public confidence, we must look at the operation of the NHS.

CURBING THE EXCESSES

Unfortunately some of the changes introduced by the Tories will have to be revised. While it will be counterproductive to embark on massive organizational reforms, the worst excesses of the internal market introduced by the Conservatives will have to be removed. Although there are advantages in splitting the functions of those who allocate resources and those who administer them, because it reduces the previous domination of providers over the distribution of NHS funding, the internal market has created an expensive paperchase in which the patient's postcode has become more important than the doctor's diagnosis.

We need to restore the patients' right to be treated at the

hospital of their choice or their GP's recommendation rather than at the hospital where their district health authority or fund holder has negotiated a contract. The bureaucratic nightmare of year-on-year contracting which has taken so much time and energy must be ended. We must cut through the costly administrative procedures spawned by the internal market and reduce unnecessary bureaucracy, while at the same time preserving the high quality management which a big and complex organization like the NHS needs to retain.

The split between purchasers and providers of health care has left many people confused about where ultimate responsibility lies. The media focus has been on hospitals and community trusts and the quality of health care which they provide. In fact health care is shaped by the contracts placed by health authorities funded according to the numbers and characteristics of their local population. So in the recent case of Jamee Bowen – 'Child B' – and her quest for care from the NHS, it was not, as might have happened in the past, a hospital which was unable to provide a service, but a purchaser, Huntingdon and Cambridgeshire Health Authority, which was unwilling to fund a treatment.

It is, therefore, crucial that health authorities command the confidence of the local communities on behalf of whom they set priorities and take decisions about the shape of local health services. Health authorities need to be reformed to bring together the views of patients, staff, professionals and local authority representatives in a constructive partnership. In the units which provide health care such as hospitals, the mixed executive/non-executive boards have made a real contribution to better management. But the boards of the health authorities with their responsibility for the allocation of large sums of public money should be wholly non-executive. It is crucial, however, that, following the Nolan Committee report, there should be greater openness and less ministerial influence in the appointment of non-executive members. The public would be alienated by a swing of the pendulum which led to one set of political appointees being replaced by another. The prime qualification for membership of health bodies needs to be a commitment to the service, not the government of the day.

Another important aspect of the reforms which needs to be changed is the GP fundholder system. General practice has been one of the jewels in the crown of our health service in the past. By its 'gate-keeping' function it has also been crucially important in limiting costs and minimizing unnecessary treatment and expenditure. Surveys now show morale amongst GPs to be at an all-time low. Meanwhile, patients' confidence is being sapped by fundholding because they suspect that money is being put before their needs. Fundholding also militates against sensible planning of services and increases transaction costs. But at the same time we must ensure that GPs remain a powerful voice locally in determining, on behalf of their patients, the priorities for local services. We should learn from successful models of GP commissioning. We should be willing to develop pilot schemes, evaluate them, and manage the service on the basis of common sense rather than the ideological approach we have seen over recent years.

ADDRESSING THE REAL ISSUES

Once public confidence has been restored and the arguments in favour of a publicly funded, publicly run service have been robustly endorsed, we will at last be able to address the real issues in health care. We need to analyse the pressures on health spending arising from increasing numbers of elderly people, advances in medical treatments and higher patient expectations, and also to adopt a broader and longer-term view of health than is customary for British governments.

The objective should not be simply to provide good medical care in times of sickness or disability. We should be seeking to maximize the good health of citizens, as well as to treat their ill health. That means looking, for example, not only at treatments for heart disease when it occurs but at ways of preventing the disease in the first place. Policies to reduce deaths from this cause go beyond the health service. Exercise, for example, is crucial. How much exercise young people take is influenced by many factors – the extent to which physical education is contained in the National Curriculum; what sports and leisure facilities at what cost are provided by local authorities; and the levels of pollution and street crime that may inhibit walking or cycling. Diet and smoking, alcohol and drug abuse, unemployment and poor housing all have huge effects on health and on the demand for health care services. The links between social class, poverty and disease were made most forcefully in recent years in Sir Douglas Black's 1980 Report on Inequality of Health; yet back in 1943 the Labour Party pointed out that 'there is hardly any activity of government that does not directly or indirectly affect health'. We need a cross-departmental government structure that looks both at the implications of non-Department of Health policies on health, and at the contributions other departments need to make to achieve health targets.

We need, too, a determination to take not only a broader, but also a longer term view. The use of tobacco not only destroys the health and lives of thousands of individuals each year but also costs the public purse millions of pounds in direct health costs, lost tax revenues and social security spending. The financial yield to government from tobacco sales is there today, however, and the health and related savings from reduced consumption are for the future. In preventive medicine, investment now will save lives and money in the decades to come. Like British industry, the health service deserves a long-term strategy.

I have argued for a return to the fundamental values and

structure of the National Health Service. We cannot pretend, however, that all was perfect with the NHS before the reforms of the 1980s or that there will not be difficult decisions to be made about the service in the future.

Any discussion of the health service has to confront the questions of pressures and priorities, resources and their use. The mantra of those pressures on a universal, free-at-point-of-access NHS has become well rehearsed: 'demography, technology, expectations'. It is worth scrutinizing each of these pressures, however, before reaching the conclusion of the 'merchants of doom' – many with an ideological or professional commitment to the private health care industry – who predict that the tax-funded service we know today will be unsustainable in the future.

The numbers of the elderly are set to continue rising, though not at the same pace as in the decades since 1950. While elderly people, especially the over-85s, do undoubtedly put a greater burden on health services, the most expensive medical care any of us will receive occurs in the six months before death *at whatever age we die*. Some estimates put the cost of that terminal care at 50 per cent of the total acute hospital expenditure in the UK. So an ageing population is not *per se* an intolerable burden on the NHS. We have coped with a 50 per cent rise in the number of people over sixty-five since 1950 without dismantling the health service: it would seem foolish to panic now.

The demographic issue which we must confront is the cost of residential and social (rather than health) care of an ageing and often isolated population. The NHS is not the appropriate body to provide that care (long-term geriatric wards were never pleasant places) and its costs would certainly prejudice the continued provision of purely medical services for the rest of the population. We need a national consensus on the best way to plan for the needs of the elderly. The relative roles of individual saving and social insurance, whether privately or state organized, must be analysed and Labour's proposed Royal Commission will need to address those issues as a matter of urgency.

Next we need to look at the effects of advances in medical treatments and technology. When the wide range of treatments now available is considered, the spectre of a catastrophic clash between infinite demand and finite resources looms large. A huge variety of treatments can be offered where in the past we had nothing – salvaging the lives of twenty-six-week-old premature babies, treating cancers that would formerly have been fatal, transplanting organs, reversing infertility. The effects of medical advances on health budgets are not *only* negative, however. Modern anaesthetic and surgical techniques have dramatically reduced the length of stay – and the costs – of many operations. Day-care cases now account for some 50 per cent of all operations. In some cases, operations have been superceded completely by drug treatments (as in the case of ulcers), by more effective diagnostic technology (as with knee complaints) and by new treatments like the uses of lasers and lithotripsy for breaking up gallstones.

Sometimes the pressures of the changes in demography and medical advances come together: the hip and knee replacement operations which are now commonplace but were unknown only a few decades ago are used predominantly by the elderly. As people live longer the demand is growing for second replacements of original hip replacement operations. These operations, however, are not simply about prolonging life; they radically change the quality of life for the elderly and can reduce the demands made on the health budget to the benefit of the community.

The last and perhaps most potent pressure on resources is the seemingly inexorable rise in public expectations. As more can be done, more is demanded: the physical conditions in which we delivered much of Britain's health care twenty years ago (Victorian buildings, inadequately maintained and unsuitable for modern treatment) are no longer acceptable. Similarly, patients rightly reject the philosophy that their time is not valuable. Waiting in serried ranks in block-booked outpatient clinics, which was common until very recently, is no longer tolerated.

Patients expect more information and more choice about their treatment, as well as shorter waits for appointments. The growth in consumerism generally has inevitably changed the attitudes of the users of public services. Sadly, the breakdown in relationships with the health service has meant that many see the only right they have been given as the right to complain after being treated badly rather than the right to be treated with competence and respect in the first place.

I am deeply opposed to calling patients 'customers'. Public services do *not* have customers with individual cash contracts. The challenge is to transform some of the staff attitudes which went with monopolistic public services in the past (summed up in the NHS joke that 'this hospital would run perfectly if only the patients didn't keep coming in and diverting everyone') so that we behave more like a service industry that really cares about quality and efficiency but without the language and values of commercialism. The ethos of a public service, combined with financial disciplines, provides the way forward for the NHS.

THE WAY FORWARD

The pressures are perhaps not so overwhelming after all. The National Health Service has survived remarkably well as it reaches its fiftieth birthday: there is no reason to believe that, with the modest incremental increase in funding each year we have seen in the past (and there is much evidence of continued and deeply rooted public support for such funding), it cannot survive into the future.

Those of us involved in the service, however, cannot be satisfied with survival. We want to improve. There are major areas which need investment – in buildings, in equipment, in training. We still keep people waiting too long for treatment; we run our acute hospitals at too high occupancy rates; we expect our doctors to see too many patients too quickly. We need to innovate, to maximize good health and reach out to people who have traditionally been neglected by conventional services.

From the early days when prescription charges were first introduced, governments have looked for extra funding for the NHS. The question is how we meet our aspirations for higher quality services if substantially increasing private expenditure on health is unacceptable either on grounds of equal access to care or efficient use of resources.

The key is in a rigorous review of how we currently treat patients and the effectiveness of those treatments. The way medicine has advanced means that much (some estimate as much as 40 per cent) of current treatment has never been evaluated or proved to be effective.

Some purchasing health authorities have tried to release the potentially large sums of money currently used to finance treatments of unproved value by issuing 'blacklists' of treatments they will not fund. Inevitably this leads to complaints about rationing, claims that the comprehensive NHS is being undermined and to controversial individual decisions. We all want the choice of taking the one in a thousand chance if it is our child who has a rare and life-threatening disease.

Crude refusal to fund categories of treatment is doomed to failure and will further alienate the public. The way to release the resources needed to improve services is to re-engage the commitment of the professionals. The last five years have sadly demoralized and demotivated doctors and nurses. We need to regain their support for a high quality NHS where professional advice is based on a scientific assessment of potential outcomes. Patients trust doctors far more than managers or politicians and they are the key to value-for-money health care. Only individual doctors can cut drug budgets and reduce unnecessary tests and procedures while taking patients with them: no secretary of state can deliver the health service we need without staff support.

In any health care system decisions have to be made about priorities – the public is not so naïve as to believe you can have something for nothing or that doctors can spin straw out of gold. We need an honest public debate about the trade-offs in health care – between accessibility and quantity, for example, between quality and responsiveness. There are competing demands. Treatments which we know work have to be weighed against a tiny number of pioneering and expensive experiments which may prove in the end ineffective. The public's affection and support for local services, and buildings is well documented. But so, too, is the fact that the chances of survival from serious illnesses like cancers are vastly improved in specialist centres which by definition cannot be located on every street corner. Other forces – like the move towards shorter working hours for junior doctors, reforms in medical education and the developing role of nurses – also contribute to the necessity for change.

We need to involve the public in deciding where the balance of benefit lies and what is most important for *them* and their communities. The public would respond positively and responsibly to such a debate if it were openly conducted by a government which was seen to be committed to making a universal, free-at-point-of-use, tax-funded NHS as great a success in the next century as it has been in this one.

12 Environment for All

Fiona Reynolds

Director of the Council for the
Protection of Rural England.

What needs to change? In the case of the environment, nothing less than for the environment to be at the heart of the decisions everyone makes; and nothing more than for us all to acknowledge its importance and to live our lives in ways that respect it.

It seems inconceivable that, by the time we reach the twenty-first century, the environment will not be one of our society's foremost concerns. From the early beginnings of environmental awareness in public health legislation to today's sophisticated concepts of sustainable development, each generation has successively shown more commitment to the environment and a greater readiness to recognize its place in the formal processes of politics and society. Today's young people are more committed than ever, and within another generation, surely, we will be seeing real results arising from its presence at the heart of policy making and implementation.

The events of recent decades have shown the environment to be subject to roller-coaster political treatment, to be in and out of fashion, to be subject to challenge from the scientific and political communities. Fundamental questions have been raised about the nature of the environmental agenda itself.

So it is impossible to look forward without also looking back, without exploring how the environment has begun to penetrate wider agendas; what has stuck and what hasn't; and how society has begun to adjust to the idea that we cannot go on living as though there were no tomorrow.

THE ENVIRONMENTAL MOVEMENT

The origins of the environmental movement in the UK lie in two distinct traditions, both with nineteenth-century roots. The first, strongly science-oriented, began with the public health legislation necessary as a result of industrial pollution. It can be tracked through the air, water and control of noxious substances legislation to today's systems of Integrated Pollution Control implemented by the new, multimedia Environment Agency incorporated by the 1995 Environment Act.

The other tradition has its roots in the nineteenth-century philosophical and aesthetic movement, personified by people like Ruskin and Morris and formalized in the establishment of such bodies as the National Trust and Open Spaces Society. This broad movement embraced elements that were science-based (such as Huxley and Tansley's pioneering work which led to the establishment of the Nature Conservancy Council in 1949) but also had an explicit social agenda. The trail here runs through the town and country planning movement of the 1930s and 1940s (with the 1947 Town and Country Planning Act being an explicit component of the new welfare state) to the National Parks legislation of 1949, the Countryside Act of 1968 and today's recognition of the countryside, in all its dimensions, as a key feature of British identity. The 1995 Rural White Paper – the first explicitly rural statement by a government since the 1942 Scott Report on Rural Areas, adopted a connected environmental and social perspective to the countryside.

In the more recent past these distinct traditions have been

caught up within a new set of issues, highlighted forcibly in the early 1970s by the oil crisis and the Club of Rome's warnings about resource exploitation. For the first time the concept of 'limits to growth' introduced a further, more serious perspective: rather than cleaning up (as pollution legislation provided for) or insulating special areas from society's 'normal' activities (as National Parks and Sites of Special Scientific Interest in essence aimed to do), society was presented with a question mark over whether it would even survive.

This was the birth of the process which culminated in the United Nations Earth Summit in Rio de Janeiro in June 1992. Until then the environment had been very much at the margins of international affairs. Although there were specific agreements on issues like ozone depletion and trade in endangered species, no environmental issue had really impacted on the wider economic and political processes of international diplomacy. But in June 1992 over a hundred world leaders gathered to declare themselves committed to sustainable development: in the words of Gro Harlem Brundtland, to using and managing the earth's resources in ways that would not compromise future generations' ability to do the same. To confirm this new commitment they signed two International Conventions, on Climate Change and Biodiversity, and a series of agreements which – although heavily criticized and much less ambitious than they had been advised was necessary – locked them and their countries into new relationships on issues such as energy, transport and land use.

Rio therefore marked a high point in political terms for the environment, representing the moment when official responsibility was accepted for the wider environmental agenda, embracing not only more familiar environmental issues like species protection and pollution, but a commitment in principle to make all aspects of the economy respect the environment and to recognise an explicit social responsibility, both within and between the different nations of the world, and between today's citizens and future generations.

But the story since Rio has been much less rewarding than its promise. Commitments made seemed to vanish into thin air, and the bubble of media fascination, political attention and even – apparently – public enthusiasm burst. Politicians returned home to life as if Rio had not happened, and before long even the language of environmental sustainability was being subtly but significantly compromised to allow business to carry on as usual. When it came to implementation, the targets agreed to carry forward the new Conventions, especially the crucial one on climate change, were unchallenging and achievable without radical changes in policy. For example, during a recession, it has been possible to plan for stabilization of carbon dioxide emissions at 1990 levels to be achieved by the year 2000 with no changes to policy, other than those that were desired for other reasons, needed at all. This has enabled all but the most committed to slip back into conventional approaches. Indeed, almost a worse scenario has emerged: one in which the environment is recognized and given superficial attention, but has little purchase on the conventional decision-making process.

Nowhere is this clearer than in the zeal for deregulation which has raced through Whitehall during the early 1990s. The environment was, in fact, one of its triggers; the European Union's enthusiasm for expensive and ambitious environmental regulation that, it was claimed, only the UK would implement properly and seriously, prompted the UK government's anxiety about the rate at which new environmental EU regulations were being brought forward. The desire for deregulation has had far more impact on public policy and practice than the desire for more effective environmental polices, demonstrating the relative lack of political will behind the latter.

The Environment Act 1995, in particular, bears the marks of deregulation. Its main purpose was to establish a new, integrated Environment Agency which should be one of the most effective in the world. But the Bill was besieged by deregulatory pressure, and the Act leaves the new Agency in an altogether less confident position than its predecessors (the National Rivers Authority and Her Majesty's Inspectorate of Pollution). Moreover, it is charged with some novel duties – for example, to take into account the costs and benefits of its actions before reaching decisions, rather than being guided primarily by environmental criteria.

BUT WHAT DO THE PEOPLE THINK?

As a corollary to this rather gloomy analysis of the way in which the environment has been treated in official circles, it is important to understand how people see the issues, and the extent to which they impact on or engage people in their normal lives. Here, a rather different and more optimistic story emerges.

There are innumerable sources of information about public attitudes to the environment: opinion polls, surveys, and qualitative research are all regularly carried out by official pollsters, industry, the environmental organizations themselves as well as by the academic community. As would be expected these have shown, over the last thirty or so years, a steadily rising commitment to and concern for the environment in all its dimensions, embracing such issues as countryside and species loss, pollution and water quality, as well as a growing level of awareness of complex global phenomena such as ozone depletion and global warming.

These concerns are now consistently and reliably a feature of polls, alongside other important contemporary issues such as unemployment, education, health and the economy. In addition increasing numbers of people who declare their support for better environmental policies are finding ways of putting their views into practice. A growing proportion of the public now regularly use recycled products, recycle goods themselves or are members of environmental pressure groups.

In recent years, two additional factors are emerging. One is a strong increase in concern for the local environment, suggesting that even if politicians can delude themselves that they are, post-Rio, dealing with the environment, such confidence is not held by the people who elect them at the local level. Indeed, some specifically local problems, such as air pollution, are getting markedly more serious and public concern about them is rising rapidly. The other phenomenon is a clear and growing disenchantment with the official process of decision making and – by implication – all those who are involved in it. Public policy is too often to deliver words, not deeds, hot air, not real solutions.

This raises important questions for the organizations that act on behalf of public interests in this field – the environmental pressure groups. In the UK there is an unprecedented number and variety of organizations with an environmental purpose, reflecting both the longevity of the movement and the strong British tradition of the campaigning charity. The movement embraces older, well-established organizations such as CPRE and the National Trust; and more radical protest groups such as Greenpeace. There are 'doing' organizations, who plant trees, clear canals and buy and manage land, such as the British Trust for Conservation Volunteers and the RSPB; and those whose sole aim is to campaign, such as Friends of the Earth. There are organizations for almost every popular species and human activity; innumerable local organizations focused on a particular area; as well as large numbers of specialist national organizations. All have distinctive styles and appeal to particular sections of the community. Not least as a result of this, the Non-Governmental Organization (NGO) movement in Britain has more supporters and members than all the political parties put together and remains a vitally important barometer of public opinion on environmental issues.

The NGOs' track record and influence is a crucial part of their success. Those such as Friends of the Earth, Greenpeace, CPRE and RSPB have played a pivotal role in the major *causes célèbres* in the environmental field: for example, re-establishing official confidence in the planning system in the middle 1980s (CPRE); securing new European Laws to protect habitats and species (RSPB and the Wildlife Trusts) and rousing public opinion and concerns about ozone depletion and global warming (Friends of the Earth and Greenpeace). All this and more has been achieved by skilful lobbying, astute use of the media and intelligent engagement with the arguments.

But the Rio summit may also prove to have marked a turning point in the evolution of the NGO movement and its relationships with the wider public. Since the Second World War, and the establishment of a strong centrally managed economy, the government – especially national government – has been the natural focus for activity and pressure. At the same time, the introduction of increasingly ambitious and sophisticated environmental legislation (including much emanating from Europe) and attempts to 'green' key sectors like agriculture, forestry and the utilities, has meant that environmental groups focused the majority of their lobbying energy at national level.

But this began to change during the 1980s and now looks very different. Structures and systems have changed so that there is now a much more complicated system of decision-making. Under a Conservative government the changes have been due to privatization, new agency and business-oriented structures within the public sector, and a shift in the role of the state from being a deliverer of services to a facilitator. These trends, while having distinct political motivations, are unlikely to change direction, whoever is in power in future, and may even be accentuated if the emphasis shifts further towards decentralization, accountability and community responsibility. It is therefore very unlikely that there will ever be a reconstitution of the pre-1979 structures of decision making.

This poses challenges to the way pressure groups have traditionally worked, and they have already begun to respond. There is a detectable shift in emphasis towards more locally based campaigning, focusing on new audiences and targets – for example the reformed local authorities, the emerging (though still informal) regional structure of government, the regionally based privatized utilities and the new Next Steps and other agencies which now have responsibility for many functions which were once the government's.

But this shift is only partly about new structures to meet new targets. It also represents a desire, and need, to connect more closely and in new ways with the people on whose behalf the NGOs speak. As anyone following public opinion on the environment will have observed during the 1990s, new levels of concern about the environment are evident. The shift to the local is both a consequence of and a response to this.

It is remarkable, looking back, that at the end of the 1980s the environment was almost wholly characterized as a global issue – climate change was the main reference point and international solutions (implicitly if not explicitly to be delivered by 'bad' countries – i.e. those who were destroying their rainforests or on the point of development of the kind we have enjoyed for decades – other than us) the answer. Mrs (now Lady) Thatcher's famous 'green' speech to the Royal Society in 1988 exemplified this moment in many ways. While it was strong on international rhetoric, it almost wholly failed to acknowledge the manifestations of the environmental problem on the ground within the UK, for which her own government was responsible.

The Rio Summit marked the point at which the wheel

reached its zenith and perhaps even gave momentum to its downward trajectory. Reaching the apparently literal summit of what politicians could and were prepared to do, the initiative has since passed back to the local level.

Two developments illustrate this clearly. First, the challenge mounted by NGOs at Rio to Western, developed governments to 'put their own houses in order' rather than lecture the developing world on the destruction of their assets, hit home. The UK and other countries were forced to recognize unsustainable national development and in the implementation of one of the summit's commitments – the preparation of a National Sustainability Plan – the connection between local and global issues has been forced more clearly into the open.

Second, another of the summit's outcomes – Agenda 21, with its emphasis on public participation and its call for local action plans for sustainable development – has passed the baton back to the people. Local authorities up and down the country, in association with local businesses, environmental groups and their own electorates, have begun to try to translate esoteric matters of global principle into meaningful activity in which ordinary citizens can participate.

It did not need a National Sustainability Plan or Agenda 21 to alert people to the deterioration of their local environments. That energy had already been unleashed. But whether these processes, combined with the growing attention of the national NGOs on local issues, can capture sufficient momentum to overturn the current lack of official interest in the environment and initiate new ways of taking the debate forward, remains to be seen.

TRANSPORT – A CASE IN POINT

The current transport debate illustrates this situation perfectly. Mobility is something everybody needs and wants, and the private car has become an icon of personal freedom and progress. Yet it pollutes and requires roads that themselves cause environmental damage when built or improved, and triggers further problems in their consequential effects: roads act as a magnet for other developments, suburbanize large tracts of countryside and stimulate an ever greater dependence on the car. All, including the government, now understand the need to break this vicious circle.

Transport has touched everyone as the one of the foremost environmental issues of the 1990s. Respectable senior citizens have shared platforms with the young and dispossessed in their outrage at the government's roads programme launched in 1989 under the provocative title *Roads for Prosperity*. As valued countryside has gone under tarmac, civic space been lost to the pervasive influence of the motor car and children's freedom to walk or cycle to school in safety been sacrificed, so more and more people, despite their own often high personal dependence on the car, have questioned a transport policy that places so much emphasis on cars and road transport and so little on people and the environment. A series of transport flashpoints, characterized by people speaking up for treasured local places about to be lost to the car, has dominated environmental news in the 1990s: Twyford Down; Solsbury Hill; the M11 extension through East London: Oxleas Wood; the Newbury by-pass – and many more.

The 'Great Transport Debate' launched by the Department of Transport in 1995 threw up some important lessons. First, there are real conflicts of interest. As road transport has become cheap and heavily subsidized by the public purse, so industry has relocated and planned its operations to take maximum advantage of it – even if this means that lorries on the move are today's warehouses and the majority of Marks & Spencer sandwiches are transported by road from a sandwich factory in the Midlands rather than being made locally. To alter these trends will need a new approach to business planning, not just stronger environmental measures. Second, solutions cannot be delivered by one player. Road travel has become a central issue of lifestyle for almost all of us and, although a new national policy framework is an absolute necessity, getting away from current car dependence also means life-style changes for us all.

POLICY INTEGRATION

What is the place of the environment in conventional economic policy? This is the real dilemma. The process of bringing environment to the centre of policy requires it to be accepted in ways that the Rio process showed politicians were not yet prepared to do.

What will change their perception? Perhaps we are nearer than we realize. For example, the road-building programme has proved impossible to deliver to time and budget because the levels of public concern are such that the consent process takes longer, expensive environmental mitigation measures have to be incorporated and much more complex consultation and negotiation undertaken than was originally foreseen. By the time a road is built, the rejected, more 'expensive' options (say of tunnelling), or the cheaper but more 'difficult' options of traffic management look far more attractive than the construction option. Other infrastructure projects like bridges, barrages, reservoirs and power stations share similar trends in budget overruns, environmental and public anxiety and long planning and commissioning time. The environmental options of demand management and minimizing impacts at source look increasingly attractive economically as well as reducing damage to the environment.

The same points are increasingly being made about jobs. The old ideas that jobs are created through massive capital investment and a commitment to new infrastructure are rapidly giving way to a recognition that the sustainable labour force of the future will be more engaged in managing the infrastructure we already have. Flexibility in the use of assets and people, and investment in services – like education – rather than bricks and mortar, is more compatible with an environmental agenda than former accepted wisdoms.

The policy formation process needs to be changed. At present, the environment is too often thought about at the last minute, by which time it is too late to do anything, when if it were brought to the heart of decision making quite different ideas and solutions might emerge.

There is some recognition of this in public policy already. In the government's 1990 White Paper on the Environment ministers responsible for environmental issues were established in each government department and an informal system of policy appraisal for the environment was initiated. There have been very few tangible results from this process, but its existence raises important questions as to how such ministers interpret their duties and what they actually do to carry them forward. So far the emphasis has been on green 'housekeeping' (e.g. energy efficiency targets within government buildings) but it could provide a platform on which to build more demanding objectives. One example would be to introduce the techniques of Strategic Environmental Assessment, a process whereby the environmental implications of a policy or plan are considered, reviewed, and, by a process of iteration and comparison of alternatives, revised so that the final choice made – which might be quite different from the starting proposition – is the 'least bad' for the environment or even delivers some positive benefits.

ENVIRONMENTAL CAPACITY

If we have learnt anything since the warnings of the Club of Rome, it is that we do not have inexhaustible supplies of primary resources; and that we as one (albeit particularly voracious) inhabitant of the planet are capable of causing devastating, irreversible damage.

The concept of sustainable development emerged precisely to address these issues. It does not deny that society wants to and will make progress, but it poses serious questions about what constitutes progress and the nature of the responsibility we owe to future generations. Sustainable development presents the challenge that it is the *environment* which is the ultimate constraint on where and how society can develop; and that it must provide the framework within which economic, social and other goals can be pursued.

This is a hard message to swallow but it is also hard to argue with. Technological innovation will only deliver partial solutions; once used, primary resources cannot be soon re-made, and irreversible changes (including everything from concreting over rural land to global warming) seriously compromise the future of life on earth.

The responsibility is on us to protect against the destruction of our world; for example, by taking preventative action before scientific proof is absolute, quarrying minerals from land which can be used for other purposes afterwards, and reclaiming derelict urban land before building on greenfield sites. In other words, we must learn to manage the resources we need to exploit in as efficient a way as possible. If we reduce our need to travel, our demands for freshly quarried aggregates and save energy, we will have both a better environment for ourselves, and will leave choices open to those yet to come.

Nowhere is this more important than in our cities, where the cumulative effect of a declining urban environment, lack of civic facilities, growing pollution and poor quality of life has caused a collapse of confidence. People are leaving the city in droves – 300 a day for the last twenty years – in search of a better existence, so the cities' problems are getting worse while the recipient areas – often the countryside – are besieged by development pressures. Seeing urban areas in a new light, as the foundation for sustainable living for the 80 per cent or so of the population who still live there, would bring immense social as well as environmental benefits.

A ROLE FOR EVERYONE

Finally, it must be stressed that this agenda does not lend itself to a manifesto approach that can be presented to – or successfully implemented by – a government alone, helpful though that would surely be.

The 1990s see us grappling with new forms of very old ideas. Jargon- and politically-loaded though they may be, a new interest in concepts such as public participation, community involvement and citizenship have exposed a real need for us to understand how environmental issues affect the lives of all people, and the importance of their positive response in the search for new life styles which are less demanding of the environment. Talking 'green' has real appeal, as both the quiet revolution of active citizenship in such activities as recycling and membership of environmental organizations, and the more outspoken road protest movements have shown, but the stronger messages still are those that make environmental connections with health, quality of life and the cultural agenda – people's sense of who they are.

For if we have learned anything else in recent decades, through the Rio process and beyond, it is that the environment cannot be compartmentalized. Those countries and regions, such as Scandinavia and some German Länder, where environmental responsibility is a more accepted part of citizenship than here, show us that the way forward depends on a deep and genuine commitment to the environment in every part of our lives.

Such a commitment is central to whether we all survive,

and, indeed, to the circumstances in which we may do so. This small planet is all we have: what needs to change is our attitude to our relationship with it.

13 Crime and Punishment

Stephen Tumim

Circuit Judge and HM's Chief Inspector
of Prisons for England and Wales from
1987–95, he is author of *Great Legal
Fiascos*.

Education and health are key problems for the end of this
century, but the first problem many people find overwhelming – particularly old people – is crime. And why is that?
Statistics are more misleading here than with most subjects,
and we do not frankly know, save for personal experience
in the streets, if crime against the person and property is
going up or down. However, whatever the figures, it affects
all ages and classes, disturbs and ruins lives.

A society suffers more from crime when people are poor
than when almost everyone is well off. Whatever the politicians publicly pronounce, there is an obvious relationship
between poverty and crime. You have only to look at the
dock in a Crown Court to see who is there. Cardinal Man-
ning put it with eloquence in the last century: 'They who
live among statistics, and have seldom, if ever, lived among
the poor, little know how poverty brings temptation, and
temptation both vice and crime . . . It would be an affecta-
tion of scepticism to say that this close relation is not by
way of cause and effect'.

So one way of reducing crime is to achieve a prosperous

society. But that is a long-term answer. Around our sad urban housing estates, how can you reduce the levels of crime here and now, how can you achieve a situation where citizens including the old can potter about safely at night? The *Daily Express* believes that harsh conditions would help. 'The very existence of prisons makes many hesitate before embarking on crime and confronts the law-abiding with the knowledge that – if only for a little while – bullies, thieves and vandals are on the receiving end of nasty experience.'

It may be that the prospective white-collar criminal, shuffling his client's papers, is put off fraud from time to time by the fear of a disagreeable prison. But although he may fear prison, I wonder if he really distinguishes, before indulging in his wrong-doing, between the toughest of prisons, such as Wandsworth, and an open prison, like Ford, as a temporary home.

I believe that judges and the courts, governors and their prisons, have a very modest and occasional influence on the commission of crime, however firmly they discharge their duties. What puts off the burglar, the vandal, the robber, is the near certainty of capture. The police are by far the most important part of a criminal justice system, and a system, I suspect, works well, where the police are known to be likely to catch the criminal.

But the function of the police is by no means limited to the catching of criminals. Direct prevention of crime by encouraging citizens to take sensible steps to protect their houses and cars combines with less direct but even more valuable prevention by community policing, by encouraging other groups in the community to reveal crime, and by flooding with officers, for a necessary period, a community which is suffering from many incidents of crime.

As I have already said, crime statistics are notoriously unreliable. Where there is difficulty – as now – in getting insurance for property, the victim of theft is far less likely to report it. There are times and places where police are more likely to record the vandalized purse as 'lost' rather than 'stolen'. There are many occasions when it suits the arrested criminal in the police station to agree to the court taking into consideration a list of offences, of which he has never heard.

I do not believe there can be any certainty about the extent to which punishment will ever seriously reduce crime. Prison can be used to replace the failed school, or to substitute, however inadequately, for the family. It keeps the serious criminal out of the way for a while, but the key question remains: where does the criminal go, what does he do, when he comes back into the community?

Punishment is inflicted by the court, which has to take into account issues of public protection, deterrence, denunciation, compensation and rehabilitation, and, above all, what is just in the circumstances. Punishment in Britain may consist of the confiscation of money, the compulsion of community service, or the deprivation of liberty. The deprivation is, as Alexander Paterson famously told us, 'as punishment', not 'for punishment'. The rate of imprisonment is higher in this country than anywhere in Western Europe and there may be a sizeable number of prisoners who could sensibly be dealt with in the community.

The media and many readers and viewers look for punishment not so much as coming from the court as from those who are carrying out the sentence of the court. In particular they look to punishment in the prisons by the Prison Service through making prison life more harsh. There are two main reasons for this. One of them is the satisfaction commonly derived by the godly from the sufferings of the ungodly. The other is the belief that if a man has a bad enough time in his sentence he will be unlikely to commit further crime. It is not a belief founded on historical experience, but both reasons raise questions which call for answers on the relationship of punishment to crime, and, for me at any rate, they are most aptly approached through the prison system.

What are prisons for? Ever since the modern concept of imprisonment was established by Jeremy Bentham around the end of the eighteenth century, prison has been the prime instrument used by the criminal justice system to attempt to reduce the rate of crime. The American Declaration of Independence, a principal event in the history of our prisons, had ended transportation to America, while South Africa and Australia were not yet used for housing convicts. Punishment became harsher with far more capital offences, and yet the crime rate went up and up. Punishment by long term deprivation of liberty, deliberately aimed at improving the behaviour of prisoners and reducing the rate of crime, came in soon after the new century.

If we are to rely on prisons to reduce the crime rate, whom do we decide to lock up? The majority of prisoners are male and well under thirty. They are young men who have failed at school or have been failed by school. They have weak (if any) family links. Their offences are mainly concerned with drink, drugs and motor cars, and stealing money to acquire more. They come from impoverished city areas. If they are violent, it is not planned, but part of their social inadequacy. Their time in prison is usually somewhere around a year and they will then return to the community from which they came. They have about half a century before them as citizens of our country.

How do we fulfil the purpose of prison to reduce the crime rate, as far as this majority is concerned? We want to make our cities safer, reduce the burglaries, and ensure there are fewer victims. If we warehouse them and simply ensure they live in custody in harsh and insanitary conditions, are we going to deter this majority from crime when their year or whatever is up? Or would such treatment – while not unreasonably pleasing to some law-abiding citizens – cause this majority of prisoners irrevocably to lose self-respect and drive them into lives of alternative crime and punishment? Idleness corrupts.

There can surely be only one answer to how we are to reduce the crime rate with this majority of prisoners. Unless we are to lock them up for their lives and not just for a year, the process must be to treat prison as an active pre-release course, so that the majority of the majority leave prison with self-respect and the capacity and intention to live as proper citizens.

This majority group urgently requires the formal education that will enable them to manage in the community. Many of them are essentially competent young men who have yet to get their acts together, and learn the dangers of unlawful drugs. There are a surprising number of young near-illiterates in prison, who, although not stupid, need support in reading, writing and arithmetic. The ratio of illiterates to other prisoners is around three times higher than would be found in their home communities. We need to re-examine the prison education curriculum, too often based on what teachers like to teach, or on an unreality as to what is needed.

The majority need the moral education they have not had in the family. They need to learn to address their offending behaviour, as our prevailing jargon calls it. In ordinary English they need to learn the difference between right and wrong and to learn how to behave. They need to understand the gravity and degrees of crime and the true suffering of victims. They need social education, in hygiene, in budgeting, about drink, drugs and AIDS. They need to learn how to conduct themselves at job interviews, and the practice of work. They need to learn that a degree of street wisdom is insufficient to enable them to lead law-abiding and useful lives.

Where possible, they should be helped to build family links. We should be establishing clusters of prisons, each cluster within one management system, so that the prisoner can be kept in his home area, yet transferred between prisons of varying regime as he progresses and where he can be provided with the necessary security and training. There is a far greater chance of imprisonment reducing the crime rate if the prisoner happens to have a law-abiding and supportive family. Inevitably there are a number of prisoners, among the majority and otherwise, who have no potential family link or only an undesirable one. There are no methods of improvement which can be applied successfully to every prisoner.

For most prisoners, including the large group I have styled the majority, custody is a comparatively short interruption, sometimes repeated, in a life of liberty. Prison regimes for short-term prisoners need not only to be about returning to liberty, but the content of the regime programmes should be drawn from the community itself. A local prison, a prison in a cluster, is part of the community. What are the conditions of education, training and employment which exist for young people in the area who are not in trouble with the law? Will non-criminal youth have trouble with unemployment? What facilities does the community make available to them? Whatever local arrangements, they need to be extended for use within the prison system, so that the prisoner on release does not enter a wholly alien world in relation to training or work. Programmes within the prison should correspond with those available in the community. On discharge, a prisoner should be able to complete a training course or work experience outside. Local employers should be asked to advise or even assist with an industrial prison by investing in work space in the prison. Preparation for release must be genuine and realistic, if prisoners are going to get work after discharge in the community. Useful prisons only come about with community support. Prisons are not separate institutions, although they separate inmates from the rest of us. They are there to reduce the crime rate largely by re-integrating the majority of prisoners into normal life.

Educating and training the majority of prisoners, running a prison as a pre-release course, calls for patience and constant devotion to duty by the Service, the education officers, chaplains and probation officers and all who work in prisons. The job of replacing the failed schools, the broken families, within what is often a matter of months rather than years, is exceedingly demanding. It will not succeed every time. It should reduce crime. It will not end it.

There are a number of guides to help not only the prison staff but management and policy makers at national and local levels in the future.

First there is the short and admirable Prison Service's *Statement of Purpose*, which is hung prominently in every prison.

> Her Majesty's Prison Service serves the public by keeping in custody those committed by the Courts. Our duty is to look after them with humanity and help them lead law-abiding and useful lives in custody and after release.

I know no other institution with a more memorable and sharp self-direction. Prisons, at any rate for the majority of prisoners, should be run as pre-release centres. From the moment the convicted criminal goes to prison he should be actively helped to lead a law-abiding and useful life. The *Statement of Purpose* is a sound text for an Inspector to apply. The bad prison is where the prisoner is in his cell and on his bed at midday. The good prison is one where the tests are not of niceness or nastiness, those sentimental qualities, but of how active the prisoner is during the day, in law-abiding and useful occupation. The Statement puts clearly the necessary case against institutionalizing the prisoner.

Second, there is the Woolf Report. After the disturbances around Easter 1990 at Strangeways and other prisons, Lord Justice Woolf investigated, with the help of counsel, the specific events; and thereafter led an examination into the problems of the prisons and the Prison Service. The result was a monumental report which both analysed the disturbances themselves and proposed solutions for the grievances of prisoners and staff which he found to be at the centre of the troubles. It remains a report of the greatest importance.

While the Woolf Report was in preparation (late 1990), the Inspectorate produced a thematic review, at the request of Ministers, on *Suicide and Self-harm in Prisons*. The report included an examination of precautions and attitudes, and a comparison between health care provision in prison and in the National Health Service. It was designed in particular to look at the anxieties, often leading to self-harm, felt by the young entering prison on remand or conviction for the first time. It made more than 100 recommendations, of which the great majority were concerned with attitudes and modest material changes capable of being put into effect without much cost.

In the autumn of 1991 were published the most important guidelines of all, namely the Government White Paper, *Custody, Care and Justice: The Way Ahead for the Prison Service*. This was the first occasion on which a British government has ever produced a full statement of long-term plans for the prisons. It was specifically stated to be a design for the rest of the century and beyond. The Government White Paper of 1991 is based on all the reports referred to above.

But there are other prisoners who do not fall within the majority, the young men who have not found their way. What about them, the other prisoners?

Let us set aside the majority, and look at the group who are the prime object of attention by the media, the most dangerous and violent prisoners. They amount to perhaps 2 or 3 per cent of the total, but it is they who make it necessary for us to pay for heavy security. The cameras and dogs, the high and strengthened walls, the electric equipment which needs – and does not always get – constant checking. Prisoners often escape not through a weakness in the hardware, but through a failure in its use. Constant searching of the cells of dangerous men, counting them on movement, continuing checking of checks themselves, require high morale among staff, encouragement and supervision.

The categorization of prisoners, following the Blake escape from Wormwood Scrubs in 1966 and the Mountbatten Report, is based on the need for security rather than control, so that every possible step is taken to see that the dangerous do not escape from the prison. Control is more an internal matter, so that staff may ensure that gangs of criminals are broken up, and that prison internal life remains under the eyes of staff. The immediate interest of the community is more in security than in control, so that the dangerous at any rate remain behind the walls and do not escape. But there are problems in ignoring the needs for control in categorizing prisoners. At Wymott in 1993, the prisoners took control from the staff, broke up the prison and terrified the weaker inmates, although there was no serious attempt at escape. The gangs needed firm control although they did not form much of a security risk in the Mountbatten sense, and were therefore put in Category C. We need to ensure proper control, as well as to maintain the necessary security, particularly among prisoners who come from the drug culture of young urban Britain.

Those on remand, the unconvicted, form in all countries a prison problem of their own. The philosophical difficulties in getting activity out of the idle, who are deemed not guilty until they are convicted, are evidenced at the Wolds, where the excellent facilities were, when I inspected, insufficiently used by prisoners who preferred to loiter. Probably a secure bail hostel is a better model than a prison for a remand centre. There is no reason why a hostel, well run, should not have rules which encourage an active life. Consideration overall is needed as to whether prisoners could not be brought more speedily to trial. I frequently meet remand prisoners who have been held for over a year. The remand population is a tempermental group, nervous about their situation, and – not surprisingly – about loss of rights.

The numbers of women prisoners are not great although they are currently increasing. Low numbers spread about the country make it more difficult to hold them in community prisons, within reasonable reach of family and friends. Some reorganization of the prison estate may be necessary to bring this population closer to home.

Young offenders constitute the biggest problem. The catchment areas are often too big so that boys from Cornwall or Liverpool are held at Feltham, near Slough, remote from their communities. The institutions are often too big. At Feltham nearly 800 teenagers are held. Our cultural attitude to the young becomes more relevant. We are fully conscious that they are offenders, but remain far less conscious that they are young. Very few staff are trained to deal specifically with teenagers: many of them have spent much of their careers with adults.

The Young Offender Institutions (YOI) are not sufficiently distinguished, save by name, from the ordinary prison. The institutions nevertheless vary vastly in quality between themselves. In all of them there is some admirable work by staff. But the job of helping the criminal teenager lead a law-abiding and useful life after release is an exceedingly demanding one. In far too many establishments the young are largely warehoused, and discharged without the skills or the self-respect which are likely to protect society from further villainy. The recidivism rates for the young remain in the area of 80 per cent reconvicted within two years of discharge. Bullies must be checked. If we bully the bullies in the course of training them, they become better trained, more efficient bullies. The outstanding model YOI at present is Lancaster Farms, in Lancashire. It shows what can be achieved.

The mentally disordered are another difficult problem. Professor John Gunn found that a very high percentage of prisoners needed psychiatric treatment which they were unable to get in prison. It is not so much a change in the provisions of the Mental Health Act 1983 which is now needed, as the improvement of attitudes to insist on transfers where medically desirable. Above all we need to train our doctors for work in prison. It has taken two years for the Prison Service to publish a most distinguished report from the three Medical Royal Colleges recommending such training. How long will it take to implement the essentials of this report?

The business of prison management must be ultimately a question for line management by the managers. All prisoners must be treated with humanity, but the balance between security and control and helping prisoners to lead law-abiding lives must turn on assessment of the prisoner. Those who escaped from Whitemoor or Parkhurst or are likely to escape are a very small minority of prisoners, but a minority which sometimes holds the attention of governments and media to the exclusion of larger minorities and the majority.

Most prisoners need to learn the practice of work, and this is not limited to what I have termed the majority. We should introduce the industrial prison.

The industrial prison is one where work comes first. Education and sport are available only at the end of a working day. The outside company employs the prisoners to make the goods. The company pays the industrial wage and provides materials and machinery. The Prison Service, which supervises the work, takes a cut, and the prisoners are paid wages in accordance with how hard and skilfully they work. The prisoners pay tax and insurance on their earnings. Their net earnings are divided, after discussion with prison officials, between their families and their own savings.

Instead of 'private cash' in small amounts being paid for prisoners by their families, the money goes the other way. Relations are improved between prisoner and family. Social security for the family may be reduced. The prisoner leaves prison with substantial savings, working skills, and the habit of work. All this to some extent happens in Germany and in other European countries. It works to the advantage of everybody, although better in a period of fairly full employment and with the agreement of the unions.

In England it has been tested out at Coldingley, where it has failed. Failure was probably due to our restriction of prisoners to pocket money. They are paid by the State a few pounds a week. They are not allowed to earn anything approaching full wages, and there are very few prisoners in England earning more than £10 weekly. Prisoners, unfortunately, will not work hard eight hours a day in order to repay their moral debt to society. If you walk into a workshop in any English prison, heads turn, the mood is one of apathy. If you go into a German prison where men are employed at acceptable wages – lower in fact than the full industrial wage – you will find the atmosphere of an efficient factory, where contract terms have to be met. If an industrial prison is to work, the prisoners will need to be paid as workers or given some other compensation, such as a substantial shortening of sentence.

Some people spend most of their lives in prison. Is it possible to develop a quality of life, a useful life, in such an environment? Long-term prisons can be productive places, where the ability to work, to earn, to give something valuable to society can be achieved. Such prisons are useful to the rest of us. Where prisoners are physically or mentally ill, the disability needs continuing assessment. Prisons need to be well integrated with other public services to ensure that proper care under the proper authorities is given to those who need it.

The approach which I find myself adopting after some

eight years independent inspection, is that education for the majority and properly paid and trained work are the keys to reducing the crime rate. But before I can put that conclusion forward, I need to look carefully at some of the counter-arguments put forward on prisons in the media debate on law and order.

The most often repeated argument has the virtue of brevity. 'Prison works', it is said. This means, I think, that while a man is held in prison, he cannot commit a crime outside. But unless all prisoners are to be held for their natural lives, the phrase seems of doubtful sense, if the aim of custody is to reduce the crime rate. 'Prison works' could have another meaning, namely that some prisons work effectively in that prisoners are discharged from them ready to lead law-abiding lives. We have, in practice, in England a number of excellent institutions. My reports for the last few years indicate a number of local and training prisons, an outstanding Young Offender Institution, a number of resettlement prisons, in all of which prison is working very well. With the resettlement prisons, the English penal system is cutting fresh ground. These prisons, starting with Blantyre House in Kent, take serious criminals with appalling records and long sentences and prepare them towards the end of the sentences for working and living in the community. Many prisoners from there go out daily to work and earn full outside wages. The sanction is that if they take drugs or misbehave they are liable to be sent to a harsher prison: it seems to work. So that if the phrase is to be construed as 'Some Prisons Can Work', my reports would strongly support it.

But the phrase 'Some Prisons Can Work' may have less public support than one might wish. There are some who would say it is inadequate: prisons hold the prisoners and it is sufficient that while inside they cannot harm innocent people and thereafter they may be deterred by the experience from the possibility of return. There are others, including many of the expert criminologists of the last thirty years, who would say that no prison works, that criminals should be treated outside. These groups have much in common. Neither believes that anything useful can be done in prison.

Another phrase reverberates through media discussion. 'We must not spend more on training and helping the criminal than we do on the non-criminal.' This appears inconsistent with the aim of imprisonment, if it is to reduce the crime rate. It may be necessary to educate or re-educate the prisoner, particularly if he comes from the majority. It seems unlikely that a man will commit a crime in order to take advantage of prison education, whether it is academic, social or moral education. But it is important to remember that if it is to be effective, the help given to prisoners must be sharp and urgent. They must be kept busy and not left lolling most of the day in their cells. Society needs here as elsewhere – in that great cant phrase of the age – to achieve value for money, VFM.

What of the cost of improvement? We already have a set of teachers in every prison. We already have a prison staff which is as responsible a set of individuals as any such staff elsewhere. The approach to education and work which is designed to reduce the rate of crime does not require the finding of overwhelming new resources. Indeed the adoption of the industrial prison should, as it does in Germany, actually produce a financial profit for the prison.

The lessons from the prisons, which I have walked about now for some eight years, is that we do indeed have a prison system capable of reducing the crime rate. But we still need to turn capacity into achievement in this as in other branches of criminal justice. Probation officers need a great deal of support after the battering of their morale suffered in recent years. Community Service needs stiffening and reorganizing if it is to gain the confidence of the courts who are to impose it. The police have problems of their own. In some respects the Prison Service has a brighter prospect than others. The

White Paper, *Custody, Care and Justice: The Way Ahead for the Prison Service*, is an admirable signpost and there is no reason I can see why it should not now be followed.

Follow the signposts, mind the gap. The view of prisoners, victims and social institutions as figures whose positions in relation to each other need adjustment, has been recently studied in a new approach, *Relational Justice*, or, as it is called in New Zealand, *Restorative Justice*. One way of dealing with convicted criminals is to keep them away from us for a very long time, lock them up, and throw away the key. Another way, and perhaps the only way with those soon to be released, is to reconcile, educate and train. On this view the Woolf Report and the White Paper and the Inspectorate report on suicide are texts of relational justice based on firm and effective resolution of grievances and the alteration of relationships.

14 Democracy in the Workplace

Robert Taylor

Employment editor of the *Financial Times*, his latest book is *The Future of the Trade Unions*.

Workers in Britain feel insecure and fearful about their future in what has become during the 1980s and 1990s an increasingly flexible and deregulated labour market. Change in the workplace has grown rapidly in response to the pressures imposed on it by technological innovation and the demands of global competitiveness. In the past it was manual workers who were the main victims of structural upheavals. But now the need to adapt has spread across the whole labour force and even into a company's management grades. At the same time inequalities in the level of earnings and wealth between workers have widened with the active encouragement of the government's regressive economic and taxation policies. Ministers are intent not on transforming Britain into a social market economy on the mainland European model but into a 'free' enterprise society comparable to the so-called 'tiger' countries around the Asian Pacific Rim. The growth of a more individualistic approach to the employment relationship between employer and workers has become the dominant objective. The government questions openly whether there is the need any longer for collective bargaining to determine wages and benefits, arguing that that familiar method of determining the employment relationship has outlived its usefulness in the new workplace where team and individual effort have apparently replaced solidarity between workers on the shopfloor.

In the words of the government's 1992 White Paper, *People, Jobs and Opportunity*: 'During the nineteen nineties successful industrial relations strategies will work with the trends in the labour market, widening individual choice and opportunity, moving away from collectivism and supporting the natural evolution of working arrangements and practices which suit both individual employees and the companies for whom they work.'

The trade unions have been disciplined and marginalized since 1979 through the imposition of eight separate and cumulatively comprehensive legislative measures. As a result the power and influence of organized labour has been substantially diminished. Today UK trade union membership has fallen to its smallest level in the workforce since the 1930s with less than a third of employees organized, while only just under half have their pay and benefits determined by collectively negotiated agreements. At the same time the government has removed many of the statutory regulations that used to protect workers from the arbitrary behaviour of employers, mostly notably with the abolition in 1993 of the tripartite Wages Councils that set minimum rates for the lowest paid and most vulnerable workers in non-unionized areas of the labour market.

Drastic changes during the 1990s in the country's employment structure have also made a profound impact on the workplace. We have seen a clear decline in the proportion of people who are employed in full-time and permanent jobs. By contrast the numbers in part-time employment, self-employment and those working on short-term fixed contracts have grown substantially. Important shifts have also taken place in the occupational pattern of the labour market with the sharp contraction in manufacturing employment in traditional industries like steel, engineering, shipbuilding and vehicle production and the expansion of the more diverse and fragmented private services sector. Small and medium-sized enterprises have increased in number as the large-scale mass production plant has declined in importance. Women now make up nearly half of the employed workforce.

These important underlying workplace trends look set to continue during the rest of the 1990s, according to independent labour market forecasts like the Institute for Employment Research at Warwick University. While the numbers of workers employed in low-skilled clerical and manual jobs are expected to continue declining, the demand for workers in skilled high technology-based occupations as well as in low-paid and labour-intensive sectors such as hotels, catering and retail distribution look set to grow.

It may be questionable whether the pace of workplace change is any greater now than in the past and some of the new features of the flexible labour market – such as the extent of part-time employment – may have been exaggerated. Moreover, the shifting occupational profile of the British workforce is a phenomenon that is not unique to this country. Across the industrialized world similar developments are apparent. The reality of an integrated global labour market may still be a long way off and the continuing strength of the nation-state should not be underestimated. But there is no doubt that the workplace is undergoing disturbingly profound change across the whole of the Western industrialized world.

As Sir Henry Phelps Brown, the eminent labour economist, explained the underlying changes taking place in late twentieth-century capitalism suggest the arrival of a new world of work which carries with it significant social consequences:

People are no longer dependent on society and bound by reciprocal obligations to it. The very notion of society is rejected. Individuals are expected to shift for themselves and those who get into difficulties are thought to have only themselves to blame. Self-reliance, acquisitive individualism, the curtailment of public expenditure, the play of market forces instead of the restraints and directives of public policy, the prerogatives of management instead of the power of trade unions, centralization of power instead of pluralism.*

We are passing through what may turn out to be the beginning of the end for the system of mass volume-production that has characterized much of this century's organization of labour. Global corporations may remain colossi in the world economy but the way they organize themselves seems likely to divide and fragment labour, making it harder to sustain strong workplace organizations to challenge the arbitrary power of capital. More than at any time during the past fifty years, a real and growing threat faces workers in their ability to retain and assert their individual as well as collective rights in the workplace. In Britain the strength of worker discontents can be found in the enormous increase in the number of complaints being reported to the independent Citizens Advice Bureaux on labour market questions by troubled individuals. The upheaval in the workplace caused mainly by radical corporate restructuring has precipitated the emergence of a divided and frightened workforce. It is true some companies operating in Britain – many of them foreign-owned enterprises – are responding to what is happening in a socially responsible way but most are not. Companies are being encouraged in the name of greater efficiency and profitability to introduce new just-in-time working methods based

* *Industrial Relations*, vol. 29, 1, Winter 1990, pp. 1–2.

on both individual and team effort and to abandon the collective approach to pay and benefits involved in bargaining with trade unions in favour of more performance-related remuneration determined without negotiation. But little evidence exists to suggest enlightened human-resource strategies are spreading across most of corporate Britain. The spread of non-unionism has led to a reimposition of managerial authority rather than to the emergence of the concept of social partnership between employers and workers that has been so successful in mainland Europe. The right to manage has grown more assertive and unilateral, although this in itself does not appear to have made any noticeably positive impact on improving productivity and overall workplace performance. Leaner and flatter organizations have also not led to the decentralization of decision-making power to workers.

The results of these dramatic trends in the workplace have proved highly disturbing for many employees, mainly because the government has made it more difficult and not easier for them to protect, let alone extend their influence, over the decisions that affect their working lives. It is true that there have been some important counter-developments in recent years that have provided workers with forms of legal protection against the worst excesses of the flexible labour market. The piecemeal and cumulative growth of specific individual employee rights enshrined in statute law has been crucial in limiting the power of companies to exercise an unquestioned authority over the workplace. To a large extent many of the new legal rights derive from the directly beneficial influence of European Union social legislation, often interpreted by the European Court of Justice in a sympathetic way to employees. In controversial areas like gender and race discrimination, unfair dismissal as well as health and safety provision, a corpus of case law has been built up in recent years to strengthen worker protections. As a result of EU pressures, the government has even been compelled to introduce regulations that require companies to create workplace representation bodies for their employees when dealing with cases of collective redundancy and the transfer of business ownership. However, the extent of individual worker rights in Britain remains inadequate particularly for the low paid, and those on short-term contracts or in part-time employment. Many workers are vulnerable because they lack access to legal aid and face cumbersome and lengthy industrial tribunal procedures as well as prohibitive legal costs that can often deter them from seeking the redress of an injustice suffered in the workplace.

The growth of individual workplace legal rights looks set to continue and this is to be welcomed. Such a development will certainly deter many companies from exercising an arbitrary authority over their employees. But it would be wrong to suggest that this will by itself provide either a satisfactory or sufficient answer to the current crisis of workplace insecurity. The mere provision of more legal rights for individual employees is not going to be enough in itself to ensure they can actually be exercised or enforced by most workers as isolated individuals. The relationship between an employer and a worker remains self-evidently not one that is based on an accepted or even implied contract of equals. A company is obliged – under current company law – to maximize its commercial performance in order to secure the approval of its shareholders while the employee remains keen to secure first and foremost higher wages and benefits as well as job security. These legitimate objectives are not necessarily compatible.

If a commitment to the provision of employee legal rights is to be effective it will require an equal commitment to the encouragement and strengthening of the right of workers to representation. It is therefore crucial that workers are able to decide for themselves how their rights at work are to be exercised and above all enforced. This means providing them with the opportunity to ensure this can be achieved through the development of a collective voice in the workplace which is clear, independent and strong. The successful assertion of a worker's legal rights will only be credibly achieved through the acceptance by employers of the principle of representation.

The debate ought to be about the different forms of employee representation that may be appropriate in helping to strengthen individual rights in the flexible workplace. Trade unions – as voluntary associations – remain the obvious institutional means available for the successful achievement of worker representation. Historically they were formed to uphold the dignity and the self-respect of workers as human beings. Through mutual protection trade unions sought to extend the issue of workplace civil rights into the public policy arena. Until recently in Britain trade unions and workers believed the best method for achieving that democratic objective was by ensuring the state and the courts were kept as much as possible at arm's length from the employment relationship. Instead they argued for a continuation of so-called voluntarism, for freely negotiated agreements between employers and trade unions that were based on trust and cooperation but lacked any legal means of enforcement. The instinctive suspicions about the use of the law to solve the often complex employment problems reflected the practical experiences of trade unions and workers alike at the hands of the common law with its concept of absolute property rights that saw collective action in the workplace as 'a restraint of trade'. However, this is no longer seen by many as a sensible way to safeguard the position of vulnerable workers in the new workplace. Instead, Britain's trade unions have dropped, in recent years, many of their remaining doubts about the introduction of legal workplace regulation and they are now looking to government for the provision of legal rights to achieve both employee representation and union recognition. There can be no exclusive legal rights for trade union members however. Belatedly trade unions accept that all workers must have access to representation and to social protection under the law whether or not they belong to a trade union.

Such a fundamental transformation in trade union attitudes has to be seen within the wider objective of establishing a social partnership in Britain between employers, workers and trade unions. A few large companies have pioneered this approach, particularly in the automobile and chemical industries. The corporatist industrial relations system based on consensus and solidarity found in northern European countries suggests the partnership approach can be successful in achieving both effective representation for workers and boosting business competitiveness. However, the obstacles to its introduction into the more fragmented and decentralized British employment scene remain formidable.

The main difficulty lies in the absence of deeply rooted, strong and effective institutions in the UK either at national level or perhaps even more importantly in local labour markets that can enable employers and trade unions to work together harmoniously for their mutual self-interest in a practical, stable and long-term way. The employer-dominated Training and Enterprise Councils are, for example, but a pale and ineffectual reflection of the statutory and comprehensive Chambers of Commerce that have helped to provide Germany with its admirable industrial craft apprenticeship system. With no compulsion to participate in them, the TECs are dependent on state support for their funding with resulting bureaucratic inefficiencies. Trade unions have a highly limited role to play in their activities. It is also questionable how representative they can be of the diverse interests in the labour market.

At the national level tripartite institutions like the Advisory, Conciliation and Arbitrary Service (better known as ACAS), the Central Arbitration Committee, the Equal

Opportunities Commission and Commission for Racial Equality continue to exist and they provide at least some semblance of authority in their respective areas of jurisdiction. But more bodies will be needed if social partnership is to remain little more than a well-meaning slogan. The promised Low Pay Commission under a Labour government may help employers and trade unions to establish a clearer common purpose in the controversial area of setting a minimum wage by agreement.

But new social institutions are also necessary in the workplace itself if worker representation is going to be effective. The most radical innovation ought to be the creation of consultation and information committees for all employees (not just trade unionists) in companies which employ more than say, a hundred and fifty people. These bodies would complement the creation of works councils that are being established at European transnational level in large companies with sizeable business operations in at least two European Union countries as a result of an EU directive. Despite Britain's opt-out from such bodies as a result of its decision not to accept the social chapter of the Maastricht Treaty, UK-owned companies are introducing them for all their workers. The new domestic plant-based committees would not be involved in any form of collective bargaining. Their purpose would be to establish a more formalized two-way flow of information over a wide range of corporate issues outside the traditional negotiating agenda between company and workplace. A growing number of larger employers have already created such forums covering their plants as part of a commitment to worker involvement, but they need to be established much more widely across companies and given clear legitimacy. The committees must also be genuinely representative of the employees who would elect their nominees from within their own workplaces. The works councils in German companies and the enterprise committees which have grown up in France since the passage of the so-called

Auroux laws in the early 1980s provide good examples of how such workplace institutions would operate in practice in helping to close the representation gap in the British workplace.

Critics on the Left who doubt the wisdom of establishing such consultative bodies by law argue they might pose a serious threat to existing collective bargaining arrangements by introducing a dual system of representation that would weaken the trade unions. But this is a risk that the trade unions should be self-confident enough to accept. If they can demonstrate in practice through professionalism and the quality of service they provide at the workplace, they ought to have nothing to fear in being able to establish themselves as an effective means of representation for workers on those bodies.

However, this will not be enough to guarantee a deeply rooted institutional presence for employee workplace representation which will help to reduce current insecurities. We also need to see the establishment of the concept of the stakeholder company in Britain. At present the short-termist strategies of most of the country's employers reflects not only a *laissez-faire* business culture that fails to think very far ahead but also their legal obligations to their shareholders under existing company law. The company's market share price is the primary focus of corporate attention. If the law was to require companies to accept they had a wider legal obligation that also extended to the wellbeing of their own employees as well as their customers this would provide a strong legal framework for the development of a more socially responsible relationship between employer and employee in the workplace.

The creation of consultative work-based employee committees and the introduction of the stakeholder company could both provide institutional expressions of social partnership between employers, workers and trade unions in Britain. However if they are to work effectively in practice they will have to accept the necessity of balance. On the one hand, workers need access to a representative voice in the flexible workplace but on the other hand they have to be prepared to adapt to the demands of commercial and technological change. Social pacts are required at workplace level that can reconcile the democratic aspiration of workers for security and fairness with reassurance to employers that there has to be a flexible acceptance of workplace change. This can only be achieved through the development of a mutual trust between company and worker that is focused on covenants and not words of good intentions. Comprehensive legal regulation will be required to provide a framework within which all sides can bargain freely to create innovative and civilized workplaces, but it should be as minimal as possible. If the development of such bargaining is left to voluntary methods, it seems unlikely that it will make much of an advance. Law is needed to provide the catalyst for necessary change. But the emphasis needs to be concentrated on the improvement of corporate performance through workplace cooperation. Workers and trade unions must accept their role as allies with employers in improving competitiveness. The achievement of strategic alliances that enable companies to carry through change with stability remains of vital importance to the benefit of both capital and labour.

Such moves to give institutional expression to social partnership will involve drastic reform in the British trade union movement which few have yet begun to realize. It will mean they will have to accept that they cannot enjoy any exclusive rights or privileges in the workplace. If trade unions hope to survive and grow again they have to adapt to the new realities. First and foremost they must recognize that a growing number of employees will need them as professional service providers. Mutual insurance through the provision of friendly society benefits was a traditional activity of trade unions when they were first established in the last century.

Now the trade unions will have to advance much further in meeting the complex and pragmatic demands of employees in the flexible workplace. This will mean not so much an extension of consumer-style attractions such as credit cards and subsidized holidays but a readiness by trade unions to increase the labour-market value of trade union members by providing them with access to training and education, a job placement service and a more effective form of legal advice. Trade unions need to respond flexibly to a segmented labour market where workers will want to enhance their employability so they will be able to move more effectively between jobs and occupations over the length of their working lives. Employees ought to be able to look to trade unions for assistance in building up their own job portfolios. There must also be an active encouragement of worker share-ownership schemes and profit sharing. The greater their say in the working of the enterprise, the greater will be employees' commitment to its success. Trade unions should further that objective. This will mean a widening of their purposes beyond the traditional collective bargaining agenda.

None of these proposed changes by themselves guarantees a future for trade unions, nor should they. It will be up to trade unions as autonomous and voluntary associations to justify their existence by effectively representing the aspirations and demands of working people in the new workplace. Of course, this will mean a shift in the balance of the existing employment relationship to allow trade unions to attract members and gain recognition from employers in a fair and impartial way. But there is enough evidence among young workers in Britain to suggest trade unions will face a difficult and up-hill task in convincing those known as Mrs Thatcher's children that belonging to a union 'makes them strong'. Collective action is no longer fashionable in an age of individualism. It is this pessimistic observation that has led a growing number on the left to question whether trade unions really have a viable future at all.

But such assertions go too far. They appear to assume that today's workplaces are benign and cooperative with no need for the involvement of any outside autonomous association to represent the views and aspirations of employees. The evidence from workplace surveys of opinion suggests this is not the case. On the contrary, workers remain discontented and frustrated because they often feel powerless to establish any influence, let alone control, over the conditions under which they have to work. The resulting 'democratic deficit' is not going to be spirited away by half-hearted and patronizing forms of human-resource management imposed from on high by employers. What is required is a dual strategy involving new legal rights for workers and the creation of social partnerships. These should not be regarded as alternative or incompatible aims but complementary, together ensuring a greater sense of security in the workplace.

The left should also reassert the importance of democratic practice in the workplace. The civil rights of the worker citizen should not end at the factory gate or office door. The arbitrary or unilateral authority of managers to manage has to be countered in a production process that claims to emphasize the need for team working, joint decision making and labour flexibility. If Britain is to see a renewal of its democratic values through the encouragement of a more active civic political culture, trade unions and workers will have to play an important role. This will mean the integration of workplace concerns into the wider debate about civil rights in the community. A recent study by Dr Neil Millward of the Policy Studies Institute suggested that there is a serious danger that the British labour market is returning to the exploitative conditions of the master-servant relationship that dominated the workplace before the creation of the trade unions. In the name of flexibility and competitiveness, millions of workers feel under threat. The creation of a practical social partnership in the workplace and in the wider labour market will guarantee nobody a job for life, but it may help to generate the kind of consent and fairness that are so vital if Britain is to combine economic efficiency with social justice and avoid a return to the harsh workplace conditions of the past.

15 Democracy as Self-Government

Geoff Mulgan

Author and former advisor to Gordon
Brown, he is Director of Demos.

When I was at school and university in the 1970s and 1980s
we were taught that Britain's system of government and
democracy was still the best in the world. Our civil service
was more efficient, our parliament less corruptible, our culture more resilient against dictators and demagogues than
any other. Only a few years later not many share these views
any more. Instead the British system is more likely to be
seen as tired and old, inefficient and illegitimate, and badly
in need of radical overhaul.

How did we get here? It may be that Britain's curse was
to get there early. In matters of democracy and government
England, and later Britain, were pioneers, and being a pioneer has its costs. Long before most other countries, Britain
had a working parliament, a semiwritten constitution, political parties and contested elections. It introduced many
civic rights, all without too many upheavals (only one civil
war and only one decapitated monarch), and without fundamental divisions over the legitimacy of the system. Indeed
its capacity to absorb opposition is usually taken to be exemplified best by the fact that all but one of the Chartists
demands (the exception is annual parliaments) are now in
place.

Much was wrong with British democracy – it ignored the poor and women, and had more than its fair share of sleaze. But it set benchmarks for others to follow. In any event few can dispute the success of the British model of government. During the nineteenth century, far from disabling government as many had forecast, parliamentary democracy enabled a small island to create a vast empire and an industrial powerhouse.

Over the last few decades this legacy has turned from a source of enormous pride into an impediment. At times it has even become an embarrassment. Sometime this century the institutions which had proven so successful seemed to lose the capacity to adapt, and previous success made it that much harder to modernize. This perhaps became clearest after 1989. Whereas a previous generation of new democracies, particularly in the Commonwealth, had opted in the 1950s and 1960s for the Westminster model, not one of the new democracies that emerged out of the collapse of the Soviet Union chose to follow Britain. For them the models were the USA and France, Germany and Spain. All wanted written constitutions, and balances of powers.

Nor have the British people themselves retained much faith in the structures which govern them. MORI has regularly polled people on their attitudes to the core institutions. Their recent results make grim reading for any supporter of the status quo. A remarkable 38 per cent of the population now agree with the statement that 'it will always be impossible to reform the system enough . . .' 80 per cent say they feel more and more remote from big political institutions and 89.3 per cent that it is time for change in Britain. Similar signs can be found in attitudes to the relationship between decision makers and the public. There is, for example, overwhelming support for referendums on particular issues, and overwhelming support for other kinds of voter input between elections.

But perhaps the most damning indictment of the current

British system of government is not that it is undemocratic but rather that it is ineffective. Parliament has proven good neither at passing well-considered legislation (the Poll Tax and the National Curriculum are just two examples) nor at overseeing government (most of the recent scandals have been uncovered either by chance or by the media).

All of this would be grounds enough for scepticism about the claims made by advocates of the status quo that the British system is marvellously adaptable, that it offers us strong and decisive government, or that the public is simply uninterested in reform.

But it would be wrong to see this solely in British terms. Although Britain has special problems that result from the special antiquity of the British system and the relative decline with which it has been associated during the course of this century, we are not alone. Even though most mainstream constitutional reformers look to other countries as models, there is a growing sense that it is not good enough to take the best of the USA in the 1970s and 1980s, or the model that Germany adopted in the 1940s. Many of these too look tired, gridlocked and illegitimate. They have undoubted virtues, notably their more effective scrutiny of the executive, their more thorough consideration of legislation, and the transparent citizens rights they uphold, but these virtues are matched by other vices. Indeed worldwide there is a questioning of many of the building blocks that the Westminster system shares with these others: the use of representative chambers of professional politicians, of occasional elections, of systems based only on parties.

Some of the reasons are long term. A more educated population has less grounds for seeing politicians as experts who are self-evidently qualified to make complex decisions. As technologies enable far easier communication it is less obvious that members of parliament need to gather together in a single chamber for long periods of time, or for that matter that voting itself needs to take the form of placing pieces of paper into metal boxes. As knowledge and information become more easily accessible it is less obvious that politicians are specially qualified to make decisions about complex issues. Many have also noticed the political parties often freeze earlier social conditions, and thus fail to represent new currents.

These are just some of the factors behind a marked disengagement from orthodox politics right across the West. This was most visible perhaps in the turn against the LDP in Japan, the crumbling of the old political establishment in Italy, the antipolitics of Ross Perot (and to an extent Newt Gingrich) in the USA. It has been manifest in Green and far Right parties in Europe.

This far-reaching alienation is perhaps the biggest reason to be worried about governance and democracy. For it not only reinforces a gap between citizens and decision makers; it also undermines the capacity of governments, as legitimate authorities, to take the long-term decisions on issues like education or the environment on which any healthy society depends. In other words we need to worry about democracy not only to empower citizens relative to government, but also so as to enable governments to function effectively.

So what is to be done? There is no shortage of reform proposals. Over the last few years in Britain many blueprints have been drawn up. Charter 88, the Institute for Public Policy Research, Tony Benn and Ferdinand Mount are amongst those who have suggested new approaches. These vary from the very general to specific proto-constitutions, drawn up by groups of lawyers and defining the powers and role of the House of Lords, regional assemblies. Although the British debate is still largely cast in these traditional terms, there is also no shortage of ideas now bubbling elsewhere about electronic town meetings, availability of legislation and policy on the Internet and so on, and dozens of new means of involving people in decisions ranging from citizens' juries (as in Germany) and Consensus

Conferences (as in Denmark), to neighbourhood forums and deliberative polls, many of which go back to the original democratic idea of using random sampling to select decision makers.

Major constitutional reform is not something to be entered into lightly. There are very real problems with many of the proposed schemes. Some are immediately vulnerable to the criticism that they would create new layers of govern-ance without properly fulfilling any new functions. Others appear to multiply new talking shops for yet more party politicians in ways that might simply exacerbate the public sense of disconnection. Others still propose new entities that do not fit with real identities or economic units.

There are also profound problems with many of the tech-nologically based schemes. There is no doubt that technolo-gies can enrich democracy around the edges. Around the world there have been many successful initiatives using com-munications technologies to make it easier for citizens to talk to and question their representatives, to study legisla-tion and mobilize for or against it. But none are yet ready to be part of the core constitution for the simple reason that penetration rates are too low. A good 60 per cent of the public believes that technologies should be used to enhance democracy. But at present barely a few hundred thousand British citizens use the Internet and even the telephone has only 90 per cent penetration, making it usable as a polling device but not as a basis for suffrage.

So what should be done about governance and the renewal of our democracy? If democracy means anything it is about self-government. It is about how collective decisions are made, reviewed, and accounted for. If there is a single core problem with our current system of governance it is that the people are disconnected from it; that it is not self-government by any meaningful definition. Instead our poli-tics is based around the idea of a fundamental divide between leaders and led, between adults and children. It is this that justifies the supreme sovereignty of parliament, official secrecy, and the shared rituals of the political class. Reversing that and recreating connections to power in ways that fit with the reality of a fairly diverse, highly educated society, is now the overwhelming priority of political reform.

We should start from the local level. More than most countries, Britain has a notoriously weak local government. Partly this has to do with the history of a strong central state. Partly it is the consequence of deliberate policies – which during the late 1970s and 1980s took discretion away from local level and effectively nationalized it, in schools, policing, health, and in overall budgetary policies, to such an extent that local councils are only in charge of about a fifth of their spending. Partly too it is the consequence of failures of local government itself. The majority of councils suffered from the ill-considered policies of a relatively small minority which have led to a significant decline in faith in local government. Today barely a quarter of the population believe local government to be honest. The proportion supporting a shift in power from national to local government is considerably less than it was in the mid 1980s, and with this loss of prestige and legitimacy has come a reduced capacity to attract the best people to become officers or councillors, particularly in the major cities.

For these reasons it would be unwise simply to pass more powers back to local government. This would give the appearance of democratization but not much more. Instead the only credible strategy would be to move on several fronts simultaneously.

The first is to pass back both power *and* responsibility to local authorities. By this I mean matching a widening of their power to set their own taxes and spending priorities on the one hand, and a widening of the means for the public to have a say on the other, by requiring referendums for budgets which are set above a pre-agreed level. In the same way, if there is to be more local government power over planning decisions let this be accompanied by requirements in disputed cases to put issues to arbitration by voter juries, small groups selected at random from the relevant population who can spend a number of days considering and deliberating over the issues, a model which has been successfully used in several German cities and in Spain.

In the long run this twin track should enhance the confidence of local government, and create the conditions in which many more people might become councillors – and in which Britain might come closer to other European countries where far higher proportions of the population serve as representatives.

But local government as an umbrella agency is no longer the full sum of local governance. Governments of all parties have increased the role of quangos, appointed boards and agencies. In some cases they have done so simply to avoid democratic oversight. But they have also sought more professionalism and more consistency, and recognized that there is also often something to be gained from an agency focused on a task, and concentrated on its relationships with its key stakeholders, rather than a general purpose council that is only accountable to the general electorate.

The challenge now is to make any such special purpose bodies accountable and democratic. Partly that involves ensuring that their members are reasonably representative, partly it means ensuring that decisions are transparent, and partly it means involving general purpose bodies in their appointment. But for me the key reform, and the best way to make them act democratically, would be to find ways to kick them out if they underperform. To achieve the first we need much clearer guidelines about open information. To achieve the latter, my own preference is for 'contestability' – the threat of removal by local electors, so that, for example, 5 per cent of the population covered by a TEC or health authority could require a referendum to be held on their dismissal. The virtue of such a scheme is that it would be rarely used, but the threat of it would force quangos to act in the interests of the local public.

At the next layer up Britain needs great diversity, or what John Major called variable geometry. Neat devisers of constitutions want consistency (this was the West Lothian question posed by Tam Dalyell). But Britain is not a consistent country. It is dominated by England, a nation that is surrounded by a series of small nations of varying degrees of coherence. Within it are regions that have strong identities and regions with almost none. In many regions, cities are more obvious bases of governance than regions, perhaps inevitably in a society that has been predominantly urban for so long.

The case for substantial devolution of powers to Scotland and Wales is overwhelming. But in my view the best model for reshaping governance in Britain would not force the English regions to mirror governance arrangements designed for the very different circumstances of Scotland. Instead I would favour a patchwork with stronger cities like Manchester, Liverpool or Leeds coordinating much of the activity in their surrounding region; with more classically European regions like the Northeast or Southwest running many of their affairs, and with the genuine nations, Wales and Scotland, gaining a significantly larger measure of autonomy including some national powers of taxation.

What about the national level? Britain has historically had a strong central state. It is this that now needs to be modernized to make it effective and legitimate. The starting point should be the House of Commons itself. By most criteria it is not an effective institution. It does not pass well-considered legislation. Nor does it act as a particularly good check on the executive – most of the really important uncoverings of government wrongdoing have come from media investigation not from MPs' questioning. And finally it does not actually represent the public very well, when its make-up is so overwhelmingly male, and so skewed to a handful of professions such as lawyers and teachers.

Not all of these deficiencies are easy to tackle. But much could be done to make Parliament more open and more effective. There could be fewer sittings of the house itself and more use of committees. These could build up a genuine strategic policy capacity. Votes could be allowed on-line or by telephone to avoid the necessity for MPs to spend so much time in Parliament (or rather in its bars). And MPs could apply to themselves what they have applied to other public services, the requirement to publish a constituents' charter spelling out precisely how they will work and how they will make themselves open to complaints about their own performance and questions from constituents.

The question of a second chamber has greatly exercised reformers. We assume that election is the only way to fill it. But my fear is that this could simply widen the space for professional politicians. There are alternatives. One would be to open up the existing House of Lords by encouraging nominations for five- or ten-year terms – so as to fill it with business people, artists, film-makers, inventors, community activists in the prime of their life rather than only at the end of it, alongside an elected component. A more radical option would be to include an element of choice by lot – the original Greek idea of democracy and still the way we choose juries.

Finally around the core institutions there will need to be far greater commitment to openness and transparency. The old assumptions of secrecy are now totally at odds with what people rightly assume is their due. Given that Britain no longer has an empire, the range of topics on which national security can legitimately be invoked is far fewer.

Openness also extends to decisions. Most of the public would like to see a far greater use of direct democracy on the really big issues. Britain has a long history of referendums, mainly at local level, on everything from Sunday opening of cinemas to rates levels. The legitimate fear of referendums is that they promote mindless decisions. But there are intermediate ways of matching the desire for public involvement with means of ensuring that decisions are not made carelessly. Demos has proposed, for example, a rule for 'post-parliamentary' referendums – opportunities for the public to call for referendums on legislation which has passed through Parliament, a model which would also cover really big constitutional changes. This would ensure that there was adequate public debate, while also serving as a check against legislation that is strongly opposed by the public.

As well as new public powers to call referendums, we could also go further to encourage what could be called the 'informal constitution' the spaces where public debate happens in practice, on television and radio. Already the media have shown far more innovation than Parliament – with deliberative polls, programmes like *You Decide* and Channel 4's *People's Parliament*, all of which have shown higher standards of debate than the formal political programmes like *Question Time* and *Any Questions*. With rapidly spreading cable television access, the scope for new fora of this kind, bringing together more specialist and local audiences, is immense.

This takes us back to the core issue. We need not only democratic forms but a democratic culture. At the heart of a democratic culture is people's ability and confidence to organize themselves. At its heart is a vitality that encourages new organizations to emerge, old organizations to die, and a healthy competition between them. Britain's system by contrast is gridlocked. It is virtually impossible to create a new party. Parliament monopolizes power and debate and it is hard for the public to break in, to float ideas, to encourage change.

As a consequence politics is drying up. In research for *Demos* we have found just how serious a problem this is becoming. Whereas thirty years ago the young were the most politically active, today eighteen- to thirty-four-year-olds are less active than any older age group, even on issues like the environment. For them politics is boring or irrelevant. Their time – the lifeblood of any democratic system – is going elsewhere. To the extent that politics is still a popular activity, it is for the rich more than the poor, men more than women, whites more than blacks.

Some celebrate the turn away from politics as wisdom. But a political system that cannot inspire people to invest time in it is likely to lose the capacity to think up a long-term way and make the difficult decisions. This is why the democratic reform agenda is not marginal but central, and why it needs to be so much wider than devising new assemblies to touch such questions as when elections are held, or even making voting mandatory to prevent the UK from following America to a situation where half the population is effectively disenfranchised.

All of this could be the challenge for the next decade. It should come naturally to us. After all Britain has a pioneering record. We have the potential to jump to a more modern system that learns from the best of other systems around the world. If we can do so we will demonstrate again the most important point about democracy, namely that governance is no longer a private possession of the political elites, but a public good, the most valuable tool whereby people govern themselves.

16 A People's Europe

Stephen Tindale

A former diplomat and policy advisor
to Chris Smith, he is Research Fellow at
the Institute for Public Policy Research.

Euro-enthusiasts display an uncritical reverence for
Europe's 'founding fathers'. Western Europe's transformation, within half a century, from an uncomfortable patchwork of warring states into at least a quasi-federation is a
tribute to Jean Monnet and his associates. But they were not
infallible – and to say this should not be taken as evidence
of hostility to the European project. The 1975 referendum
settled the pro- or anti-Europe question (despite the Labour
Party's ill-judged and electorally disastrous reversion to an
anti-Market position in the early 1980s). For those of us
too young to have voted in 1975, the issue is not whether
or not we wish to belong, but what sort of Europe we want.
It is possible – indeed essential – to criticize the existing
model of European integration without aligning oneself with
the Bruggist little Englanders.

Since the signing of the Maastricht Treaty the European
project has faced its most severe crisis. Through de Gaulle's
confrontations with the EC institutions in the 1960s, the
failure of monetary experiments in the 1970s, the Euro-
sclerosis of the 1980s, pro-Europeans could console themselves with the knowledge that public opinion in the key

countries – France and Germany – was solidly behind closer integration. The French referendum, which came within a couple of percentage points of wrecking Maastricht altogether, and the German public's scepticism about giving up the Deutschmark make the 1990s difficulties a challenge of a different magnitude. One reaction has been to suggest that pro-Europeans needed to be more outspoken in defence of their beliefs. Roy Jenkins, integrationist par excellence, accepts that 'the pro-European case has been allowed to go by default', due to a 'loss of nerve' by supporters. More outspoken – and more honest – argument in favour of closer integration would certainly help reverse the decline in public enthusiasm. But the last thing we need is more lofty, meaningless rhetoric about 'our European destiny', 'being at the heart of Europe' and so on. The case has certainly been badly presented in recent years, but this does not go to the root of the problem. European integration does not need to be relaunched, but rethought.

The 1996 Inter-Governmental Conference is being billed as a minor tidying-up operation. It must be more than that. There need to be fundamental changes to the way Europe is organized, and a thorough reappraisal of the objectives of integration. If these changes are to provide lasting foundations, they need to be presented openly to the people of Europe. A settlement drawn up by diplomats and politicians alone will be at best worthless, and quite possibly undermine the entire project.

We need now to refocus on our political vision for Europe. Our objectives should be to increase the wellbeing of Europe's citizens on the basis of a European model of capitalism, with high social and environmental standards, in contrast to the casino capitalism of the Anglo-American model, and to support peace, democracy and respect for human rights throughout the continent. In other words, we need to build the social dimension of European integration and enlarge the membership of the Union. These are concrete goals, unlike nebulous concepts such as 'ever closer union' which tell us nothing about what or why we want to unite. They may in some respects be difficult to reconcile, but they are not incompatible as long as we are open-minded in our assessment of institutions and policies. Existing and projected EU activities should be measured against these two objectives, and those which stand in the way of reaching them should be abandoned. The concept of an *acquis communautaire* or an accepted body of community legislation must be rejected.

A PEOPLE'S EUROPE

When Jacques Delors became President of the European Commission he took the decision to kick-start European integration through the Single Market programme. Some years later he launched the 'Social Charter', in the realization that people could not be expected to feel warmly about a technocratic programme of internal trade liberalization. The EU's social policies are a means of increasing support for Brussels among citizens. Delors never gave environmental policies the same emphasis, which was a significant tactical error, since European environmental policy is consistently popular with European public opinion, perhaps because this is self-evidently a policy area which cannot be addressed by nation-states acting alone.

We should emphasize the social and environmental dimensions of integration, not just to win greater support from the public, but also because these are essential to the European model of capitalism. We want trade and economic activity to be on the basis of respect for social standards and a high level of environmental protection. This is partly to avoid 'social and environmental dumping' – producers taking advantage of lax standards in parts of a free trade area to drive down standards everywhere. Though the term is a loaded one, we could say that we want trade to be fair

as well as free. But it is also a political point: high social
and environmental standards are part of our core objective.
From a social democratic perspective, the single market is
not an end but a means – the goal being increased welfare.
Higher economic growth built on lower social and environmental standards would represent not progress but exploitation.

Policies on employment can be seen in much the same
light. The EU should do more to promote employment
partly because there are steps which can best be undertaken
in harmony with all EU countries, such as shifting taxation
off labour and onto pollution. This would help convince
public opinion that 'Brussels' was addressing real concerns
rather than arcane matters like the shape of cucumbers.
And a high level of employment is an essential part of the
European model – continuing mass unemployment is a
waste of people's lives and will eventually destroy the
social fabric upon which the welfare system is dependent.
A Labour government should vigorously pursue European
policies on employment, and support the proposal by
the Swedish government to write full employment into the
Treaty. The latter would be of mainly symbolic importance
– but symbolism is important in the task of building new
political entities.

The stock response from the right is that social and
environmental protection increases business costs, that we
have to choose between maintaining or raising standards
and making profits. The low cost Asian model, we are told,
had elbowed aside the higher cost European model. The
picture of Asian success which is presented is a partial one,
and ignores the considerable government involvement in
long-term economic planning. But the essential argument is
that Europe needs to drive down its costs in order to compete with the likes of Thailand and Vietnam. But there is
little evidence that the Social Charter will increase costs. It
provides a floor not a means of raising standards. We need

to decide if Europe wants to enter a downward spiral of costs and social provision to compete with low-wage economic rivals. If we cut costs and wages now to compete with Thailand, we will have to do so again in ten years' time to compete with China, and again ten years later to compete with Brazil, Indonesia or India. And so the spiral will continue. This is hardly an attractive prospect for advanced liberal democracies – indeed it is in danger of belatedly validating Marx's vision of the increasing immiseration of the working class, leading to capitalism's collapse under the weight of its own immorality. The way forward is to compete on the basis of higher productivity not by slashing social costs.

Nor is it true that environmental regulations damage economic progress. The most successful postwar Asian tiger, Japan, has built its success on a combination of long-term planning and high standards which force its industry to be more efficient, more innovative and thus more competitive. Environmental improvements often save money – by reducing the energy bill or cutting the amount of waste which needs to be sent for disposal – as well as improving public health and quality of life. One of the little-noted aspects of the Maastricht Treaty is that it extended the use of majority voting into environmental matters. The institutional arrangements are therefore in place for a major EU-wide crusade to improve environmental standards, repairing some of the ravages of the Industrial Revolution, but at the same time boosting the efficiency of European industry and ensuring that it can compete into the twenty-first century.

FROM EU-ROPE TO EUROPE

But the EU alone, as currently constituted, cannot tackle Europe's environmental crisis, for the simple reason that it covers only half the continent – and the less polluted half at that. It is a truism that pollution does not respect national boundaries – and it is no more respectful towards the Union's lines of demarcation. German and Austrian children continue to suffer because of air pollution from the Czech Republic and Poland. The reality of environmental inter-dependence is one compelling reason why the EU must be enlarged.

But it is not, of course, the only reason. As with the social dimension, practical considerations are underpinned by political principles. We must enlarge what Timothy Garton Ash calls EU-rope to include all European democracies. This is what the Treaty of Rome promises, and the promise has been reiterated in dealings between the EU and Eastern Europe since the end of Communism. It must be delivered. There is a moral imperative – what justification can there be for excluding fellow Europeans from the club simply because they were unlucky enough to fall within the Soviet sphere of influence in 1945? But there are also strong security and economic reasons. The liberalizing forces in Eastern Europe have made the 'return to Europe' a central part of their appeal, and a rebuff would strengthen the hand of anti-democrats. The greatest contribution the West can make to the stability and prosperity of the new democracies is to welcome them into the European main-stream.

One of the least appealing aspects of European integration so far has been the way in which it has built the prosperity of member states at the expense of those outside by adopting protectionist policies such as the Common Agricultural Policy. Trade is far more significant to developing or transitional economies than aid can ever be. The EU has made significant moves in the direction of trade liberalization with Poland, Hungary, the Czech Republic, Slovakia and, more recently, the Baltic States. But these fall short of open access, and exclude most agricultural produce, which is precisely what most Eastern European states are best placed to export.

It would be possible simply to sign comprehensive free-trade agreements with these states, without letting them into the EU. But we want to ensure that they respect social and environmental standards, to ensure that trade is fair as well as free, and to spread our vision of a European model of capitalism as widely as possible. If something is good – and the European model is good – why not seek to export it? The European model rests on the fact that the single market is regulated by a set of commonly agreed rules. And fairness demands that Eastern European states should be allowed to participate in setting those rules.

But would this mean that we would be forced to accept lower standards in order to accommodate the newcomers? Is there a tension between maintaining or strengthening the European model and exporting it to the East? Clearly Eastern European states are not in a position to adopt Western levels of social and environmental protection overnight; they will need a transitional period and financial, technical and political support to get there (as Greece, Spain and Portugal had on joining). But if we see the European Union as being primarily a free-trade area based on high social and environmental standards, there is no reason why this should not cover the whole continent. Indeed, the more widely we can spread respect for social rights and the environment the better. The difficulty comes if the EU moves beyond this to EMU, defence or fiscal union. Here there is a tension between widening and deepening. Before considering how to deal with it, we need to look at how wide the Union might become. Who should be allowed to join?

THE RULES OF MEMBERSHIP

Poland, Hungary, the Czech Republic and the Baltic States are relatively straightforward cases. They are clearly European and, at least at the moment, clearly democratic. Other applicants are more problematic. Romania and Bulgaria, for example, are keen to join. There are strong reasons for wanting them in, to strengthen their democracies and to avoid the impression that the EU is intent, in David Marquand's phrase, on recreating 'Catholic Europe' – the area which recognized the authority of the medieval papacy. This might appeal to some Christian Democrats, but surely should not do so to Social Democrats.

The European Union must not have a 'state church' or favoured religion, which would alienate many of its citizens. But this is not the same as saying that it should have no moral basis or should fall into the trap of cultural relativism. Democracy and respect for human rights should be the foundations of European integration. So states like Romania should only be admitted if they are liberal democracies. There is a convenient yardstick against which to judge this in the European Convention on Human Rights which, though nothing to do with the EU at present (it was drawn up by the much wider Council of Europe), may develop into the Union's Bill of Rights. States which respect the Convention should be admitted; those which do not should be excluded. This provides a useful carrot with which to influence the behaviour of governments with despotic tendencies, and a powerful stick – temporary suspension or expulsion – for states which are in the EU.

Being democratic is only half the test laid down in the Treaty. The other requirement is that states must be European. This means that we must eventually consider the likes of Ukraine, Moldova and Albania as members. But what of the two semi-European states, Turkey and Russia? Turkey first applied to join in the 1960s, and though it has not exactly been encouraged, it has never been turned down either. It is a member of NATO, and since its participation in the Gulf War has been seen as a respectable interlocutor again. A customs union for manufactured goods has been negotiated for 1996. But full membership is thought to be impossible: Turkey has a terrible human rights record, it is far too poor, and the Greeks would veto its application anyway. The first point is certainly a barrier to membership today – and rightly so. But the same logic can be applied to Turkey as is used in Eastern Europe. Membership or potential membership should be used to strengthen the forces of liberalism, democracy and secularism, and to insist on proper treatment for Kurdish dissidents. The Turkish government recently introduced a series of constitutional reforms aimed at strengthening the functioning of democracy. They were opposed only by the most anti-European party, a group of religious fundamentalists. Our vision of Europe ought to mark Turkey as a potential member, though attaining membership will be very difficult.

Russia could be more problematic still. It has not submitted an application, and may never do so. Post-imperial pride and its self-image as a superpower may lead it towards its own economic block with Belarus and other former Soviet Republics. But some of the players in the complex mosaic of Russian politics have stated their ambition to 'return to Europe' by joining the EU. If the application comes, and if the country is by then a liberal democracy, can it legitimately be refused? Russia is historically and culturally a part of Europe, though much of its territory is in Asia. In many ways it is analogous to Britain, a power which has traditionally combined Continental involvement with wider, non-European interests.

BRUGES AND BEYOND

The main argument used against Russian membership (on the rare occasions when it is even considered) is that it is simply too powerful and too big; its inclusion would make the EU unworkable. This begs the question of what work we want the EU to do. The Thatcherite vision of Europe as a loose collection of nation-states would have no difficulty with the notion of widening the membership – preferably to include North America as well. So how does the conception of Europe envisaged here differ from that of the Bruges speech?

The first point of contrast with the Thatcherite project is that I am arguing for a European fair-trade area, with high social and environmental standards, not simply a free-trade one. This requires strong central institutions setting the standards, not a collection of states indulging in competitive downbidding. The wider the membership, the greater the importance of operating on the federal principle of majority voting rather than the intergovernmental one of unanimity. And since the refusal to meet high social and environmental standards by one country will threaten the maintenance of standards in the others – the free-rider problem – no opt-outs should be allowed in these areas. The Conservatives' refusal to participate in the social chapter is damaging to working people not only in Britain but throughout the EU. It must be reversed.

The second major difference lies in the attitude to the single market. While Thatcherites regard this as the overriding priority, Social Democrats should see it as a useful means of increasing prosperity, but not something to be used to reduce the rights of member states to protect social or environmental standards. Common standards agreed at European level should be a floor, not a ceiling, and states should have the right to adopt higher levels of protection. This could result in hidden protectionism, but need not do so as long as there are strong central institutions able to police developments, and an impartial body to judge whether a measure is aimed at protection or protectionism. Again this points to developing European institutions, not emasculating them as the Right would like to do.

Third, a Social Democratic approach to Europe would recognize the need for common European policies to ensure that economic activity within the EU develops in a sustainable way. Without common action, the growth resulting from the single market will take a heavy toll on the environment, primarily because most of the increase in traffic will travel by road. A European transport policy should develop railways and inland waterways, rather than the Trans-European motorways which are short-sightedly being planned at present. A European energy policy should set the framework to reduce the continent's reliance on fossil fuels and nuclear power. Both energy and transport are areas which could be used to build links between the EU and its neighbours, in particular by building the infrastructure which would enable Western Europe to use more Eastern European natural gas. This would benefit both parties, and the global and local environment.

Finally, Social Democrats recognize that it is desirable to redistribute wealth between regions as between individuals. There are obvious political constraints – the familiar difficulty of whether taxpayers in Basingstoke are prepared to subsidize the unemployed in Galicia. Expansion to include Eastern Europe will exacerbate the difficulty, partly by increasing demand for support and partly because there may be even less 'fellow-feeling' between rich Western European taxpayers and poor Eastern European peasants (although we probably have more in common, culturally, historically and economically, with many of the applicant countries than we do with Greece). We need nevertheless to argue the case that it is right in principle to help areas declining due to the inevitable changes which occur in a market economy. An increased role for the EU's main redistributive mechanism, the structural funds, is much to be desired.

It would be possible to achieve this without increasing the overall EU budget, but only if common sense was at last allowed to prevail in agricultural policy. James Meade once wrote that he refrained from discussing the CAP 'to avoid the apoplectic fit which I might suffer if I started to do so'. I share this sentiment. It is now widely accepted that the price support on which the CAP is based, which has led to absurd levels of overproduction, can no longer be justified.

CLUBS WITHIN CLUBS

A Social Democratic vision for Europe, then, envisages the EU expanding at least to the Russian border, and possibly beyond. It seeks a European fair-trade area based on free movement of goods, services and capital, though not necessarily of labour, and high standards of social and environmental protection. It involves common policies on transport and energy, to ensure that economic growth is sustainable, and redistribution through the structural funds. This is, it seems to me, a worthwhile and ambitious vision. But where does it leave the more dramatic aspects of integration which some are seeking, notably economic and monetary union (EMU) and a common foreign and security policy which might or might not lead in time to common defence policy?

It is obvious that the notion of all member-states moving together towards the same goals would be impossible under this scenario. 'Multispeed Europe' would be inevitable. But this is the case whether the EU enlarges or not – indeed we have multispeed Europe at the moment. Not all member-states take part in the Exchange Rate Mechanism, the Schengen Agreement or the Western European Union. John Major succinctly and accurately summed up the suggestion that all fifteen members would take part in EMU in 1999 as 'Eurocrap'.

The question which remains to be decided is whether all member-states, though moving at different speeds, are all committed to arriving at the same destination. Pro-Europeans are keen on insisting that everyone should sign up to an undefined but uniform *politique finale*. But the British and Danish opt-outs from EMU have destroyed this hope: these two countries have not committed themselves to anything on the EMU front. And this is surely a desirable situation. EMU is not like social or environmental policy, where the failure by one member to participate will undermine the efforts of all the others. There may be a fear of competitive devaluations, but presumably those who join EMU will do so in the belief that the gains in terms of stability will outweigh the loss of the exchange-rate weapon. And it is likely that some states will want, for economic or political reasons, to remain outside EMU indefinitely.

Defence cooperation is a similar case. It is not yet clear whether any states will want to move towards a genuine European defence policy, perhaps using the WEU as an adjunct to or replacement for NATO. What is clear is that not all states would want to do so, now or in the future. Four of the fifteen member-states are neutral, and others might well have practical or political reservations. While it might be desirable to have everybody participating, the disadvantages of non-participation by some are not great enough to justify making a common defence policy compulsory. Indeed, since it is likely that such a sensitive area for national sovereignty will continue to operate on a consensus basis (as NATO does), a restricted membership has obvious advantages.

Membership of the EU cannot therefore be taken to imply any commitment to EMU or a common defence policy, even in the long term. So the notion of an agreed *politique finale*, like the *acquis communautaire*, must now be abandoned. Instead we should recognize explicitly that some member-states will want to integrate more than others, for sensible and practical reasons. This will, one hopes, put an end to all the silly rhetoric about missing the bus or being in the slow lane. There is nothing wrong with missing the bus if it is not going in the direction one wishes to travel.

This recognition could lead to a two-tier Europe, with a central core operating EMU and a common defence policy and an outer ring taking part only in a regulated single market. But it is more likely that it would lead to a Europe of overlapping circles, or a series of clubs within clubs. The likely members of EMU include at least one neutral, Austria, and possibly also Sweden and Finland. The possible participants in a common defence policy include countries which are members of NATO but not the EU, let alone being candidates for EMU: Norway, Iceland and Turkey. It is also likely that Italy and Spain would want to participate in defence arrangements, since they are likely to be excluded from EMU. One of the secondary advantages of the 'overlapping circles' approach is that it would enable these countries to maintain their pro-European pride despite failing the Maastricht criteria for EMU.

THE UK: AT THE HEART OF EUROPE?

Where should the UK position itself in this new Europe? Clearly a Labour-led Britain would play a much more constructive role in the core questions of regulating the single market. Should it also take part in EMU and a common defence policy?

The economic arguments for EMU appear to be finely balanced – exchange-rate stability and lower transaction costs against the loss of the exchange-rate weapon to adjust to shocks. There are also political arguments for and against: a European Central Bank would be unaccountable, but having control of monetary policy has done little good for past Labour governments – indeed it was at the heart of the difficulties of both the Attlee and the Wilson governments. On balance, it seems to me that the fear of being constrained in the future by central bankers is less compelling than the knowledge that we have been sunk in the past by speculators. EMU could benefit the Social Democratic project by enabling states to undertake more radical or imaginative policies without being whipped back into line by the currency markets. The evidence that devaluations do not in the long run help our economy also seems strong. Britain should therefore participate in EMU, with two provisos. First, conditions at the time or the design of the institutions could tip the balance the other way. Britain's EMU opt-out, unlike the social chapter opt-out, should remain in force. Second, it must be recognized openly that EMU would be a significant step towards genuine union, not a functional issue with a few broader ramifications. It would be a change of major constitutional import, and so should be taken only after a referendum. We cannot create a people's Europe without the people's consent.

The arguments for closer defence cooperation are more clear cut. It would strengthen the European pillar of the Atlantic Alliance in response to the American's post-Cold War disengagement. It would increase the capacity of European powers to act in regional conflicts such as Bosnia, where Western policy was constrained until mid-1995 by American unwillingness to get involved. And it could eventually make possible significant reductions in defence expenditure as duplication became unnecessary. Britain has little to lose from enthusiastic participation in European defence cooperation, which offers a means of ending our long post-imperial decline into insignificance.

EU OR UTOPIA?

How practical is this vision? Is there any possibility that a Europe resembling this model will emerge from the 1996 Inter-Governmental Conference? the IGC will surely confirm the existence of a multispeed European Union, and may extend it into the field of defence. Eventual membership has already been promised to Poland, Hungary, the Czech Republic and Slovakia. We already have majority voting for the two key areas where the single market needs regulation to ensure fair trade: social and environmental protection (though Britain does not participate in the former). So we are not in fact as far from this model as much of the anti-Europe rhetoric suggests.

Labour Britain should ally itself with Germany in pushing for early enlargement and greater powers for the European Parliament in social and environmental affairs. To France we should offer support for closer defence integration and a more positive line on EMU. The great stumbling block will be the CAP. Here Germany will have to choose between its traditional willingness to appease the French (and its own farmers) and its strong wish to expand the EU eastward. The two are simply not compatible. So the conditions may at last be right to break the Franco-German front on CAP and secure sensible reform. It may require a crude financial settlement giving France enough money to allow it to go on subsidizing its own farmers – this would be a prize worth paying, at least on a transitional basis. CAP reform would then make possible the rapid expansion of the EU to the east.

It used to be said of the Holy Roman Empire that it was neither Holy nor Roman nor an Empire. We now have a European Union which is neither European nor a Union. 'Union' implies centralized government and the abolition of lower tiers of parliament (as in the Act of Union of 1707 between England and Scotland). European implies that it covers the whole continent. What we have today is a Western European community which is in some respects federal, (since member-states have pooled sovereignty in areas where policies are decided by majority). Whether we want a Union, let alone an ever closer one, is debatable. But we should undoubtedly seek to make this strange club to which we belong genuinely European. Helmut Kohl has spoken of letting the first of the Eastern European states join by the year 2000, and this should be adopted as the goal of a Labour government. It will by then be a decade since the fall of Communism, which is roughly the time Spain was made to wait after the death of Franco. Within this broader federation there will be room for defence and monetary unions to emerge, and Britain should participate in both. This would be a messy but workable solution; surely better than one which is neat yet fatally flawed.

PART THREE
Past and Present

17 1945

Michael Young

As well as writing the 1945 Labour
Manifesto, he founded the Consumers'
Association, and was the first to
advocate the idea of the Open
University.

I wrote most of the Labour Party's 1945 election manifesto,
Let Us Face the Future. Herbert Morrison, Patrick Gordon
Walker and Ellen Wilkinson all supplied some paragraphs
but it did not hang together too well, and the task of giving
the document some cohesion fell to me.

Early in 1945 Morgan Phillips had been promoted from
being research secretary to being secretary of the party, so
there was a vacancy. At that time, I was Director of Political
and Economic Planning (PEP) which was a broadly based
think-tank. PEP had been doing a lot of work on what
was called 'Postwar Reconstruction'. It had produced good
studies on unemployment, town planning, and the health
service and, in my view, had given the best evidence there
was to the Beveridge Committee. So I was well up in current
politics and economics, and, when Morgan Phillips offered
me the job, I accepted. My appointment was endorsed by
the policy committee and I moved straight in. I think the
only doubter was Aneurin Bevan who said I had an old
head on young shoulders.

WRITING THE MANIFESTO

If the Labour Party had a decent organization, I would never have found myself writing the manifesto. I was paid £6.00 a week, and was given an empty office and a secretary. I found myself responsible not only for policy but also for political propaganda. There was time pressure. The Labour Party was not prepared for an election; indeed several of the leaders did not even think there was going to be one. There was division about whether the coalition government should be continued at least until the end of the Japanese war, and some people thought for even longer. Then suddenly everything began to accelerate and things that would ordinarily take years happened in weeks. I had the good luck to be in a pivotal position for a few months.

Let Us Face the Future almost wrote itself. The bits on full employment, on social security, on the National Health Service, for example, had been virtually prepared not only by organizations like Political and Economic Planning but also by Whitehall during the war. For the first time, the civil service was in effect helping with the Labour Party programme. The most rushed bits were the ones on nationalization because these were Labour commitments rather than Coalition government policy. Unfortunately, the only model for public ownership was Herbert Morrison's London Passenger Transport Board. I was very doubtful about that model being universally appropriate. But there was not the time to go into detail. The only serious discussion we had was about the title. The first title was *Let's Face the Future*. Then somebody said (it might have been me) it would be much stronger if we dropped the apostrophe: it then became *Let Us Face the Future* which was thought to be a better formulation.

Labour's 1945 manifesto is soggily written and certainly not easy to read right through. Indeed I doubt whether many people did read it. Many of the most influential documents are not read – their reputation springs off the cover, as it were, because they appear at the right time. And the mood in 1945 was such that anything produced by the Labour Party was going to be rapturously received.

WHY LABOUR WON

Unlike some of the party leaders, I was certain that Labour was going to win. I had been a local candidate for St Pancras Canal before the war and so was able to compare canvassing in 1943 and 1944 with what the same sort of voters had been saying in the 1930s. An extraordinary swing to Labour had taken place. People, especially the young, had completely changed their views. I used this piece of mini-research at a conference at Dartington in 1944 to persuade Stafford Cripps that he should stay with Labour rather than joining the Common Wealth Party.

The main reason why we won was the unpopularity of the Conservative Party, though not of Churchill. The Tories were rightly blamed for the 1930s – for unemployment and poverty. By contrast, Labour had gained credibility during the war. Labour had been part of the wartime coalition and had important ministers, such as Ernest Bevin and Herbert Morrison, in the government. These attracted some of the reflected glory of the success in the war. With Churchill, they had become patriotic symbols and their success in government erased memories of Labour's failures in 1929–31.

Linked to this and perhaps even more important was a widespread belief in the authority of government. Authority in general was still respected and Labour benefited from being part of the society that it was condemning. People were prepared to trust government and to believe that when government ministers, especially Labour ones, said that they were going to do this, that and the other, they would carry out their promises. People knew from experience that things had worked much better in the war. There had been full employment, there had been a planned economy, and, above all as far as Labour was concerned, there had been 'fair shares'.

There was general agreement that equality had contributed to national solidarity during the war. Rationing was popular. Everyone acknowledged that the health of the nation was better than it had ever been, or has been since. Few wanted to go back to 'devil take the hindmost'. They wanted the fair shares system of war time to be continued into the peace. And it was Labour who benefited. If Churchill stood for the military side of the war effort, the Labour Party stood for the fair shares side. 'Fair shares' was Labour's big idea in the 1945 election.

Except in certain parts of the country, such as the coalfields, we did not play up nationalization. But there was a feeling that the private utilities were in a bit of a mess, much of the electricity supply industry was already under public control, and the railways had, in any case, been virtually nationalized during the war. So there was little opposition to the pragmatic, piecemeal public ownership which we proposed.

THE 'THREE' COALITIONS

It seems to me that three 'coalitions' were constructed.

The first was the coalition of 'ideas'. Labour's great strength in 1945 was that it was drawing on a raft of ideas and policies which had been floating around in the 1930s and which had then been seriously examined and worked on during the war. These ideas came not only from the left: Keynes and Beveridge after all were Liberals, while PEP's research groups were run by managers, experts and professionals. Apart from public ownership, Labour supplied the practical experience of the working class – the desire for decent homes, for jobs and for social security. Nineteen forty-five was Beveridge plus Keynes plus Socialism. The socialist working-class tradition gave a cutting edge to it all.

The second coalition was the coalition between radicalism and patriotism. Amazingly, the patriotism which centred on Churchill was turned on its head and went the way of Labour. There was a real sense in 1945, one which was well understood by the voters, that it was the Labour Party's leaders, not Churchill, who were speaking for the nation and its concerns. *Let Us Face the Future* was a patriotic document because it proposed to provide homes, jobs and security for a people which had fought so hard to win the war and now wanted a decent peace. *Now Let Us Win the Peace* was Labour's powerful rallying cry.

The third coalition was the one between intellectuals, thinkers and planners on the one hand, and practical politicians on the other. During the war the reputation of intellectuals increased remarkably. The Fabian Society was highly respected – people in and around the Society as well as a whole lot of other people were mobilized; there was a great feeling of movement back and forth between freelance intellectuals and civil servants and ministers. There was real trust of the intellectuals by the politicians and Whitehall – and by the general public too. They deserved that trust because they worked so hard and were generally constructive.

After the end of 1942, when the Coalition government began to consider postwar reconstruction, the ideas of the intellectuals, for example for a welfare state and a National Health Service, were polished, worked over and made more or less operational by civil servants. If it had not been for that, the Labour government could not have done all that was done in that five-year period after the war. Starting from scratch in 1945 they could not have done the preparation and then put the legislation through and implemented it. Two or three years of the work of the Labour

government was done by the Coalition government before
the Labour government was installed.

LESSONS FOR LABOUR

The conditions of 1945 were uniquely favourable – the pre-
war failure of the Tories, the success of Labour ministers
in the wartime coalition, the desire for 'fair shares' to continue in peacetime, the fact that Labour spoke for a national
consensus. So much has changed since 1945, and especially
since 1979. There are the global changes (described elsewhere in the book); there are the changes introduced by
Mrs Thatcher. The Thatcher regime laid waste the moral
economy, putting profit and loss before the human account.
Peoples' ways of thinking have altered dramatically – to
some extent, attitudes have been privatized. The media is
so much more powerful in its ability to challenge the authority of politicians and also of the experts generally – politics
in a sense has become a branch of the media.

Yet, as in 1945, there is now a feeling that the tide has
turned. All the emphasis on the market, and on productivity
and competitiveness has a clear downside in creating more
unemployment and more insecurity, so that many people
who thought they had reasonably secure jobs do not think
so any longer. There is a real conflict between the big
increase in short-term work, casual work and the rapid turnover of jobs and people's long-term commitments for mortgages, pensions and life insurance. Many people are in a
velvet trap. The Tory project has begun to unwind.

Turning to the three coalitions which mattered so much
in 1945, the first one – the coalition of ideas – is to some
extent already in place. The unexpected success of Will
Hutton's book, *The State We're In*, with its call for constitutional as well as economic and social reform, is just one
indication of the hunger for an alternative to the Conservatives. At the level of policy, there is considerable overlap,

not always acknowledged, between the opposition parties, and at local-council level the Labour Party and the Liberals have often worked together to implement agreed programmes.

More work needs to be done, however, if the two other coalitions, which were so successful in 1945, are to be recreated. I have talked of the coalition between radicalism and patriotism. On the issue of radicalism, I am not yet convinced that the Left has faced up to the extent of changes both globally and in our own society, or to the radical policies that will be needed to provide more jobs and greater security. If we are to get back to full employment, it will probably be on a two-tier basis. There will be first, an internationally competitive economy and then a second, mainly local service economy. As far ahead as one can see, there are likely to be millions of people who are not employed in the first economy and they cannot be left to rot. I envisage a revived local government being largely responsible for seeing that there are jobs available in the second economy. I am very keen, for example, on the idea of compulsory civilian service for youngsters, as well as a voluntary service for those, who, like policemen, have been forced into early retirement.

Turning to patriotism, it was very strong in 1945 and it can still be a powerful force. It is a question of Chinese boxes. If people are proud of the place where they live, Durham or Tower Hamlets, that's the beginning, as I see it, of patriotism. If you are proud of Durham, you are also proud of Durham within the country of which it is part; and then there is no reason why you should not also be proud of the country within the even larger unity of which it is also part. There is no conflict between being proud of Durham and being proud of Britain and so there is no conflict between being proud of Britain and being proud of being European. I may be a much better European if I am sufficiently proud of Britain to think that it is going to play a very constructive, leading part on the European scene. Indeed it would be much easier to be proud of Britain if one thought that patriotism did not stop at the boundaries of one country.

The third coalition – the one between the intellectuals and the politicians – is crucial. With today's media, there is always a temptation for politicians, for understandable reasons, to keep their cards close to their chest. Yet, unless they are prepared to open up the debate, to bring in the intellectuals without necessarily making any commitments to their findings, then much of the detailed work which will both help Labour win the election and sustain it once in power will simply not get done. Of course, you do not have to think of preparing for what the government might do just in terms of the manifesto. There can be very important issues which are not going to appear in the manifesto at all. What you need here is the ideas, the detailed work, consideration of options and people sitting down for months and months actually battering their heads against the serious problems, and they are severe. There could be many versions of the Social Justice Commission on matters of policy and it could, even now, become much more like what was done for 1945. The Labour leadership needs to have the self-confidence to use intellectuals in a constructive way.

If Labour is to win, the programme needs to be radical. And it needs to be in tune with the popular mood. That mood can in part be created by the right kind of political leadership, bringing together the radical and patriotic, and using the work of intellectuals to make the programme more incisive, and capable of winning another peace.

18 1964

Giles Radice

Labour MP for North Durham and
Chairman of the Commons Public Service
Select Committee, he is the author of
The New Revisionism, Offshore and
The New Germans.

Nineteen sixty-four was a time of hope. But, despite the
electoral successes of the Labour Party in 1964 and 1966,
the Wilson government disappointed its supporters.
Although the world of the 1990s is very different from that
of the 1960s, what happened to Labour then has lessons
for the party today.

In 1964, standing for the first time in a parliamentary
election, I was the Labour candidate for the Chippenham
constituency in Wiltshire. Chippenham was normally a safe
Conservative seat but at a by-election in 1962 the Tories
had only narrowly beaten the Liberals, with Labour dropping back to third place. The combination of the fall in the
Tory vote, my own political inexperience and, above all,
the heady sense of change in the air was enough to persuade
me that I could bring off an improbable victory even in
rural Wiltshire.

THE CHANGING MOOD

The background to the 1964 election was highly favourable to the Labour Party. By 1963, the Macmillan government, so triumphant at the 1959 election, had run out of steam. The economy was faltering, the government's attempts to join the Common Market had been humiliatingly rebuffed by General de Gaulle, and Macmillan himself was made to look out of touch by the Profumo scandal, when the Minister for War was forced to resign because he had lied to the Commons about an affair with a call girl. Macmillan's successor, Sir Alec Douglas-Home, who renounced his earldom to become Prime Minister, seemed bumbling and amateur, a figure from another age. His unguarded admission in a newspaper interview that he used matchsticks to work out economic problems appeared to highlight what an inappropriate choice he was for a modern British Prime Minister.

The 1960s was the time when the chattering classes suddenly woke up to the nation's relative decline. There was a strong feeling at Westminster, in Whitehall and in the media that Britain had not done as well since the war as her European neighbours. Critics pointed to our comparatively slow rate of growth, our class-ridden society and our antiquated institutions. Penguin published an influential series of 'specials' with titles like *What's Wrong with British Industry?*, *What's Wrong with the Unions?*, *What's Wrong with Parliament?*, *What's Wrong with the Church?*

Three books in particular made an impact on me. The first was *The Stagnant Society* by Michael Shanks, then industrial editor of the *Financial Times*. Shanks argued that our outdated industrial relations and class systems were holding the country back and that we would only be economically successful if we became a more open, mobile and classless society. 'Only when we feel ourselves to be genuinely one nation and one people will we be able to tap to the full the wonderful vein of courage, enterprise and initiative which lies hidden in the British personality.'

The second was *British Government Observed* by Brian Chapman, Professor of Government at Manchester University. The opening words of his preface were scathing: 'I take it that there is little doubt that Britain has now reached her lowest point in international prestige for many a long year. Her haughty exclusion from the European Common Market is not the beginning of a new situation, but the culmination of a series of disastrous diplomatic, military and economic policies.' In Chapman's view, the main reason for these failures was that British government was too amateur; he believed that there was much that we could learn from the greater professionalism of Continental administrations, especially that of France.

In my view the most convincing and comprehensive of the three works was *The Conservative Enemy*, a collection of essays by Anthony Crosland. At that stage, Crosland was not the prominent politician he later became but Labour's leading revisionist intellectual, breathtakingly intelligent and extremely bold in his judgments. Here is Crosland on Britain: 'A dogged resistance to change now blankets every segment of national life. A middle-aged conservatism, parochial and complacent, has settled over the country; and it is hard to find a single sphere in which Britain is predominantly in the forefront.' He goes on in words which still find their echo today: 'we cling to every outmoded scrap of national sovereignty, play the obsolete role of an imperial power, and fail to adjust to the new, dynamic Europe ... wherever innovation is required, we see a frightful paralysis of the will. The cause is partly our oppressive, traditional pattern of class relations, partly the psychological difficulty of adapting from great-power to second-rate international status, partly the complacent ignorance bred by an insular tradition.'

It was to this impatient mood that Harold Wilson, the

new leader of the Labour Party, was appealing when he put forward his agenda for a 'New Britain' in the run up to the 1964 election.

WILSON'S NEW BRITAIN

As leader of the opposition, Harold Wilson was a political phenomenon. I was a Gaitskellite, who strongly supported Hugh Gaitskell's attempt to modernize the Labour Party and grieved at his sudden death. But only the churlish could deny the energy and ability of Gaitskell's successor. In marked contrast to Douglas-Home, Wilson seemed the personification of the dynamic, meritocratic Britain which he wanted to create. He was fluent, assured and well briefed, a professional to his fingertips. At the time, many of the younger generation saw him as a British version of the charismatic President of the United States, John Kennedy.

Wilson was on top form when he spoke to his first conference as party leader. Reading the speech today, it seems overlong, somewhat didactic in tone, and excessively *dirigiste*. But that October morning in Scarborough, it was inspirational, providing the link that was so badly needed between socialism and Britain in the 1960s, between Labour and the national mood.

The concentration on science and the need to harness its application to industrial production established Labour's credentials as a modern party. 'The Britain that is going to be forged in the white heat of this revolution,' said Wilson, 'will be no place for restrictive practices or for outdated methods on either side of industry.' The emphasis on educational reform – on abolishing the eleven-plus, expanding the universities and creating 'a university of the air' – demonstrated that Labour was the party of opportunity. And Wilson's vision of a classless, mobile society, open to the talents, promoted Labour as a national party, able to appeal beyond its traditional strength to new sources of support.

After the applause had died down, Dick Taverne, then Labour MP for Lincoln, said to me 'Wilson has just won the election'.

In the spring of 1964, he followed up his Scarborough address with a series of speeches on specific topics (published later that year by Penguin as *The New Britain*): These covered economy, science and technology, housing, employment, law reform and foreign policy. As at Scarborough, the underlying themes were modernization and breaking down the barriers of class and privilege. Wilson committed a Labour government to replacing 'the closed, exclusive society by an open society in which all have an opportunity to work and serve, in which brains will take precedence over blue blood, and craftsmanship will be more important than caste. Labour wants to streamline our institutions, modernize methods of government, bring the entire nation into a working partnership with the state.' It was stirring stuff.

But as spring turned to summer, the economy improved and the Labour lead in the polls, which we all followed avidly, began to slip. Nothing much happened in August. As the sun shone, Sir Alec took to the grouse moors, Harold Wilson relaxed in his cottage on the Scilly Isles, while the prospective Labour candidate for Chippenham waited nervously for action to begin. When NOP put the Tories fractionally ahead at the end of August, it seemed that the Conservative tactics of postponing the election until the last possible moment was paying off.

The election campaign was a rollercoaster. If Labour went into the election as narrow favourites, the three main polling organizations put the Tories ahead at some stage during the weeks that followed. Our great advantage was that Wilson was a much better campaigner than Douglas-Home. There was also a strong feeling on the doorstep that it was time for a change. On the other hand, Labour had been out of office for so long that for many voters actually making the change seemed a big gamble.

Labour started the campaign well. There was a splendid rally at Wembley on 12 September at which Harold Wilson gave a Kennedy-style call to get the country moving again: he wanted people with 'fire in their bellies, compassion in their hearts'. The manifesto *The New Britain*, mostly written by Peter Shore, argued for faster growth and effective economic planning and was well received. Labour posters, with the slogan 'Let's go with Labour and we'll get things done', were attractive and positive. As I got home after my village meetings, I watched Labour politicians, especially Wilson, perform effectively on television.

But, as the election day drew nearer, there were moments, even in remote Wiltshire, when I felt that the Labour campaign was not as well focused as it had been earlier. Wilson's speeches were often too diffuse, and Labour's election broadcasts too scrappy. And in the last few days, as Harold Wilson left London for Merseyside, the momentum seemed to go out of Labour's efforts. It was almost as if we had lost our nerve at the prospect of victory.

The election night of 12 October was nail biting. By then I had reconciled myself to defeat at Chippenham and I finished in third place, 7000 votes behind the victorious Conservative. However, from the results coming in on my portable radio, it was clear that Labour was gaining seats elsewhere. But would it be enough to give Labour an overall majority? Wilson, who travelled back to London by train on Friday morning without being certain of victory, said to a journalist, 'It's getting more like the Kennedy story . . . We'll get the result from Cook County soon.' It was not until 2.48 p.m. on Friday afternoon when Labour held Brecon and Radnor that he was sure of an overall majority. It was a wonderful moment. But, despite all our advantages and Wilson's tremendous personal contribution, Labour had only just scraped in. The final figures were Labour 317, the Conservatives 304 and the Liberals 9.

'YOU KNOW THAT LABOUR GOVERNMENT WORKS'

Labour's small majority meant that Harold Wilson was forced to devote the period between October 1964 and the March 1966 election to demonstrating that Labour could provide an effective government and, therefore, deserved to be re-elected (whenever Wilson decided that the timing was propitious) with a decent majority. He was triumphantly successful in achieving his objective. Denis Healey, who was highly critical of his second premiership, says that Wilson's first two years as Prime Minister were 'brilliant'.

Looking at the Labour government from outside, Wilson appeared to be in almost total command – of his Cabinet, of Parliament, and of the national political scene. In Kennedy mode, he promised a 'hundred days of dynamic action' and was able to tell the December party conference that the government had already carried out some of its pledges, including increasing old age pensions and social benefits. He was always making news. Whenever you opened the newspaper or turned on the TV, Wilson dominated the headlines. In his first eighteen months, he gave five interviews on *Panorama* and made six ministerial broadcasts.

In contrast to Douglas-Home's administration, the Wilson government seemed to be a 'ministry of all the talents'. George Brown, exceptionally able though temperamentally flawed, was First Secretary of the newly established Department of Economic Affairs: his role was balanced politically and administratively by James Callaghan, the apparently unflappable and sensible Chancellor of the Exchequer. From the Left, there was Richard Crossman, intellectually gifted if sometimes unreliable, and Barbara Castle, who had star quality. Wilson sensibly promoted the brightest of the Gaiteskellites: Denis Healey was appointed Defence Secretary in October 1964, and, during 1965, both Anthony Crosland and Roy Jenkins became Cabinet Ministers, the former as Education Secretary and the latter as Home Secretary. Despite Labour's thirteen years out of office, it was a government of which party supporters could be proud.

The symbol of Wilson's first administration was the National Plan. Thirty years later it is hard to recall the excitement which many people felt when George Brown launched it in September 1965. 'Indicative planning' was an idea which had been successful in France and which politicians, civil servants, academics and even businessmen believed could work in this country. By announcing a growth target of 3.8 per cent per year and coordinating resources and investment, it would be possible, so Brown and his supporters argued, to improve economic performance. I was so impressed that I arranged to have a photograph taken with George Brown at that year's party conference for inclusion in my electoral address under the caption 'Giles Radice discusses Wiltshire's place in the National Plan with George Brown'.

Wilson called the election for 31 March 1966. I had been persuaded by the local party to fight Chippenham again. Although I now knew there was no chance of winning, I was determined to hold on to the Labour vote, which was in danger of being squeezed by the Liberals. The Butler and King survey of the 1966 general election reports that I compensated for the weakness of my party organization by having the loudest loudspeaker. My message was a simple one: 'A vote for Giles Radice is a vote for Harold Wilson and the Labour government'. Harold Wilson's authority and popularity as Prime Minister, which enabled me to keep up the Labour vote in Chippenham, swept Labour to an overwhelming victory, with a majority of 97. Ben Pimlott, Wilson's biographer, is right to conclude that 'Wilson's achievement was a breathtaking one and a clear political vindication of his premiership.'

THE BALANCE SHEET

Wilson's triumph was, however, short-lived. In July 1966, a run on the pound forced the government to introduce an austerity package, including cuts in public spending and a wages freeze – a move which meant the abandonment of the National Plan growth targets. In November 1967, following a similar crisis, the pound was devalued. Labour never really recovered. Despite a temporary lead for the party in the polls in the run-up to the election, the Tories under Heath won comfortably in June 1970.

In the summer of 1968, I took part in a Young Fabian debate on the Wilson government. I argued the case for: Phillip Whitehead, later MP for Derby and now an MEP, put the case against. My side was roundly defeated, partly because of Whitehead's superior eloquence but even more because few of us any longer believed in either the Labour government or Harold Wilson. With hindsight, it is clear that the majority Young Fabian view, one which was shared by many young people at the time especially on university campuses, was far too harsh.

The Wilson governments of the 1960s had substantial achievements to their credit. In education, Labour was committed to abolishing the eleven-plus exam and establishing comprehensive secondary schools. The famous Department of Education circular, 10/65, was issued to local authorities asking them to draw up plans for comprehensive schools, and by 1970, the proportion of pupils in comprehensives had increased from 10 to 32 per cent, a change which was carried much further by Margaret Thatcher, when she was Education Secretary in Edward Heath's government. In recent years, there has been criticism of educational standards in comprehensive schools, some of it justified. It is noticeable, however, that Conservative Secretaries of State for Education have never called for a return of the eleven-plus exam. This exam was deservedly extremely unpopular because it not only divided children into academic and non-academic streams at a ridiculously early age but also condemned the vast majority of children to inferior 'secondary modern' schools. Labour's measures gave that majority a chance for the first time. The Labour government also carried through the major expansion of university education recommended by the Robbins Report, created twenty-nine polytechnics (now universities), and set up the Open University, an initiative which was strongly supported by Harold Wilson and has been an outstanding success. Labour's reforms marked the beginning of mass higher education in Britain.

As Home Secretary, Roy Jenkins encouraged radical changes in the laws on homosexuality, divorce and abortion as well as preparing race relations legislation banning discrimination in housing and employment. Arguably, these liberal reforms, which both reflected changes in social values and provided a new framework for more civilized behaviour, helped usher in the modern age.

In terms of its more traditional objectives, Labour's record on social justice was praiseworthy. There was a substantial increase in spending on health and education. Pensioners, large families and the unemployed gained more in real disposable income than the rest of the population. One authority, the economist Michael Stewart, concluded: 'To have promoted a measurable improvement in the distribution of income against the background of the deplorably slow rate of growth . . . was one of the Labour government's main achievements.'

However, the Wilson governments of the 1960s failed in their central aim which was to improve the rate of growth. Admittedly the growth in domestic output of 2.3 per cent a year between 1964 and 1970 looks better in retrospect than it did at the time. But if output had been greater, there would have been more for both consumption and public spending. Higher and sustained growth would have also led to increased investment and a strengthening of the economy at a time when the opportunities for British industry in world markets were extremely promising.

The conventional explanation of Labour's relative economic failure is still the right one. The decision not to devalue immediately on taking office or at the latest in July 1966 meant that the government was forced to squeeze the economy and sacrifice growth in order to maintain the value of sterling – a parity which, in the end, proved unsustainable. As it was, Labour used up all its credit with the unions and its working-class supporters without being able to deliver the fruits of growth. If the government had devalued earlier, there would have been the chance of nearly four years of export-led growth instead of two and the Labour Party might well have won the 1970 election.

In external affairs, the government's record is also open to attack. There was the ineffective handling of the admittedly intractable issue of Rhodesia. There was the support for America intervention in Vietnam. And it was only because of financial pressure that the government was persuaded to abandon its 'East of Suez' role, with the Prime Minister being on his own admission a 'late convert'. It was, after all, Harold Wilson who said in his Guildhall speech in November 1964: 'We are a world power, and a world influence, or we are nothing'. In 1967, after Wilson and Brown as Foreign Secretary had toured Continental capitals, the Labour government applied for entry into the EEC, only to be brutally rejected, as Macmillan had been earlier, by de Gaulle. But if Labour, like the Conservatives, had begun to come to terms with Britain's reduced status as a medium-sized European power, Wilson remained ambivalent on the question of Europe, as his stance in opposition after 1970 demonstrated.

LESSONS FOR BLAIR'S LABOUR PARTY

Both the successes and failures of Wilson's Labour Party in the 1960s have lessons for Blair's Labour Party in the 1990s.

Much has altered since the 1960s. The power of governments has been considerably diminished by the growth of world markets. 'Corporatist' policies have far less relevance today. And social change has transformed the political landscape. Indeed, despite the emphasis on modernization, the 1960s are closer to the 1940s than to the 1990s, not just in time but also in spirit.

Even so, there are obvious political parallels. As in the 1960s, there is an unpopular Conservative government. As in the 1960s, the Tories are faced by a Labour Party, which, though it has been out of power for a long time, is, under charismatic leadership, making a strong bid for power. And there is also much the same desire for change amongst the voters now as there was then.

Harold Wilson's outstanding performance as leader of the opposition provides a good model for Tony Blair in the run up to the next election. It was not just that he dominated Parliament and the media. Even more important he put forward a credible alternative agenda and succeeded, to a considerable extent, in making that agenda the battleground of the 1964 election. The lack of focus during the actual election campaign as well as the fading away at the end of it which nearly cost Labour the election underlines how important it is to keep Labour's effort going until polling day.

Wilson was, in many ways, a supremely well-equipped Prime Minister. He was both literate and numerate; and, as a former civil servant, he knew his way around Whitehall. A Cabinet Minister at thirty-one, chairman of the Public Accounts Committee, and both a former Shadow Chancellor and Shadow Foreign Minister, he had a thorough grasp of the issues. And he had the good sense to appoint the most able men and women in the party to his cabinet and the skill to weld them together into an effective team. If he may have sometimes interfered too much during the first two years of his premiership and later have become paranoid about plots to depose him, he was generally loyal to and supportive of his colleagues, especially in a crisis.

The crucial decision not to devalue earlier was, however, very much a personal policy of Harold Wilson. Though the initial reluctance in October 1964 was understandable given the administration's inexperience and small majority, the failure to grasp the nettle in July 1966 effectively undermined the underlying purpose of the Labour government. The moral of the story is that incoming governments should try and face up to the unpleasant decisions straightaway.

On trade union reform, Harold Wilson was on the side of the angels. He backed *In Place of Strife*, Barbara Castle's White Paper which gave the Employment Secretary limited powers to intervene in industrial disputes. After Mrs Thatcher's legislation, *In Place of Strife* seems very mild and eminently sensible. Yet his policy was opposed by the unions, rejected by the NEC, and, in the end, disowned by his cabinet. Roy Jenkins wrote, 'It was a sad story from which he and Barbara Castle emerged with more credit than the rest of us.' The issue of Labour's relations with the unions remained unresolved and was to re-emerge disastrously in 1979 with the 'Winter of Discontent'. Tony Blair's insistence that trade unions should not expect special favours from his government will stand the party in good stead if it wins the next election.

In terms of party reform, Wilson was a traditionalist. He opposed Gaitskell's attempt to revise Clause IV on the grounds that it was unnecessary and divisive. 'You don't have to be a fundamentalist to say that Genesis is part of the Bible', he explained to an interviewer. The problem with such a pragmatic approach was that, once the National Plan had been effectively abandoned after July 1966, there was little left in which the party could believe, unless it was Clause IV fundamentalism. The revision of the clause in 1995 gives Tony Blair a much stronger platform on which to base his policies.

Although Harold Wilson was a decent and humane man with little side or pretension, he acquired the reputation of deviousness and opportunism, as the quotations most associated with him demonstrate: 'It does not mean that the pound in your pocket has been devalued' (after devaluation), 'I won't take no for an answer' (before de Gaulle vetoed British entry to the Common Market), 'months rather than years' (predicting the collapse of Rhodesia's independence), 'a week is a long time in politics' (a dictum which he often repeated). Wilson's image undermined his authority with his party, in Parliament and with the voters. As Tony Blair well understands, it is essential to be honest with the voters and not to make promises which cannot be kept. Trust is a political prize which once lost is almost impossible to recover.

Like Harold Wilson before him, Tony Blair wants to make Labour the main party of government. The experience of the 1960s shows how crucial it is for Labour to have a credible project that will not only help win elections but sustain the party in power. Once it loses its long-term strategy, as happened with the Wilson government after July 1966, a government of the centre left is at the mercy of events and is likely to be driven from office.

19   1997

Yvette Cooper

An economist who has worked as a
leader writer for the *Independent*, she has
been an adviser to John Smith and
Gordon Brown.

When I cast my vote in the next general election, I will be
one of millions of voters under the age of forty who has
never had a chance to vote for a victorious Labour government. For the eighteen-year-olds who voted for the last
Labour government in 1974 will be forty by the time the
next election happens. The Conservative Party will have
been in power for eighteen years if they run to the full term
in 1997 – that really is a whole lifetime for some of those
casting their first vote this time.

Yet it has happened before – Labour sweeping into office
after more than a decade out of power. When my grandmother voted for the first time in 1945, there had been no
Labour Prime Minister since 1931, even though Labour
Ministers had been partners in the wartime Coalition
government. And when my mother as a student watched
Harold Wilson on the hustings in 1964, Labour had been
out of power for thirteen years.

But the political lessons from previous Labour victories
and defeats are of limited use in persuading the young voters
of 1997. Labour needs to recognize how much has changed

in economics, in society and in people's attitudes to politics since 1945 and 1964. My generation lead very different lives to those of our parents and grandparents. Many of those changes have been for the better, particularly for women, even though they have created new problems.

One of the biggest changes – and most difficult challenges for Labour – is the growth in scepticism and disgust for politics generally among young people. If the caricatures of the Thatcher generation are to be believed, we are self-centred and cynical; we are not interested in political projects to help others, and we don't believe that politicians could ever make them work.

I believe it is essential to confront this apparent alienation among young people. Although some of it is merely the overblown rhetoric of the media, much is a direct response to the failure of politicians in the 1980s and 1990s. Labour understands that they have, in the past, contributed to the current youth malaise about politics, and take seriously their responsibility to rebuild the credibility of politics. Labour will need to build a consensus among all young people, if it is to have any chance of tackling the problems that divide them and that will blight them in the next century.

For we are not all equally equipped to cope with change. What for some has meant increasing opportunities and freedoms, for others has meant greater insecurity and hardship. Even among twenty-year-olds, the extremes of income, employment chances and education are shocking. And the extent of the divide, and the increasing isolation of a core of young people threatens the cohesion of the whole society. We need to extend education and opportunities to everyone in society – both for moral egalitarian reasons, and in the self-interest of every member of the community.

In 1997 Labour faces a serious challenge in attempting to win over the young generation. They must persuade them to abandon their 1980s allegiance to the Conservatives, to reject the self-centred values they supposedly hold, and above all to overcome their cynical distrust of government and politics. To win, and to have an agenda worth winning for, in 1997, Labour needs to inspire both trust and hope in the younger generation.

CHANGE ACROSS THREE GENERATIONS: 1945, 1964 AND 1997

On 8 July 1945, my grandmother voted for the first time in her life. I imagine her pushing her two-week-old baby – my mother – in the pram to the polling station in the local school and marking a cross by the Labour candidate's name. Her daughters believe winning the war made little immediate difference to their family; my grandmother's father, husband and brothers all worked in the pits in Whitehaven, and the hardships and rationing of war were little different from the poverty of peacetime. Winning the peace changed everything. The postwar Labour government built a free NHS; tragically in the past members of her family had died from curable illnesses because they could not pay medical bills. And they began a programme of house-building which lifted my grandmother's family out of rat-ridden slums and into prefabs.

In 1964 my mother, a student in South London, went to hear Harold Wilson speak on the hustings. She was too young to vote. The first Wimpey bars had just opened, so had the first boutiques on the King's Road. Wilson's government heralded a huge expansion of higher education with the building of new universities. Battersea College of Advanced Technology, where my mother was studying, turned into Surrey University and moved out to Guildford. For those who could not leave jobs or home to study, there was now an Open University to learn by correspondence.

If I compare my life today with that of my mother voting in 1964, or my grandmother voting in 1945, the contrasts are striking. Like many other women of my generation, I have had far more chances and far more freedom than my mother or grandmother before me. Yet the legacy of the last fifty years is mixed, for the new opportunities I enjoy have still not been extended to everyone, and the strong communities that supported members of my family in the past now seem to be lost.

Richer than any generation before us, we have benefited from decades of economic growth – even where that growth has been slower and more turbulent than in other countries. Income per head has doubled since 1964 and tripled since 1945. Two thirds of households have cars, twice the proportion that had them thirty years ago. In 1964, hardly anyone had central heating, today 82 per cent of us have it in our houses. Most people have video recorders, and one house in five has a home computer.

I have been able to take advantage of far more opportunities than my mother or grandmother. Starting at a local comprehensive, I have studied at universities in Britain and the US. I have travelled all over the world, where my grandmother only left Britain once on a day-trip to Calais. And I am better paid already as a young economist than my mother is as a teacher of twenty years' experience.

It has taken two generations to liberate most women from the sole role of housewife and mother, and to give them the chance to enter the workplace on their own terms. In Whitehaven in 1945, full employment meant work for all the men of the town. Of course my grandmother did not go out to work. She said for her to go out to work would have been unacceptable – 'What would the neighbours say?' Yet according to her daughters she was desperately bored and frustrated at home.

When my mother first started work as a statistician in a paper mill in Scotland in 1966 – well before the Equal Pay Act – she was paid less than her male colleagues. And when she returned after having children, she found it hard going in a workplace designed for men, where leaving early to look after a sickly child was deeply frowned upon. Today, my mother is an extremely successful head of a huge maths department in a Hampshire sixth-form college – if her staff, men or women, have child-care problems they simply bring the kids into work with them. Twenty years later, I expect to have it all! I want to be able to work all my life in stimulating jobs, but I expect to be able to choose terms which are compatible with having a family too – perhaps working part-time for a while if I want.

Women are choosing and needing to work in greater numbers than ever. Over 70 per cent of women are now in the workforce. And work for women matters not just for the sake of equal opportunities, but as an economic necessity. The economy needs the talents and skills of well-educated women, and women need the security of being able to earn an independent wage. Unlike our grandparents' generation, women cannot count on a husband for life, and an ever-present father for their children to support them as they grow. The divorce rate is high. And one in five families are being brought up by one parent alone. Not surprisingly, the modern labour market is having to adapt in order to make best use of women's abilities.

The arrival of women is not the only big change in the workplace since my grandfather and father started their first jobs. Technological advances mean there is much less demand for unskilled labour in the economy today, and much more demand for highly skilled and extremely adaptable workers. Competing in a global market reinforces the intensity of change, because if a British company does not adopt the latest available methods and techniques, you can guarantee someone else, somewhere else will. And they will sell their more modern, better quality, and cheaper products to British consumers and push that lethargic British company right out of the market. So businesses have to adapt fast or go under. Jobs change and adapt or they are destroyed. And people have to change and adapt too or they will be left unemployed. Simply finding a lower paid, unskilled job is no longer much of an option. In a global market, Britain can never compete with developing countries to provide cheap labour, and we should not be trying to.

It is a world which to our grandparents would sound horribly insecure. For there are no jobs for life, few relationships for life, and few neighbours for life, as people move around the country to be educated and to find new work. It is a world of changing jobs, changing careers and short-term contracts. Young women are working just as much as men. It is a world of part-time work as much as full-time. And the highly educated who pick up the newest techniques can earn huge amounts of money.

For many people these changes are extremely positive. For the consumer, this is certainly good news, for competition provides us with variety, high quality and low costs. And for many young workers, the new labour market is a liberation. Young mothers are increasingly able to find part-time jobs where in the past they could not work at all. And for the highly skilled young people who want a variety of different experiences, short-term contracts are extremely convenient. For example, highly skilled computer analysts will rarely find short-term contracts a problem because their skills are in such high demand they know they can easily find another job, and the short-term nature of their contract actually allows them to bid up their wages.

Unfortunately, 'flexibility' is not liberating for everyone. In fact for many it is extremely threatening. Unless you are highly qualified and know that you have the chance to take new courses to reskill when necessary, you have little confidence about finding the next job when the current one runs out. The supermarket shop assistants on zero-hours contracts who never know from one week to the next how many hours they will be working or at what time of day, are left with no power at all in the flexible labour market.

Week by week they do not know how big their pay packet will be, or whether they will be able to pick the children up from school.

The problem is that we are not all equally equipped to deal with change. And the new opportunities young people have today have still not been extended to everyone. As the consequences of missing out and failing to get qualifications or jobs become ever more harsh, social divisions have become sharper and communities weaker. Communities have not simply become less supportive, they have become actively threatening. In northeast London, where I live, I know few of my neighbours and I am afraid to walk home from the bus stop alone. And crime has increased in villages and towns as well as in the cities over the last twenty years.

On the streets, in the work place and in the family, there is no reason why the changes that have taken place need be destructive and pernicious. The problem is that the changes divide us. For the well-educated woman living in London, able to choose when and how to work, secure in the knowledge that she can leave her husband if he cheats on her and support herself, with a community of friends of similar interests networking across the city – things are looking pretty good. For the badly educated woman struck in a block of flats nearby with a two-year-old to bring up alone, living far from her family – things are looking grim.

A GENERATION DIVIDED

The Thatcher generation of voters under forty is divided. We face deep disparities in our income – the young rich and young poor are farther apart than ever. We are split in our job opportunities, with unemployment increasingly concentrated among a small group of young people who stay out of work for years. Our life chances are still very different if we are men or women, and the disadvantage for young blacks in terms of education, jobs and pay are still immense.

It is an often heard refrain; the rich have got richer and the poor poorer. What is shocking is how early in life the gaps starts widening. For among twenty-year-olds, not long out of school or university, the gap in their living standards is far wider than it was thirty years ago. Despite a common international culture of music, fashion, video and consumer brand names, the cash they have to play with, and the circumstances of their lives are polarizing. The 1980s gave a lot of young people a chance to get rich, at the same time as cutting benefits for under-twenty-fives, pushing up youth employment, and raising homelessness among teenagers.

But so what if there is diversity in the lives young people lead and the jobs or careers they pursue? The problem is that the people who are stuck in low-paid insecure jobs at twenty are unlikely to be on a well-paid career trajectory by thirty. And youngsters out of work for a year or more are less likely to have found a steady job five years later. For the low-paid and out-of-work youth are predominantly those with no qualifications – something that will haunt them all of their working lives.

Those who do not get good educations do not get well-paid jobs. Increasingly, they don't get jobs at all. No qualifications, no job, no money, no independence, and not much chance of breaking out. And still, despite all the rhetoric of the classless society, the poorly educated are the children of the working classes.

Youth unemployment remains concentrated among unskilled men in cities who remain out of work for years at a time. The problem is even worse among young black men – 60 per cent of those living in London are unemployed. In 1992, 90 per cent of men in their twenties with degrees have got jobs, compared to only 60 per cent of those with no qualifications. And the figures are even more striking for women. Eighty-eight per cent of women in their twenties with degrees have got jobs, compared with only 33 per cent of their counterparts who have no qualifications. The difference between the twenty-something men and women who left school without certificates is that the men are usually registered unemployed, while most of the women are looking after children.

The key to finding and keeping work and earning respectable wages in the 1990s is education. The most important determinant of children's career chances and standards of living today is the education they receive. Graduate men, for example, earn almost twice as much on average as men who have no qualifications at all.

But this makes it all the more outrageous that education remains so unfairly distributed. Higher education is still expanding. As higher education expands, and as salaried jobs expand, so the chance of someone from a working-class family becoming a professional as my mother did has grown. But family advantage still makes a difference – both to the qualifications you pick up and to what you do with them afterwards. Research done by Gordon Marshall and Adam Swift shows that people like me with professional parents have a much better chance of getting those crucial academic qualifications than our classmates whose parents have no qualifications at all. And as even stronger evidence of the persistence of the class system in Britain, they find that a degree from a working-class family still will not get you as far in life as a degree from a middle-class family.

The British education system is failing many people. Still, in the mid 1990s, too many teenagers are leaving school with no qualifications. Many have serious literacy and numeracy problems; 15 per cent of sixteen-year-olds cannot calculate how much change they should get in a shop – the kinds of skills you would expect from a seven-year-old. Twenty-four per cent cannot manage to interpret a video-recorder instruction manual. And this is the generation that needs to be fluent with computers to survive. What chance have that 24 per cent got?

Education matters more today than it did for our parents and grandparents. In the 1940s and 1950s, if you did not get a good education, you might still get an apprenticeship. If not, there was plenty of unskilled manual labour to be done. Unskilled men could still get a job, and unskilled women could find a working husband to support them whilst they brought up children. Not so in the 1990s and the twenty-first century.

Long-term unemployment of unskilled young people – and the unfair distribution of opportunities that it represents – will be one of the biggest issues facing the governments of the next millennium. New opportunities are needed for the most disadvantaged young people in society: better basic education, real opportunities to retrain later on, and opportunities to work. The urgency of the case is without question; for moral reasons we must attack the unfair distribution of life chances by accident of birth and local school, and in the name of social cohesion we need to avoid the growth of an alienated, excluded underclass.

But providing these opportunities will not be easy. For giving real opportunities to the most disadvantaged young people, providing them with jobs, and sorting out the worst schools in the country will all cost money, money that has to come from elsewhere – either from the pockets of the programmes which go primarily to middle-class youth. All the other young people need to be persuaded that this is a price worth paying. Only by overcoming social divisions will we generate social cohesion. Yet only by building a consensus that the community has an obligation towards all of its members will we be able to pay for extending opportunities. Building this kind of consensus among the Thatcher generation will be a difficult task.

THE ANTI-POLITICS GENERATION?

The young generation pose a difficult problem for Labour in 1997. For the biggest economic and social issues of the future are already evident in the insecurity and divisions which haunt young people's lives. To tackle the insecurity and heal the divisions, Labour needs the support of the whole generation – yet this is not obviously forthcoming. For the voters under forty have predominantly voted Conservative rather than Labour in the past. We are accused of having self-centred individualistic values which inhibit us from supporting projects to help others or the community as a whole. And we are perceived as too cynical and distrustful of government to believe that any political project could make much difference, no matter how worthy its aims.

We have all heard the laments about the alienation of this generation from politics and society. Cynical, and selfish, we are accused of registering rarely and voting grudgingly. After all, government cannot do much for us, parties are out of touch with our lives and our concerns, and our single vote certainly makes no difference at all. Two aspects of this apparent 'alienation' matter for Labour. First, there may be generational value changes taking place – and this could be particularly important if they are values that Labour has not traditionally identified with. And second, Labour needs to understand the extent and the causes of the current antagonism towards politics.

During the 1980s the Conservatives managed to crack the old stereotype of young people as idealistic left-wingers who move to the right as they age. Consistently since 1979 even the youngest voters have been more likely to vote Conservative than Labour. The result is that most of the generation under forty have never voted Labour in a general election in their lives before. Even in the 1992 general election when Labour made a significant recovery, more young men voted for Major than for Kinnock. Women under twenty-five were the only group who were more likely to vote Labour than Conservative.

The question is whether this change in voting preferences reveals a deeper shift across the generations away from traditional Labour values. In particular, have young people become so selfish during the Thatcher years, that it will be hard to persuade them to take part in a project to help others or the community as a whole?

Certainly we want more freedom and choices in our lives than our parents ever had. Alongside our increase in material wealth we want ever more choices about the way we spend it and ever more control over our own lives. Helen Wilkinson argues in research done for Demos that there has been a generational value shift towards greater appreciation of personal autonomy and away from respect for tradition and authority. But there is no evidence that these preferences for greater individual choice necessarily mean we are part of an irretrievably selfish society.

What we do know is that young people are fed up with politics from any party. Ours is the apathetic generation: according to a BBC/NOP poll, only 6 per cent of those under thirty-five describe themselves as 'very interested in politics'. One in five young people aged between eighteen and twenty-four are not registered to vote. Party membership remains concentrated among older voters, particularly in the Conservative Party, where the average age of party participants is over sixty-five. Meanwhile we apparently have little respect for existing political institutions, or for other aspects of authority or the establishment. We are more likely than older generations to be involved in alternative forms of protest, ranging from demonstrations against animal exports to picketing the path of the M11.

I believe, however, that the apocalyptic vision of politics and the next generation is wrong. Most young voters are not irreconcilably alienated from politics. Like generations before them they simply have more interesting, cool and sexy things to do right now. Politics has never been a widespread popular preoccupation particularly among the young – apart from among a few angry young students who are as active today as they ever were, and who still tend to prefer to remain outside mainstream forms of protest just as they did in the 1960s. Young activists lament the rise of apathy among their peers, but it is worth noting that the student politicians of thirty years ago were doing exactly the same thing. And that same BBC/NOP poll which supposedly proves how few of us are very interested in politics, shows in fact that most young people do feel that politics is relevant to their lives.

This is not to say that young people are not more sceptical about politics than they were when my mother first voted. Much of it is the extremely healthy and inevitable result of subjecting politicians – warts and all – to the scrutiny of television, beamed into every home, alongside a societywide decline in respect for authority and traditional institutions including the church and the monarchy. Shaking up politics with radical institutional reform would certainly get at the complacency and absurd rituals that any ruling class is wont to adopt.

But it will not be enough to revive young people's perceptions that government actually can and should make a difference. For during the 1990s, they have been pushed to the limits of their credulity by the betrayal of the expectations and political promises of the 1980s. In the 1980s boom, the generation under forty expected – indeed were promised – great jobs, ever rising wages, ever rising wealth (as house prices escalated), and ever falling taxes without damaging public services. The widespread disillusion as all those expectations came crashing down is not just disillusion with the Conservatives; it is a cynicism for the whole currency of political promises and government potential.

Labour has its own credibility problems. For although it was a Conservative government that has so debased the language of political promises in the last five years, young voters do not yet believe Labour can deliver either. And Labour's politics and campaigns in the 1980s and 1990s – as well as the distortions of them in the tabloid press – must take some of the blame. In 1992 Labour went to the election with a long list of potential policy reforms. Conservative Central office attached a price tag to every one, totted them up to create a headline figure of £35 billion, and then found the tax bill to match: £1,000 per person per year.

It is true that if you implemented all those policies in one year it would cost billions of pounds. But in politics today, it just is not good enough to say, well we wouldn't have done it all in one year, we would have done it gradually as the economy could afford it. It gave us the worst of all worlds. On the one hand, the list of proposals lent credibility to the Tories' ludicrous campaign to convince people we would double their taxes. And on the other, we seemed to be making promises on policies we could not keep and raising expectations we could not deliver on.

What is more worrying, and more difficult to tackle than general cynicism, is the fact that young people are divided in their attitudes to politics in the same way as they are divided in their lives. Twenty-four per cent of blacks are not registered to vote. If those who don't vote and have most suspicion about politics are also those who have fewest chances in life, then we have disenfranchised those the Labour Party grew up to speak for.

Even so this is not a whole generation irrevocably alienated from politics and society. Some young people are clearly excluded from the mainstream way of life. Without adequate education, qualifications and opportunities, they feel that Britain has little to offer them, and it is hardly surprising that they reject conventional politics too. But for everyone else, the most important factor contributing to their cynicism and disgust is their betrayal by Conservative politicians in the 1980s and 1990s. Rebuilding public confidence in politics and government will form an essential part of the task for Labour during the rest of this century.

THE TASK FOR LABOUR

The Labour Party in 1997 faces a serious challenge; overcoming the cynicism and winning the hearts of the young generation of voters. They need to persuade us that it is in all of our interests, as well as morally just, to extend opportunities for prosperity and security to everyone. And they need to convince us that they have the integrity and the ability to make these opportunities a reality. It is only when we feel we can trust the promises politicians make that we will allow ourselves to believe in a better future.

Labour under Tony Blair has already done much to respond to the concerns of young voters and the Party needs to build on its growing youth membership.

But the responsibility on the Labour Party is immense. For Labour has not been out of power this long in its entire existence. If the party succeeds, this election could prove a historical turning point. If it fails, it will have blown its last chance. My grandmother voted Labour in 1945. She died not long after I was born. If current demographic trends are anything to go by, I could still be voting in 2045. I hope that Labour can build a programme to persuade my generation to vote for them this time. Whether it be through far-sighted self-interest or moral purpose, we must start the next century as we mean to go on.

20 The Prospects for a Labour Government

Peter Hennessy

Professor of Contemporary History at
Queen Mary and Westfield College,
London, he is author of *Cabinet,
Whitehall* and *The Hidden Wiring.*

With an unpopular government and with a revived and
modernized Labour Party under Tony Blair, the centre left
in Britain has potentially, as in 1945 and in 1964, another
historic opportunity.

THE POLITICS OF PESSIMISM

There is, however, one very big difference in the political
ecology of mid 1990s Britain, compared to mid '60s or mid
'40s Britain. In contrast to those earlier periods, we are now
locked into the politics of pessimism. Both 1945 and 1964
were moments enthused with genuine hope, hope that well-
designed schemes drawn up by sensible politicians, officials
and intellectuals would be the beneficial escalator to necessary change, higher productivity and greater social justice.

In 1945, we were war winners and still a world power. In
terms of wealth, we were well ahead of France and Germany
whose economies had been severely damaged by the war.

In 1964, though Germany had passed us four years earlier, in terms of wealth per head we did not feel we had fallen irretrievably behind. In fact, Labour politicians, seeing the success of indicative planning in France, felt that, if they could get rid of over-extended defence and financial commitments, Britain would be able to catch up.

Today people are far more pessimistic. Government has lost much of its authority, both at home and externally. Our relative economic position is much worse. In OECD terms, we are nineteenth and falling. The old alibis for relative economic failure – sterling's reserve currency status, excessive defence expenditure, the power of the unions – have been removed without halting our relative decline. The politics of pessimism means that marginal changes in income tax have become the preoccupation of the hour instead of the long-term need to lay down procedures for careful and cumulative economic and institutional reform and building up human and infrastructural capital for the future.

Yet Mr Blair and the Labour Party have one priceless advantage and that is that expectations are so low. Compared to 1945 and 1964, politics is almost an 'illusion-free zone'. Expectations of the incoming Labour government were very high indeed in 1945 – and to a considerable extent, the government was able to fulfil those expectations. Expectations were also high in 1964: Wilson's rhetoric, the language of modernity and technological change, the meritocratic impulse aroused enormous expectations, as did the persona of Wilson himself. When the disappointments crowded in, as they did in battalions from July 1966 onwards, popular disillusionment was very profound.

Now many voters are hopeful that a Blair government would make a difference but Tony Blair has not allowed expectations to get out of hand. So if, despite Britain's relative economic position, the neglected human infrastructure and the lack of social cohesion, year on year things get a little better, it would seem almost miraculous.

R. H. TAWNEY AND WINDOWS

The key issue is education and training. Labour has to focus on the problem that was already sapping Britain's economic and industrial vitality even before there was a Labour Representation Committee, let alone a Labour Party. In the 1860s and 1870s reports and Royal Commissions were already telling us that our education and training was inadequate. Now, in the age of the information revolution, education is even more vital.

Paradoxically, though we lost out in earlier races in the nineteenth and at the beginning of the twentieth century and later again in the 1950s and 1960s, the transformation in information technology gives us a new opportunity. If we could make a supreme act of determination and will as a nation, then the catch-up phenomenon could work in our favour.

What Labour has to do is make education and training the priority. If you like, it has to marry the vision of R. H. Tawney with the opportunities of 'windows' – Tawney + Windows = New Britain. It has to make its case clearly and honestly to the British electorate. Tony Blair has to say straightforwardly that he cannot offer instant promises of gains in living standards but that he can and will invest in education and training and then protect that investment for short-term ups and downs in the money markets by ring-fencing it if faced by pressures for spending cuts. In other words, it will be a government for the long term – for 2030 as much as for 1997.

Of course, this is a risky political strategy. In wartime, it is much easier to confront people with the truth. In peacetime, especially with 80 per cent of the population in work, it is much harder to sustain the sense of danger. People have to be persuaded that is necessary to put deferred before instant gratification, investment before consumption. It is partly about finding the right kind of language. Labour needs to warn that we are already reaping the whirlwind of the failure to invest properly in education in the past and that, unless we sustain that investment over a number of years, we shall continue to fall behind as a nation. What makes great trading nations formidable is not a little twiddle on the income tax here, a little fiddling on the VAT there, plus a bit more conspicuous consumption but long-term commitment to education, innovation and investment.

LABOUR'S RELATIONSHIP WITH THE INTELLECTUALS

In his essay, Michael Young writes of the 1945 coalition between politicians and intellectuals. The position of the intellectuals today is very different from that of 1945. In 1945, they were the territorial army of the state in Whitehall and also well dug in in think-tanks like Political and Economic Planning (PEP) and the Fabian Society. Today the intellectuals are dispersed and a large portion of them are not in public or political life. Nor should they be. Many of them are not even in the universities. They are in the information business, in consultancies and some of the very best of them are in the media.

However, media people have, to a great extent, rubbed their noses in trivia and fad and fashion. And they have become cynical. Scepticism is the necessary intellectual condition for improvement; cynicism is waving the white flag. William Waldegrave has talked of a politico-media complex driving contemporary government. Both the politico bit and the media bit have the attention span of a gnat.

Even the think-tanks are in danger of allowing themselves to be driven by the short term. The real purpose of intellectuals in a society is to hold up evidence and truth to those in power, to provide the inconvenient analysis to those who want the swift and metricious solution. When think-tanks are driven by 'niching' and marketing themselves, they spend too much time hyping up their own influence and spotting the next trend rather than thinking seriously about the issues.

What Tony Blair needs to do, if he has not done it already, is to create his own personal think-tank. The people who staff it could draw on their own networks – in the universities, industry, the city, the media and so on. Their job would be to provide information and present the options. Of course, there will be leaks sometimes but that must not stop the process of thinking. My advice to Mr Blair is to use the advice of intellectuals where it is useful – and not to be put off by the media.

PREPARING FOR GOVERNMENT

In opposition Labour must start to prepare for government, especially for its coming into office. It is essential that, during its first few days, a Labour government is not forced into rushed decisions on vital matters which subsequently are difficult to reverse.

Phillip Whitehead and I interviewed James Callaghan for a television programme on cabinet government in the mid 1980s. Callaghan was almost word perfect twenty-two years on, on the brief waiting for him in No. 11 Downing Street on the evening of Friday 16 October 1964: 'We greet the Chancellor and welcome him. We have to record there will be a deficit of £750 million in the balance of payments'.

I found that file recently at the Public Record Office. The deficit was an even more chilling one of £800 million. And tucked away at the back was a section on what some in the new Wilson cabinet of 1964 called 'the great unmentionable'-devaluation. 'Of all the expedients for dealing with a deficit in the balance of payments,' the Treasury told him, 'devaluation is the most drastic. Circumstances are conceivable in which we might have little or no option; but it should be an important object of policy to avoid allowing such a situation to arise.'

The following morning Callaghan met Harold Wilson and George Brown in the Cabinet Room. They ruled out devaluation before the civil servants came in to take a note at the first Cabinet Committee meeting of that government on economic affairs so that the dreaded D-word did not appear in the minutes. Some have claimed that by 11 a.m. on the morning of Saturday 17 October 1964 the future of the Labour government was sealed, thanks to the impossibility of keeping the pound at $2.80.

What the Labour opposition must do is to reduce the shock of that Friday evening and Saturday morning. From the beginning of this year, Mr Blair and his shadows have been able to consult the permanent secretaries about the machinery of government and to indicate any changes they might wish to make in the direction of policy. But such chats are only a minor part of the preparation the leader of the opposition and his colleagues will need.

The key requirement, in my view, is a kind of cabinet office or central policy review staff in waiting to prepare a tough, comprehensive and regularly updated audit of reality for Mr Blair and his colleagues. They need people who can keep them up to speed on international affairs, the linkage with the international economy and the world money markets as well as what is happening in the domestic economy, in the training programmes and the classrooms. Such intellectual, analytical and practical R&D ahead of election day will repay every pound spent many times over when the bone-tiring slog of government begins to drain pre-election aspirations of their vitality. It will focus would-be ministers' minds on things as they really are and help train them to take decisions on the basis of knowledge and evidence.

MACHINERY OF GOVERNMENT

It is essential that the Labour Party thinks about the instrument of state in advance. A Labour government will be dependent on the civil service, the people and the systems of the state as well as the £260 billion it will inherit in public expenditure terms to carry out its policies. The cabinet minutes will say that the cabinet invited the Secretary of State to do X but if there is no wiring behind that minute, no mechanism for making it happen, it does not happen. Labour has to get to know how the Whitehall machine works, so that it can get the best from it.

Despite everything that has happened under the Conservatives, the civil service remains, in the words of the Treasury and Civil Service Committee's report on the role of the civil service, 'a great national asset'. There are not many other countries in the world where an incoming set of ministers would be able to inherit such a corruption-free, intelligent, effective and non-partisan body of civil servants. Many of them are looking forward, if only for professional reasons, to serving a Labour government.

The managerial reforms introduced by the Conservatives have had a major impact on Whitehall. An incoming Labour government would certainly need to re-examine some of the post-1992 market-orientated changes – market testing, contracting out and privatization. But the agency revolution which now covers two-thirds of the civil service is politically 'neutral'. These agencies were specially designed, partly at the suggestion of the Treasury Select Committee, so that their governing 'framework' agreements could be changed to reflect different public and policy purposes.

Labour will, however, need to look at the policy analysis capacity of the civil service. For too long, under Conservative governments, the quality of policy advice has been ignored. If politics is ideology- rather than evidence-driven, there is the strong temptation to say, 'I know what the policies are. Do not give me the alternatives. Just tell me how to do it.' Civil servants whose intellectual and public policy salad days should have been the 1980s are the saddest people in Whitehall. They too have been in opposition not in the political sense but in terms of their careers because they have not been properly stretched. A Labour government would need to put that right.

I am in favour of allowing each Cabinet Minister a British version of a French style *cabinet* in the form of an enhanced Private Office of up to eight: half career civil service, half irregulars with a leavening of real outside experts as opposed to political fixers of the usual special adviser type. When a Cabinet Minister recruits temporary civil servants, he (or she) should choose people because they know something rather than because they believe something. One commodity that is never in short supply is political prejudice. What ministers really need are outside experts who know about the issues which will drive key legislation and early decisions facing incoming ministers and can say, 'Hang on, it is not that easy but I can see a way around the difficulty.'

The Prime Minister, above all, needs strategic back-up. Writing about Peel when British government in the mid nineteenth century was very small beer indeed, Walter Bagehot said that the Prime Minister needs a 'mind in reserve'. In a very real sense, the Prime Minister is the Queen's only Minister for Strategy. So Labour needs to create a central policy review staff in waiting which can be converted into the real thing on day one of government. In addition Mr Blair may have to strengthen the No. 10 back-up at his disposal.

It is crucial that Tony Blair should confront the occupational disease that has afflicted every set of cabinet ministers that has occupied the Cabinet Room since 1939 – overload. If he could come in with determination, a true sense of the strategic and the measures to make and keep thinking space in the *mêlée* of governance, he will increase the chances of those ghastly pressures of history and inheritance being tackled and make it that bit more manageable.

CONCLUSION

It is essential that the centre-left succeeds this time. For most of this century, the possibility of a centre-left alternative has kept the right decent and socially minded, for fear of the competition beating it. The British political system, quite apart from the Labour Party itself, cannot risk the centre-left being tainted once more (and perhaps permanently) by the stain of drift and incompetence.

CONCLUSION:

The New Agenda

Giles Radice

This book demonstrates very clearly that, for the first time
for a generation, there is now an agenda which unites a
broad spectrum of thinking on the centre and left. This is
potentially a development of the greatest importance. It is
a truism that governments lose elections. But it is also the
case that, if oppositions are to gain power and establish
themselves securely in government as a force for change,
they have to be able, as with Labour in 1945 and in 1964
and the Conservatives in 1979, to draw not so much on a
set of detailed policies as on a common pool of ideas and
themes, relevant to the concerns and needs of the times. The
ideas which run so powerfully through these essays – the
need to equip ourselves through education and training for
social, economic and technological change, the need for
social cohesion, the need to decentralize and democratize
power, the need to cooperate with our European and other
neighbours on the basis of a modern definition of patriotism,
the need for a new politics, founded on values, openness
and trust – could both provide the catalyst for a decisive
change in British politics and inspire a successful centre-left
government.

THE FAILURE OF THATCHERISM

Thatcherism, defined as an assortment of firmly held but loosely linked right-wing ideas such as privatization, deregulation, reduced public spending, and tax cuts, dominated the political agenda of the 1980s, just as Mrs Thatcher dominated the political scene. But by the end of the decade, it had become clear that, like its progenitor, it had failed.

For all its political success in the 1980s, Thatcherism was a remarkably limited doctrine. With its crude laisser-faire economics, it did not provide convincing solutions to such deep-seated problems as Britain's woefully inadequate system of education and training, the poor record in civil research and development and the relative weakness in high technology industries. The run down of health and education services, the cuts in welfare benefits and the overall deterioration in state services graphically demonstrated the paucity of Thatcherism as a public philosophy.

But perhaps the most glaring indictment of Thatcherite Conservatism was its divisiveness. In an unequal world the spirit of competitive individualism characteristic of Mrs Thatcher's approach derived the need for one person to care for or think of the needs of others. It could not provide a cohesive society in which all citizens had a stake. It had nothing to say to the unemployed, the poor or the sick. It had nothing to say to the inner cities or to the ethnic minorities. It had nothing to say to the northern half of the British Isles. So it could not offer convincing answers to crime, poverty, racial tensions or discrimination, inner-city deprivation or regional inequalities.

The nearest surrogate to a unifying theme was the unattractively strident form of insular nationalism which became such a feature of Mrs Thatcher's leadership, especially at the time of the Falklands War and in her policy towards the European Community. The effect of this aggressive approach was to damage Britain's relations with its European partners and to marginalize its influence on the Continent.

But, despite its glaring failures, there was still, at the beginning of the 1990s, a feeling, even on the left, that there was no real alternative model to the market triumphalism of Thatcherism. One reason for this pessimism was the exhaustion of the old social democratic model of the 1960s and 1970s. If in retrospect the achievements of those Labour governments seem more substantial than they did at the time, it is simply not possible to go back to a world of planning, incomes policy and 'corporatism', let alone to the 'socialism in one country' version proposed by the hard left. That world was politically undermined by the widespread industrial disputes of 1978–79, the so-called 'winter of discontent', which was such an important factor in Labour's defeat at the 1979 general election.

At the same time, the increase in the spread and impact of global markets has circumscribed the ability of individual governments to control their own economies. The power of these global forces has became more and more obvious. In the early 1980s, the Mitterand government in France was forced by a run on the franc to abandon its Keynesian experiment, while in 1992 the British Conservative government was driven out of the ERM by similar forces. So, even if it so desired, it is impossible for Labour to return to the economic ideas of the 1960s and 1970s.

The collapse of the Soviet Union was also crucial. Social Democrats and Democratic Socialists had been amongst the strongest critics of the Soviet regime. But inevitably the catastrophic failure of the command economies of the Communist empire rubbed off on them because, for a time, it seemed to discredit the very idea of government intervention.

THE TIDE TURNS

In the mid-1990s, the tide turned. John Major, who had succeeded Mrs Thatcher at the beginning of the decade, could never decide whether he should continue on the course which Mrs Thatcher had chosen or return to a more humane form of Conservatism. Instead, he tried unsuccessfully to straddle the two positions. His government proved itself incompetent and became deeply unpopular. By 1996, it had totally run out of steam, not just physically tired but bereft of ideas for the future.

At the same time, alternative themes were emerging on the centre and the left. As in the early 1960s, when intellectuals like Brian Chapman, Anthony Crosland and Michael Shanks were writing scathing accounts of their Britain, books were influential in this development. Will Hutton's *The State We're In*, a lucid argument for economic and political reform, became a surprise bestseller in 1995. Andrew Marr's *Ruling Britannia*, part description, part polemic, put forward the case for democratic change, while Simon Jenkins' *Accountable to None* castigated the centralization which had taken place under the Conservatives.

Two independent commissions, one set up by John Smith, leader of the Labour Party from 1992 until his tragic death in 1994, the other by Paddy Ashdown, leader of the Liberal Party, proposed new directions. The first, the Social Justice Commission chaired by Gordon Borrie, was the most comprehensive analysis of social welfare since the Beveridge report and put forward policies to adapt the welfare state to change, especially in the labour market, and in the position of women and the elderly. The second was the Dahrendorf Commission which examined the dilemma for modern societies of how to combine wealth creation with social cohesion. It strongly supported the idea of a 'stakeholder' society. As Lord Dahrendorf put it in his 1995 Churchill Lecture: 'Wealth is more than GDP growth; economic development has to be sustainable not only in environmental but also in social terms; inclusion is not an optional extra but a condition of long-term wealth creation; stakeholders are as important for companies, communities and countries as shareholders; the public domain with its values of service continues to have a significant place even in a globally competitive economy.'

However, the most important reason for the change of ideological climate was the election of Tony Blair as leader of the Labour Party in the summer of 1994. Mr Blair is not only interested in ideas but convinced of their crucial political importance. Hence his successful campaign to replace the old Clause IV of Labour's constitution, which committed the party to a command economy, by a modern version, based on ethical values. His speech to the 1995 party conference at Brighton, arguably the most successful by a Labour leader since Harold Wilson's address to the Scarborough conference in 1963, outlined an alternative political agenda, the principles of which he discusses in the introduction to this book. He sums up his vision succinctly: 'My vision is of a Britain that is truly one nation; where we work together to prepare ourselves for massive economic and technological change; to extend opportunity in a world of deep insecurity; to create a genuine civil society where everyone has a stake, where everyone has a responsibility, and where power is pushed down towards the people instead of being hoarded centrally; and to secure our place in the world as a nation cooperating with others in Europe and elsewhere.'

THE UNDERLYING THEMES

Few of the contributors to this book are directly party political. Some are not even committed Labour Party supporters. They have been chosen for their intellectual distinction and authority on the issues covered in this book. It is, therefore, all the more striking how far their essays reflect and expand on the themes contained in Tony Blair's opening statements. As this book shows, an alternative political, economic and social agenda has emerged which Tony Blair is articulating with eloquence and passion.

It is not just that Mr Blair has caught the intellectual tide. Unusually for a politician, he is helping shape it by his speeches, articles, interviews and broadcasts. And, if Labour wins the next election, his government will be the instrument for making a reality of the new agenda about which these authors write with such clarity and vigour and to which their essays in this book make such a notable contribution.

This agenda reflects the realities of the times. Charles Handy, Denis Healey, Patricia Hewitt, David Marquand and Robert Taylor spell out the profound changes that are shaping our lives – the information revolution, transformations in technology, global markets in finance, business and investment, dramatic shifts in labour markets and changes at work and in the family. These developments are much too profound to be reversed or be resisted, especially by individual governments. But that does not mean that everything should or has to be left to the market. Global rules can be established by global institutions; national advantage can be pursued in different ways; above all, citizens can – and must – be equipped to manage their lives in this new world.

Charles Handy warns that, unless governments act, 'we could end up with an even more divided society – the fortunate minority, the knowledge workers, the professionals and the managers, on the one hand; and, on the other hand, all the rest who will be increasingly impoverished and cut off from the opportunities of this new world.' Hence the argument for government involvement, especially over education and training. For these essayists, education is a big idea of the millennium – the new commanding heights of the economy. It is not only the key to economic and industrial success; it gives individuals the tools to survive and prosper in the global market. It, therefore, needs to be given the highest priority and managed both with rigour and imagination.

If these global changes make education and training even more essential than before, the information revolution, perhaps the most important of these changes, provides, as Tim Brighouse points out, new ways to improve educational skills. David Puttnam argues that it could also offer fresh chances for the British to develop their creative talents, to the benefit both of themselves individually and of the country. Already considerably more workers are employed by the audio-visual industries than make cars and car components. So the information revolution is not just a challenge; it also provides enormous opportunity.

The need to create social cohesion is also at the heart of the new agenda. David Marquand says that to pursue wealth creation without at the same time pursuing community values is 'a contradiction in terms' and that a nation 'wracked by crime, unemployment, decrepit public services and social exclusion is, by definition, unsuccessful'. Tony Blair and other essayists understand that a 'stakeholder' economy is central to this argument. Firms are not just a bundle of assets owned by shareholders but living communities united by common aspirations whose future depends increasingly on the skills and commitment of the whole workforce. Hence the case for fair treatment and rights as well as responsibilities for employees. A healthy economy is one in which opportunity is available to all, advancement is through merit, and from which no group or class is set apart or excluded.

Success will require that the relationship of trust and inclusion is fostered throughout society. If people feel they have no stake in society, they feel little responsibility towards it and little inclination to work for its success. That is why our essayists argue for an education system which encourages excellence for all; for welfare reform to help people back into work and give people a stake in their own benefits; for a national health service which continues to serve all the people; for a penal policy based on more effective community policing and prison reform to help criminals become useful members of society; and for a realistic programme to strengthen the modern family as the basis for a healthy society.

The argument about social cohesion is linked to another key idea of this book – that of decentralizing and democratizing power. Under the Conservatives, Britain has become the most centralized nation in Western Europe. In the name of their market ideology, the Thatcherites have sought to tame, curb, or reconstruct the intermediate institutions of civil society, including local government, trade unions, universities, and professional bodies. This ruthless centralization, combined with the impact of global markets, has undermined community to the detriment of society. Our essayists are passionate believers in 'subsidiarity' – the Continental Christian Democrat idea that issues are best dealt with at the most local level or, as Charles Handy puts it, 'small where things matter to be small and big where it counts'. Denis Healey argues that devolution is the only way of satisfying the pressure for more autonomy, especially in Scotland, without creating a separate state, and David Marquand believes that many of the policies needed 'to restart social capital and protect community in the new economic era are best carried out by localities and regions'. To promote subsidiarity, Geoff Mulgan puts forward ideas to strengthen local and regional government, to make the quangos, which have become so characteristic a feature of Conservative Britain, more accountable and introduce more referenda, while Robert Taylor sees a key role for a reformed workplace trade unionism.

The new agenda calls for a modern definition of what it means to be British. Over thirty years ago, the shrewd former American Secretary of State, Dean Acheson, drew attention to British identity problems: 'Great Britain has lost an empire and not yet found a role.' In the 1980s, the Thatcherites tried to provide an answer to this dilemma by an assertion of an anachronistic 'Little Englander' nationalism, combined with an unconvincing globalism. No wonder, as Neal Ascherson says, that the British feel a deep sense of uncertainty about their role in the world.

Tony Blair has rightly refused to allow the Tories to walk away with the patriotic card. But he draws a distinction between the immature xenophobia displayed by Michael Portillo, the Conservative Defence Secretary, at the 1995 Conservative party conference and 'one-nation' patriotism: 'A country with high ambitions and high ideals for itself but also outward looking and tolerant of others: That is patriotism for the new millennium.' Much of the answer, as he and other essayists argue, lies in a more positive attitude to British membership of the European Union. A Britain which was able to play a more constructive and effective role in Europe would be a Britain of which it would be easier to be proud.

The tone of the book is positively European, inspired not by fanaticism but by national interest and good sense. As David Sainsbury points out, Britain needs, for straightforward commercial reasons, to play a central role in the development of the European Union; Stephen Tindale, a member of the younger generation who takes British membership for granted, sets out a programme to expand the European social dimension and enlarge the membership of the EU and argues for strong British involvement in such a programme, while Denis Healey wants the European Union, under British influence, to lead an international initiative to tackle problems of global security and prosperity.

An equally important theme of the book is the need for a new politics. Yvette Cooper warns of the alienation from politics of the young generation. Tony Blair shows that he too is acutely aware of the disillusion with politics and politicians. Hence his refusal to make promises that cannot be kept in government. The lesson of the 1964 government's experience is that it is essential to retain credibility. Expectations were high in 1964: once disappointments crowded in and Harold Wilson acquired a reputation for opportunism, popular disillusionment was correspondingly profound.

It is, therefore, essential, as David Lipsey argues, that Labour does not make spending commitments it is not certain of keeping. It is noticeable that the authors, even though they are not party politicians, are cautious about putting forward uncosted proposals. However, as Peter Hennessy notes, compared to 1945 and 1964, politics is almost an 'illusion-free zone'. If a Labour government could actually deliver on those promises it made, 'it would seem almost miraculous'.

The British are grown-up people who understand, often from personal experience, the pressures facing their governments. But pure pragmatism will not be enough to retain the commitment of Labour's supporters or the enthusiasm of the voters. That is why the value-based approach to politics set out in Clause IV, as well as the relevance of the new agenda, is so important. A Blair administration could transform political life by being at the same time principled and open and honest about problems and difficulties.

THE NEED FOR IDEAS

In his Introduction, Tony Blair says that the role of intellectuals and thinkers is crucial to the regeneration of politics. He wants the Labour Party to be able to 'draw on a coalition of thinkers, including people outside the party'. Such a 'coalition of thinkers' will be as valuable in government as in opposition.

Of course both politicians and intellectuals are well aware of the difficulties. Negative campaigning and a hostile and often trivializing media mean that any proposal put forward by someone known to be connected even tenuously with the Labour Party is immediately misrepresented as Labour Party policy. The intellectual community itself is far more diverse and dispersed than it was in 1945 or even in 1964 and Peter Hennessy warns that those who are in the information business or the media are in danger of becoming too short-term and cynical. Charles Handy points out too that politicians and intellectuals have different functions: The task of politicians is to articulate popular aspirations, while the role of free-standing thinkers is to 'come up with views of how the world is going or ought to go'.

All the same it is essential, as Michael Young argues, that intellectual thinkers and experts are able to make their contribution to the renaissance of progressive politics in Britain. Young proposes the setting up of more commissions on the lines of the Social Justice Commission, while Hennessy suggests the creation of a shadow central policy review body. I would add that it is also important in the run up to the election and beyond to use to the full existing 'think tanks', which like the Fabian Society and the Institute for Public Policy Research are either linked to or favourable to the party, as well as reaching out to other bodies.

This book, inconceivable five years ago, is itself part of the process of involving intellectuals and is, as Tony Blair says, 'a testimony to the rebirth of confidence and new thinking on the left-of-centre of British politics'. Equally important, it sets out a new political economic and social agenda for Britain which is relevant to the needs and concerns of the new millennium, an agenda of great significance because it unites a broad spread of non-Conservative opinion across the country and could inspire a new Labour government.

Index